The Trans-Evangelist

SECOND EDITION

7-7-20
To DINAH
– a gift from AARON KILGORE
– blessings!!
SISTER Paula

The Trans-Evangelist

SECOND EDITION

The Life and Times of A Transgender Pentecostal Preacher

by

Sister Paula Nielsen

One Spirit Press
Portland, Oregon

Printed in the USA

ISBN: ISBN-13: 978-1547134823
ISBN-10: 1547134828
Cover and Book Design Spirit Press, LLC
Alice Firpo Designer

One Spirit Press,
onespiritpress@gmail.com
www.onespiritpress.com

Portland, Oregon

This book is dedicated to the memory
of four women whose influence played a strong role
in shaping the person I am today:

Sophie Tucker
Aimee Semple McPherson
Kathryn Kuhlman
Janis Joplin

Table of Contents

Foreword	2
Introduction...	5
One: Growing Up In the 40's...	9
Two: Finding God In the 50's...	55
Three: Cataclysmic Changes of the 60's...	115
Four: Sins of the 70's...	177
Five: Shifting Priorities of the 80's...	219
Six: The Gay 90's...	265
Seven: New Beginnings in a New Century...	287
Epilogue...	313
Afterword...	315

The author would like to point out that the landscape and vocabulary of the trans community has changed considerably since the decades and years that are recounted in the telling of this story.

The words and phrases used herein reflect the idioms of speech of the particular years and decades in which these events transpired.

Acknowledgments

The author would like to acknowledge with special thanks those who helped in the preparation of the manscript of this book.

David Grant Kohl, local historian, went over all of the chapter drafts, gave his insight that made each chapter come alive.

Dr. David Wheeler, American Baptist pastor and theologian, generously gave his time to review the manuscript for spelling, grammar, and sentence structure.

Suzanne Deakins of Spirit Press donated her time and talents in the formatting and publishing of this book.

And a special word of thanks to Daniel Spiro, Producer of my television program and film documentary of my life and ministry. All expenses came out of his own pocket.

Without the help of these wonderful people, this book never would have been written.

Foreword

I first heard about Sister Paula when I came across a youtube video for my radio show The Sir Darryl Radio Experience. Sister Paula was proudly proclaiming her support for Hillary Clinton for President of The United States. Her endorsement was so bold i was intrigued to learn more about her so I invited her to be a guest on my show and she has been a regular contributor ever since.

To call Sister Paula's story interesting might be the understatement of the decade. To navigate through life trapped in the wrong body must be on the same level as being sentenced to life in prison for a crime that you did not commit. To decide to challenge social norms and go against what society has established is proper for men and women must be on the same level as planning your escape from the same prison. Sister Paula has experienced both and shockingly has come out of the experience with a stronger faith than she had before going thru it.

Sister Paula has given us a look into a world that most people would never see. Her insight is not just that of a gay man but as a transgender woman who then went on to become a preacher. This destroys the mindset that limitations are put on us because of our orientation. Sister Paula is the living proof the only limitations we are truly subject to is the limitation of thought. Sister Paula did not believe that being transgender is a reason to not become a preacher therefore it was no road block for her.

Over the past few years I have had countless conversations with Paula about her childhood, her parents, discovering she was transgender and the issues that come with transitioning. Sister Paula has never held back or been too shy to tell me about her experiences. I have sat in my radio studio countless times in awe of her ability to recall the details of experiences with her mother and her father as well as her willingness to share with the world some of the most painful and happiest moments of her life.

This book will serve as a motivation NOT JUST to those who have this struggle, but it will serve as a motivation to any of us who have struggles in our lives. You can lay down and quit or you can take the Paula method and stand up, move forward and be all that your being allows.

This is the story of a survivor. This is the story of a dreamer. This is the story of a WINNER.

I invite you to learn more about Sister Paula thru this book. Listen to her story. Hear Her Song!

Sir Darryl

Drag preacher can't change image

"I don't really like the term 'drag evangelist,' but so far it's all I've come up with to call myself," says Paula Nielsen.

"On my TV show I just call myself 'Sister Paula.'"

For as long as Paula can remember — even back when she was a little boy named Larry — she has been driven to do two things: "live as the woman I know I really am, and preach the gospel of the Lord."

Paula, a transsexual, has lived as a woman since 1963. For a number of years in the '60s, she worked as church secretary in a fundamentalist church in San Diego. No one suspected she was anything other than the woman who answered the phone and did the typing.

Her life as a woman and her faith are closely linked in Paula's life.

"When I was growing up, I knew I was different, but I thought I was the only one like me. My one-on-one relationship with God got me through all the teasing and cruelty in school. Now I feel the call to help others."

Late last year, after appearing as a guest on a religious cable television program, Paula was asked to be host of her own Christian broadcast. After a great deal of prayer, she accepted the offer.

Paula called her show "Changing the Image," after her favorite Christian song.

"It just seemed right. Not only would it be the name of the show, it would be the central idea of the show."

"Changing the Image" premiered on cable TV Dec. 7 in the Portland area.

Nancy Harmon was definitely not as happy about Paula's program. Nancy is the head of Love Special Inc. Outreach Ministries. She's a Christian composer and singer and the author of the song "Changing the Image."

After Paula's program had been on the air for nine weeks, she received a letter from Nancy Harmon, claiming Paula had violated copyright laws by calling the program "Changing the Image," by playing Nancy's recording of the song at the end of every program, and by singing the song herself on the fourth show.

Paula called her lawyer. He did some investigation and said it looked like Paula could continue to use the name "Changing the Image." Another lawyer said Paula could use the song itself, as long as she paid royalties.

But Paula felt uncomfortable.

"Here is a woman who writes wonderful, wonderful songs. The holy spirit gives her those songs. And she was asking me not to use one of them."

After more prayer, Paula sent Nancy a letter, agreeing to change the name of any future programs and to stop any use of the song "Changing the Image." She could not, however, edit out the name and song from the programs which had already aired, and which might be aired again. She hoped Nancy would understand.

Nancy didn't. Nancy's lawyer, Lawrence Sherris, responded.

"I represent Love Special, World Outreach Ministries Inc. and Nancy Harmon," wrote Sherris.

"My clients, as Christians, find the connection of Mrs. Harmon and her song with a television show dealing with abnormal sexuality morally repugnant and personally embarrassing."

The letter ended: "We insist . . . if any of the previously broadcast programs are rebroadcast, all use of Mrs. Harmon's voice, song, song title or name be deleted."

"That's the letter that made me mad," says Paula. "My television show does not deal with 'abnormal sexuality,' nor does it describe any 'sexual practices,' abnormal or otherwise. I talk about the holy spirit."

Nevertheless, Paula has agreed to "go the extra mile" and remove all traces of Nancy Harmon's song from the TV show. The next 10-week series of shows will be called "Sister Paula."

The Oregonian 1988

INTRODUCTION

"So Sister Paula is going to tell all?" The rumble coming over the telephone wires wasn't the bombs bursting on Washington, it was a long time friend having himself a belly laugh.

"You may be shocked by some of it," I fired back.

"I takes a lot to shock me."

Just the same, take this from me, "you ain't heard nothing yet."

Go to it, Paula. For years, I have been waiting to be told how you survived for more than seven decades. There's not another person like you on the planet. I can count on you to tell the truth.

Two things have gotten me through: God's protection and my sense of humor."

This book is the life journey of a transsexual seeking acceptance. There are some things, I would just as soon not tell. Joan Rivers once told a guest on her network television show: "No one can smear you if you have told the story yourself." Authors of the Bible did not cover up the sins and mistakes of individuals who were mightily used of God. A researcher won't have to look far to discover the sins of Sister Paula. Yet, the greater fact is that the historian will also discover many wonderful spiritual victories of Sister Paula. Through it all, God's hand has remained on my life.

While on this journey, I have made a few poor choices. However, I have never regretted the decision to change my identity from Larry to Paula. Paula is who I am. I am not "confused" about my gender identity. In my growing up years I was expected to dress and act a certain way and participate in specific activities. Many of my innate desires went contrary to those expectations. Somehow I had the courage to be me.

Shortly after I started the Sister Paula public access television program a man wrote me a letter that said: "I am shocked to see a female impersonator on TV pretending to be a God fearing woman of God." He was wrong. I am not "impersonating" anybody nor am I "pretending" to be anything. Someone once told me that I can be an entertainer or a preacher, but I cannot be both. I respond to this with a Chinese proverb: "Those who say it cannot be done should not interrupt the person doing it."

Four things I have never questioned: (1) my born again experience and baptism with the Holy Spirit, (2) my call to preach the gospel, (3) my being transsexual, and (4) the angelic protection on my life as promised in Psalms 91:3 & 11.

In this book there are shared experiences that readers will have to believe because no one could possibly make then up.

This is my story exactly as I remember it.

1939

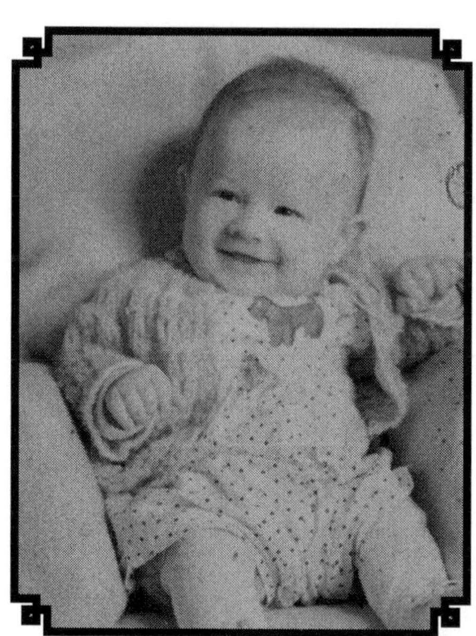

Years As Larry

Growing Up in yhe 40's

1944

1948

A Star Is Born
1938-1943

I made my first appearance into this world on July 13, 1938 at St. Vincent's Hospital in Portland, Oregon. I was destined to become a public figure. My baby picture appeared in the local newspaper when my parents entered me into a baby contest. My full given name was Larry Maclean Nielsen.

In 1942, my sister, Teresa Sue, came along. I vividly recall Mom bringing home the newborn baby girl, wrapped in a blanket. She was called "Terry Sue." Dad affectionately called her "Sue, Sue."

My earliest childhood memories go back to when I was four years old. I loved my tricycle and had a spirit of adventure, which often got me into trouble. For his entire working life, my father was a longshoreman. He was 6' tall, and had a loud booming voice, which I inherited from him. I also inherited my father's height.

All of my life I was told: "You have your mother's brown eyes." Years later, when performing as a drag entertainer, I quipped the line: "I was born with my mother's features, and father's fixtures." Coming at it from a Biblical standpoint, in the Genesis account of creation, the woman was made from the man. On a scale of 1 to 10 -- 1 being "masculine" and 10 being "feminine", I rate myself 8.

As I grew older, my grandmother on father's side, nicknamed Fussbudget, told Mom that her brother in "The Old Country," Scotland, acted just like me. Fussbudget's maiden name was Maclean.

Our home was situated in suburban SE Portland. My bedroom was located in the back portion of the house, just off the kitchen. When in bed I could see the refrigerator door. Late at night, I would often awaken and see Dad standing at the open refrigerator door, guzzling down milk, out of the bottle.

Throughout my growing up years, my role models were all heterosexual. And yet, I was born biologically male, with innate feminine mannerisms far outweighing the masculine. On the other hand, I know straight-laced heterosexual people who were raised by gay parents. Biologically siring children does not necessarily result in good parenting skills. The sexuality of one's parents has nothing to do with the sexuality of the child. It is important that children be raised with love and understanding, being allowed to evolve into who they are.

This was during the turbulent post World War II era. In those days, the enemies of America were called Germans and Japs, two terms that Dad used often. On the Ross Island bridge, which crossed the Willamette River, dividing Portland's east and west side; I recall two life size effigies called Hitler and The Jap. Each day the effigies were pushed out, on a diving board, further and further, until one day they went into the waters of the river.

Throughout most of the decade of the 1940's, post war government rationing came into play. Among other things, cigarettes were rationed. Mom and Dad were smokers. I can still see people lined up for blocks outside the Fred Meyer store on SE 82nd & Foster to buy cigarettes.

As a tyke, I was always getting into mischief. I got poison oak from wandering into the wrong bushes. I sported a swollen lower lip when I put a flower to my mouth and blew into it. This resulted in my being stung by a honeybee. I experienced the excruciating pain of being burned when I put my hand on a hot iron. According to my mother, I raised hell.

Following my father's example, I learned to cuss at an early age. Yelling out: "You sunny-bitch" got me a spanking. Throughout my lifetime, swearing when angry has been the sin that does so easily beset me. (Hebrews 12:1) When I do it in public, folk within a city block radius can hear me.

My greatest adventure during those years was when I ventured away from our house, walking 15 blocks to SE 82nd & Powell, into a Piggly Wiggly grocery store. I walked in and helped myself to the ice cream bars in the display case. The store manager called the police. Mom had also called the police to report that I was missing. While feasting on this cornucopia of frozen goodies, the police officers found me with ice cream smeared all over my face. They took me home. The "rod of correction" was applied to my backside.

While my parents were not churchgoers, they practiced the scriptural admonition "spare the rod and spoil the child." When I did something wrong, I got a spanking. However, I insist that this was not abuse. A spanking, applied to an erring child's backside, is not corporal punishment. There are adults in prisons today, who would be living productive lives had their parents corrected them in this fashion throughout their formative years. (Hebrews 12:5-8)

Fussbudget had four children; my Dad, Alex, Uncle Donald, Aunt Ann and Aunt Margie. During my early childhood, I especially loved Aunt Margie. She was very pretty, and was married to a handsome man named Lester. Sometimes I would spend the night at Aunt Margie's house.

Mom and Dad lectured me about wetting the bed. Rather than spanking me, they laid down the law that I could not spend the night with Aunt Margie until I stopped wetting the bed. The ploy worked. I have never wet the bed since.

In the fall of 1943 came my first day in school at Kellogg Grade School, located close to our home. This day remains crystal clear in memory. It marked a turning point when I first realized that I was different.

The rough and rocky road of life lay before me.

Childhood Lessons

1943-1946

My early grade school years taught me more than just the lessons of "readin', writin', and 'rithmetic."

At five years old I was enrolled in kindergarten at Kellogg Grade School. This brick structure on SE Powell in Portland, with its large playground in front, is still there. The memory of my first day of school, walking up the cement steps to the entrance of the school, is etched vividly in my mind. While I was walking up the steps, a group of kids my age were running along beside me, pointing at me, and laughing in derision. I do not recall what they said. I only knew they were laughing at me. At the conclusion of that first day of school, while I was walking across the playground on my way home, a group of kids chased after me, laughing and mocking. It was then that I first realized I was "different."

This was my first experience with prejudice. I was confused. I could not understand why they were bullying me. Thoughts raced through my mind: "What did I do wrong?" and "What did I ever do to them?" My young mind couldn't comprehend their being mean to me for no reason. This is the insidious evil of bigotry, which escalates into hate crimes, people harassing people who have done nothing to them.

I grew up under this societal structure. In 1943 I had no idea that boys were supposed to act a certain way, and girls another. My natural and innate mannerisms were what society mandated for girls. There was nothing I could do to change that -- it was just who I am. All my life I have envied folk who fit into family and peer expectations, and can blend in with the crowd. This I have never been able to do.

Throughout my lifetime, I stood out in public. Because of that, I was subjected to ridicule. Most of the time I can ignore it. Yet, every time it happens, I still feel deep inner pain; smiling on the outside, hurting on the inside. Born to be different. Born to be hurt.

In 1944, I learned that prejudice has no age limitation, and that adults and children alike are sometimes cruel to those who are "different." My first grade teacher, Mrs. Nelson, was a stern old lady. (The word for someone like her is used regularly in dog kennels). I did not like her, and she did not like me. Consequently, I was always raising hell in her classroom. Mrs. Nelson was nice to the other kids; she was abrupt and abrasive with me.

On the first day of school, Mrs. Nelson told us that if we needed to go to the restroom, to raise our hand and ask to be excused. One day I raised my hand for permission to go to the bathroom. When Mrs. Nelson saw me raise my hand she ignored me. As a result, I peed in my pants. Mom was not amused when I came home all wet.

Another time, when the kids were leaving for lunch, Mrs. Nelson told me to remain at my desk. I do not recall why. With me sitting in an empty classroom, she got up, as if I were not there, and walked out, locking the classroom door behind her. I was trapped there for the duration of the lunch period. Living close by, I normally went home for lunch. When I did not show up, my mother complained to the school principal about this harsh treatment. On another occasion I stormed out of the classroom and went home. I told Mom: "I am never going back there again." Mom escorted me back to the school.

In the fall of 1945 I started the second grade. Unlike Mrs. Nelson, my second grade teacher was very nice to me, and treated me the same as the other kids. I cannot recall her name. We liked each other. I never got into trouble that school year.

Mom and Dad's marriage was beginning to sour. Dad was a womanizer and a boozer. Their relationship was becoming more and more turbulent. Somewhere in between the first and second grade, our family moved out of our small house on SE 67th. Our new home was a larger Victorian type structure, a few blocks north on the same street, on the other side of SE Powell. Unlike our previous home, this one had a large front porch, a spacious living room, next to a large dining area. Behind the dining area, south of the kitchen, was my bedroom.

Two blocks north of our home was a large white wooden church. It was there that I attended Sunday School for the first time. I was taught the story of Jesus. That year, I was in the Sunday School Christmas program. Mom and Dad were not church-goers, but they did come for special events. I enjoyed standing on the platform with the other kids, with Mom and Dad in the audience, as we sang:

Away in a manger, no crib for a bed,
The little Lord Jesus lay down His sweet head.
The stars in the sky looked down where he lay,
The little Lord Jesus, asleep in the hay.

Often, Dad's brother, Uncle Donald, and his red headed wife, Dorothy, came over to play pinochle with my parents. Dorothy's maiden name was Hotchkiss. The family nicknamed her "Hotchee." One such family social visit was on Christmas Eve of 1945. I wanted to stay up and be present when Santa Clause delivered my gifts.

Suddenly, there was a sound on the front porch. Dad looked out the large living room window, and announced that it was Santa Claus. He carried on a conversation with the mythical character. Dad told me that Santa would not deliver my Christmas presents until I was in bed, sound asleep, and that Santa Claus was preparing to leave. Dad said to old St. Nick: "If Larry goes to bed, will you come back with his presents?" Dad told me that Santa agreed to this. In the meantime, he would deliver gifts to other kids in the neighborhood, and then return to see if I had gone to bed. The ploy worked. I promptly went to bed. Mom, Dad, Uncle Donald and Hotchee resumed their pinochle game with no more interruptions from me. When I awoke on Christmas morning, there were my gifts under the Christmas tree. Santa kept his word.

While living in this house, in 1946, I first learned the painful lesson of death and dying. My beloved Aunt Margie was hospitalized with health issues, complicated by double pneumonia. She never came home from the hospital. I will never forget the evening when Dad came to my bedroom to tell me that Aunt Margie had died, and that we would never see her again. The emotional pain was indescribable. I cried myself to sleep that night. This was my first encounter with the pain of sorrow that comes from the loss of a loved one. I couldn't understand why God would take a person I loved, and who treated me with kindness, away from me. I learned the lesson that:

There is no love without sorrow,
and no sorrow without love.

My parents would soon get a divorce. Our days in the Victorian house in SE Portland were ending. Another phase of my life was about to begin. There were more lessons for me to learn.

Guilds Lake
1946-1947

Located in the far NW section of Portland is an industrial section called "Guilds Lake." Guilds Lake was the site of the 1905 Lewis and Clark Exposition and Fair, which brought great prosperity to Portland. The buildings and grounds of the fair were almost immediately turned into an industrial area when the Fair closed The giant retailer Montgomery Ward established their mail order catalog headquarters near Guilds Lake. (Dad always called it: "Monkey Ward's"). Their building is now a business park, called Montgomery Park. (Hence, the big neon sign atop the structure only needed two letters changed...from Ward to Park). In 1946,

Guilds Lake was a post-war "defense housing" project -- long duplex type complex apartments. Workers in the Kaiser shipyards also resided in these buildings.

Mom, getting ready to divorce Dad, got him to sell the Victorian house in SE Portland. When my parents separated in 1946, Mom, my sister Teresa, and I, moved to Guilds Lake. Aunt Lorraine (Mom's sister) and Uncle Bob (Potter) already lived there with my cousins Jimmy, Richard, Doreen, Annette, and Terry. At first, we stayed with Aunt Lorraine and Uncle Bob. Eventually, Mom rented her own apartment in Guilds Lake. Dad had moved to a rented room downtown at the Gilmore Hotel on 18th & West Burnside. Mom went to business school and landed a clerical bookkeeping job at Davidson's Bakery, a leading producer of retail bread and various baked goods.

Uncle Bob was a heavy boozer. While living with them, I recall a time when Bob came home in a drunken rage, and was mean to Aunt Lorraine, even to the point of choking her. While he was never abusive to his kids and he treated me okay, he was abusive to his wife. And he cheated on her. And yet, Lorraine stayed with him until his death in 1963 when he, while intoxicated, slipped off a Columbia River dock and drowned.

When turning 8 years old in 1946, I looked forward to my tenth birthday. I thought that would make me grownup. One day I told Uncle Bob that I had no muscles (biceps) on my arms. (My arms and legs have always been very feminine). Charles Atlas, the muscle man/body builder, was featured in comic books and in the Sunday newspapers. He was a public personification of masculinity. I asked Uncle Bob why I didn't look like Charles Atlas. He told me that I needed to go outside every day, pick up a heavy object, and exercise with it. I picked up everything from tools to an ax, big rocks, bricks – you name it. My efforts to develop biceps were short lived. To this day I have maintained my feminine arms and legs.

My parents' separation, which led to a divorce, was Mom's idea. No longer would she tolerate Dad's loose lifestyle of drinking, carousing, and one night stands. Dad did not want the divorce. While Mom, Teresa, and I were still living at Aunt Lorraine's, Dad often visited us. One day, with tears streaming down his face, he begged Mom to give him another chance. About my sister, Teresa and I he said: "They are the best kids on earth." He was 30 years old at the time.

In his attempts to get back into Mom's good graces, Dad did two things: First, he got religion for a short time. He attended Hinson Memorial Baptist Church, in SE Portland. Albert Johnson was the pastor. At Dad's request, the pastor called on Mom, beseeching her to give Dad another chance. The pastor's plea fell on deaf ears. Hinson's Sunday night services were broadcast over the radio. While driving, Dad listened to the church service on his car radio. Without revealing Dad's identity, the pastor told how Dad begged Mom to give him another chance. The pastor asked his congregants and radio listeners to pray that their marriage might be salvaged. It didn't happen.

Second, Dad started taking Teresa and me out to movies, to dinner, and he bought us toys, clothes, etc -- anything we wanted, we got. Not wanting my parents to split up, I tried to talk Mom into taking him back. It didn't matter. Her mind was made up. She proceeded with, and got, the divorce.

Most of my third grade was spent at Guilds Lake Grade School. Here was another teacher with whom I just didn't get along. Why, I don't know. She was a middle-aged woman and her name was Mrs. Hinshaw. As with Mrs. Nelson in the first grade, in Mrs. Hinshaw's third grade class I raised hell. I interrupted her, refused to do things she asked, and even one day physically fought her, pounding at her shoulders. More than once she sent me to the principal's office for reprimanding. She gave me low grades on my report card. (Looking ahead briefly, I finished out the third grade at Sherwood Grade School. Had this not happened Mrs.

Hinshaw probably would have flunked me, and I would have had to take the third grade over). Under the comments section of my report card, Mrs. Hinshaw wrote: "Larry does not give attention to his studies, does not do what he is told, and acts like someone half his age." I asked Dad what that meant. "It means you act like a four year old."

I got into major trouble twice - both times influenced by Aunt Lorraine's oldest son, my cousin, Jimmy. One afternoon, during recess on the school playground, Jimmy came up to me and said: "When the bell rings let's just leave and not go back in." Being unhappy at that school, I was easily influenced. This happened a couple of times until the principal notified Mom what was going on. The swift correction of the rod was again applied to my backside. My career in playing hooky came to an abrupt halt.

Another time, at a small grocery store in Guilds Lake, Jimmy taught me how to shoplift. Langendorf chocolate, cream -filled cupcakes sold in packages of two for a nickel. I developed a habit of walking into the store and picking up a package of cupcakes. Then, while walking around, I would slip the package into my coat pocket, and then exit the store without paying for them. This crime caper was short lived. One day, outside the store, a clerk came up from behind me and said: "I'll take that nickel." He swiftly removed the cupcakes from my coat pocket. The police were called. I was terrified of being taken to jail. The cops took me home.

Years later, in talking about this incident with Mom, I recalled how frightened I was of going to jail. She said: "You got a darn good spanking. Do you remember that?" I do not recall the spanking but then, I got lots of them in those days. All I remember was how frightened I was of going to jail.

Dad's brother, Uncle Donald, and his wife, Aunt Hotchee also lived at Guilds Lake. Hotchee would send my cousin Jimmy and me to the Safeway Store – located next door to Monkey Ward's

– giving us money to buy her groceries. One day, when the groceries were loaded up in the shopping cart, Jimmy said to me: "We are going to walk out of here without paying for this." We split the money that Hotchee gave us. If asked, we would say we "lost" the sales slip.

We got away with it for a short time, UNTIL: When we got meat from the butcher, he would put a price slip on it. When the meat was paid for at the front cashier's counter, this slip would be removed from the package of meat. When we took the groceries to Hotchee, she noticed that the slip was still on the meat package. She caught on to what we were doing, and confronted us about not paying for the groceries. Jimmy denied it. I can still hear him saying: "Honest, Hotchee. When we went through the front line, there were a lot of people, and they were very busy. They must have forgotten to tear the slip off." Hotchee did not believe him. She never asked us to go grocery shopping for her again.

The "rod of correction" was teaching me important Biblical principles of right and wrong. This remains with me to this very day. The scriptures declare: "Train up a child in the way he should go, and when he is old he will not depart from it". (Proverbs 22:6) It is important that kids be taught right from wrong in their formative years. "God's Ten Rules For Living", The Ten Commandments, declare: "Thou Shalt Not Steal." When these rules are followed early on in the lives of children, they are less likely to become criminals when they reach adulthood.

I also recall a Bible class in the home of a lady in a Guilds Lake complex apartment. She told Bible stories with flannel-graph materials. Two Bible stories I learned there are the Old Testament story of Joseph who was treated unjustly by his jealous brothers and sold into slavery; and the New Testament account of Jesus, who travailed in intercessory prayer in the Garden of Gethsemane, and sweat drops of blood. At this young age the Holy Spirit was planting seeds in my heart which would soon evolve into my salvation and call to preach the Gospel.

At Guilds Lake Grade School, I developed a puppy love crush on one of the boys in my third grade class. His name was Cary. I did not understand my feelings for him. All I knew was that I thought about him most of the time. On the playground, when he would be friendly with the other kids, especially the girls, I would feel strong jealousy. This was the beginning of a pattern, which would follow me throughout my grade and high school years. Every time we moved to a new school, there would be another boy I would develop strong feelings for.

The fondest memory of my Guilds Lake days was the discovery of going to the movies. Cousin Jimmy told me about the Blue Mouse Theater downtown on SW 11th and Washington. Jimmy, Richard, and I went there on Saturday afternoons. And I have been an avid movie buff ever since. For years, I had a fantasy/dream of owning my own chain of movie palace theaters. In the 1920's, the Blue Mouse had been one of the first theaters to show talkies, like Al Jolson in The Jazz Singer. I loved that theater, with all of its fancy decorations and huge posters of coming attractions. Little did I know that in the late 1950's and 60's it was to become a popular spot for gay men seeking anonymous amour. Even in the 1940's, straight teenagers would neck and carry on in the balcony.

Mom would give me 50 cents to go to the movies. If I had a whole dollar, I felt wealthy. 20 cents fare for the electric trolley streetcar (10 cents each way), 20 cents for admission to the show, with a dime left over for a bag of popcorn. The aroma of popcorn hit people's nostrils the second they walked into the lobby.

This was before the advent of television. In the 1940's the Blue Mouse specialized in movies for kids Every Saturday afternoon, the theater would be jam packed with screaming kids. We were in seventh heaven with two black & white westerns, six technicolor cartoons, a newsreel, topped off by a cliffhanger serial. The cartoons included Walt Disney caricatures, Donald Duck, Mickey Mouse, et al. and Looney Tunes favorites Bugs Bunny, Porky Pig, et al.

Singing cowboys were in their heyday. The biggest of the singing western stars were Roy Rogers and Dale Evans, billed as The King of the Cowboys and Queen of the West, with Roy's horse Trigger, and their gray-bearded comedy sidekick, Gabby Hayes. I idolized Roy and Dale – they were my role models. As I grew older, my love for them increased. Another top singing cowboy was Gene Autry, with his comedy sidekick, Smiley Burnett. Other movies on the Blue Mouse bill included cowboy stars The Lone Ranger, with his horse Silver, and Indian sidekick Tonto; Red Ryder, and of course, William Boyd as Hop-along Cassidy.

The westerns had heroes and villains, good guys and the bad guys. Of course, the good guys were the cowboy stars, the heroes. At the end of the movie, the good guys always won out over the bad guys. Good always triumphed in the final reel. Movies of this decade usually had happy endings. They portrayed life as we would like it to be.

The 20-minute serials would end each week with a hero in a precarious situation – anything from a train coming at them, being on a conveyor belt about to be sawed in half by a buzz saw; and then continued until next week. From week-to-week I lived to see the next chapter. Hence, they were classified cliffhangers.

While we were living in Guilds Lake Mom remarried. Her second husband was a handsome man named Frank Young. Frank worked as an electrical lineman, and his work required that he relocate in Northern California. Since my sister Teresa had not yet started school, she went with Mom and Frank to California. Consequently, I went to live with Grandma Hazel (Mom's mother), and her husband Joe, on their farm in Sherwood, Oregon. Dad still lived in the Gilmore Hotel. I was 9 years old – the year was 1947. The path of my life journey was about to take me from being a city slicker into the world of a farm boy, complete with overalls.

Sunbonnet Sally or Overall Jim?

1947-1948

So far on my life journey I had lived in urban areas of Portland. From there I went to live on a farm. No longer was I a "city slicker". I became a country boy. I missed life in the big city. Looking back, it was on the farm where I discovered the true meaning of love from animals. It was there that I learned many of life's important lessons that I would not appreciate today had I not lived on Grandma's farm.

In 1946/47 Sherwood was a small farming town, located about 25 miles southwest of Portland. Folks grew crops and raised livestock. Today it has evolved into suburban shopping malls and modern housing/apartment projects. Little farmland still exists.

US Highway 99 linked Sherwood with Portland at an intersection called Six Corners. The one-mile road between Six Corners and Sherwood was paved with cement. Two miles father west from the intersection was a dirt road leading to Grandma Hazel and Joe's farm. From that dirt road, our dirt driveway led to a complex of house, barn, and a few other buildings. Past our farm, the road wound further up into the heavily wooded hills. A little wooden country church stood overlooking our farm at the top of the west facing slope.

Grandma was a very industrious, hard working woman. Born in 1900, she passed on in 1970. A song from her generation, that she loved to sing, was, Pack up your troubles in your old kit bag, and smile, smile, smile.

Grandma and Joe's livelihood came from the livestock and crops on the farm. The farming was also for our own food consumption. Grandma often said: "Most of the food on our table is raised right here on the ranch." She baked bread and biscuits and she whipped cream and butter from the fresh cream produced by the cows. I especially remember the homemade strawberry shortcake with whipped cream. To this day I have never eaten any desert that topped this. And my cousin Richard still says, "That woman made the best homemade apple pie."

The farmhouse was a small two-bedroom ranch style home. The cooking was done on an old-fashioned wood stove. Part of my chores was to help Joe chop wood for the stove, which also provided our heat. Hot water for bathing and washing clothes was also heated up on the stove. Grandma washed our clothes in a big brass tub with a scrub board, hanging them out to dry on the clothesline. Having no bathroom facilities, we bathed in the same big brass tub. Behind the house was an outhouse. I still remember having to get up in the middle of the night to go to the bathroom, walking in the blustery winter cold to the outhouse and back.

West of the house, between the driveway and the cow pasture was a large garden where Grandma grew strawberries, potatoes, carrots, and tomatoes. We even had an apple tree. Behind the outhouse was a barn that housed the cows; behind that, a rabbit hutch, a chicken coupe, and a pigpen. We also had two goats, and ducks. I helped with milking the cows. East of the driveway was a corn patch that bordered another road which also lead to the church.

West of the dirt driveway, and the portion in front of our house, was the cow pasture. We had eight cows, two of which stand out in my mind. Shirley was a redheaded type of cow with small protruding horns. When Shirley lowered her head and pointed at you with her horns, in warning, this meant you had better veer off. And then, there was my beloved Daisy, a large, gentle, motherly brown cow whom I would snuggle up for hours. I promised Daisy that, when I moved back to the city she would come with me. She became ill with a swollen udder and died. I don't recall if she was put to sleep, or what. I only remember the sorrow I experienced when Daisy left us.

It was at this time of my life that I became keenly aware of my love for animals. Animals do not know prejudice and bigotry. They are loving creatures who instinctively know who loves them. They respond to, and return, love. It doesn't matter if you are lesbian, gay, straight, bisexual, or transgender. An animal's love is totally unconditional. Throughout my lifetime, I have received love from my pets when people didn't like me. This has helped get me through a long and difficult life.

An old cabaret song says:

Like the farmer said, the other day,
to keep the milk pails full,
You've got to have contented cows,
and one contented bull.

I am not sure how many bulls we had. I do remember one. He wouldn't bother you if you didn't bother him. Like Shirley, when he lowered his head, pointing at you with his horns, you backed off. He must have been contented – the cows reproduced. I recall one day when my cousin Jimmy came to visit, I rushed out, greeted him excitedly, and exclaimed, "Shirley had her calf."

My earliest experience as an entertainer was on the Sherwood farm. Out in the cow pastures were tree stumps. Often in the afternoon, I would use a tree stump as a stage and empty coffee can as a microphone, and re-enact movies, entertaining the cows. The cows were a captive audience as they grazed nonchalantly, chewing their cuds, without a care in the world.

In listing the animals on the farm, I have saved the best for the last: Grandma's rust colored mutt, a playful, loving, and affectionate dog, named Mugsy. I loved Mugsy and he loved me. We did everything together. Mugsy slept with me. Often I would wake up to Mugsy licking my face. When I traveled up and down the dusty country roads, riding my red and white Schwinn bike that Mom had sent me from California, Mugsy ran along beside me, smiling, and barking happily. Just as Jody, in the movie The Yearling, dreamed about his childhood days running across the open fields with his pet fawn, Flag -- even so I dream of my carefree childhood days, back home on the farm, with Mugsy running along beside me. Among all my childhood memories, I cherish this one the most.

Grandma and Joe did not go to church. Some deeply religious neighbor farmers, the Abershires, took me to church with them. It was there I developed my first crush on a man. He was not a boy, like the one in Guilds Lake, but a dishwater blond, handsome man in his 20's. His name was Wally. Wally was a deacon at the little white country church, located on the hill above our farm. Wally, in his Sunday go to meeting, striped zoot suit was so good looking. I kept my feelings for Wally a secret. My lifelong dream of being a preacher's wife probably started the first time I saw Wally.

It was also at this church that I experienced my very first church potluck supper. Everybody brought food. I went crazy when surrounded by that enormous cornucopia of delectable goodies – fried chicken, comfort food casseroles, salads, and deserts filled the long table in the church basement dining area. Even after everybody else had stopped eating, and were listening to a guest speaker, I was still pushing down food. I couldn't get enough of it.

One luxury we did have in the farmhouse was a radio. Night-after-night I sat by the radio listening to the programs. My entertainment included comedy shows such as Fibber McGee and Molly, Jack Benny with his sidekick Rochester, The Great Gildersleeve, Our Miss Brooks, Judy Canova, and Baby Snooks, a little girl character played by that wonderful veteran vaudeville comedienne extraordinaire, Fanny Brice. And then, there were the spooky radio shows such as Inner Sanctum (the squeaking door), and The Whistler. And game shows such as It Pays To Be Ignorant. The song went, "To be dumb, to be dense, to be ignorant."

I loved to imitate the radio commercials. A sponsor of Baby Snooks was Jello and Jello pudding. The commercial went: J E L L ---O. Another jingle went: "F A, Franco American" (canned spaghetti). And, cigarette commercial tunes: "C A M E L -- S" (I'd walk a mile for a Camel), LSMFT (Lucky Strike means fine tobacco), and the cute bellboy's slogan, "Call for Phillip Maur-ees" (Morris). Then there was a detergent commercial tune: "DUZ does everything". Often, when riding in the back of the pick up truck, I would sing and re-enact those commercials. Oh yes! Those were the days. My love to entertain started during my year on the farm.

I always looked forward to Dad's visits from downtown Portland. He usually took me to the movies. Sometimes we went to downtown Portland when I would insist on going to the Blue Mouse. He also took me to the Robin Hood Theater in Sherwood. My fondest memory of this theater was the MGM classic The Yearling starring Gregory Peck, Jane Wyman, and the child star Claude Jarman, Jr. A heartwarming story of a boy and his pet fawn, that movie made me cry then, and still does every time I view it on television or video. Another movie my Dad took me to see in nearby Newberg at the Francis Theater was Walt Disney's Bambi, another classic that makes me cry every time I see it. These wonderful movie family classics will never be duplicated.

I spent the remainder of the third grade, and the entire fourth grade, at Sherwood Grade School. The grade and high schools were about two blocks apart. The same school bus transported kids to both schools. On her 18th birthday, I told a girl on the bus: "Now you are a woman." She found that amusing, and often told her peers what I had said.

Unlike Mrs. Hinshaw at Guilds Lake, my third grade teacher liked me. My grades improved and I passed the third grade. I also fondly recall my fourth grade teacher, Mrs. Keitcher. She was a very caring and compassionate Christian woman, and a middle age plump motherly type. She always treated me with kindness and respect. I cherish her memory.

In 1947 there was a post-war rationing of paper products, such as paper towels and drinking straws. We were only allowed to have one drinking straw each. During a lunch period, I took two straws. Mrs. Keitcher came over to me at the cafeteria table and kindly asked: "How come two straws?" After that, I only used one.

It is noteworthy how the role models one has in their growing up years affect their entire life. This is especially true of the example set by schoolteachers. Interestingly enough, when I liked my teacher, I got good grades. When I disliked a teacher, my grades dropped.

During the fourth grade, I first became aware of my desire to wear girls' clothes. I literally loathed the Levi overalls, with the bib, that I had to wear. I thought overalls were ugly. There was a girl classmate, who sat across the aisle from me, named Gertrude. Her parents were prominent and wealthy citizens in the community. Gertrude wore the prettiest colorful ruffled dresses. I would sit at my desk, looking at her, and I yearned to be able to dress like that.

It was also at this time that I became aware that I hated participating in boys' sports activities. I preferred to play hopscotch and jump rope with the girls. In those days, surprisingly enough, jump rope was considered effeminate. This was in spite of the fact that grown muscled athletic men jump rope to keep in shape.

I was expected to engage in sports with the other boys. During recess on the school playground I would migrate to the girls. Sometimes they wouldn't let me play with them. And so I started stealing money from Grandma's purse to buy candy bars for the girls so they would accept me into their playground activities.

It wasn't long before Grandma discovered money missing from her purse. She questioned me about it. At first, I denied it. This denial was followed with a guilty conscience. Finally, I confessed I took the money. I told Grandma why I did it, and promised it wouldn't happen again. This time I did not get a spanking. I learned the painful lesson that you cannot buy friendship and acceptance.

Once I was part of a performance given during a school program. The skit was called Sunbonnet Sally & Overall Jim. Three boy/girl couples were chosen for the routine. Since I always wore overalls, I was one chosen for the part of overall Jim. I came right out and said to Mrs. Keitcher: "I don't WANT to be overall Jim; I would rather be Sunbonnet Sally!". Of course, my request was not granted. The teacher gently said, "no."

One summer afternoon, after the fourth grade was over, I was lounging in bathing trunks on a blanket in the front yard, thinking about Mom. Lo and behold, a car came racing down the dirt driveway. It was Mom, Frank, and my sister Teresa. Also, a new family member was included in the entourage. From her marriage to Frank Mom had a new baby boy, named Dennis. They stayed with us on the farm for a short time. Mom was so happy to have all of her kids together again.

Frank's dad lived in Kelso, Washington, about 50 miles north of Portland. And so, by autumn, before starting the fifth grade, Mom, Frank, Teresa, Dennis, and I loaded up the car and off to Kelso we went. My days on Grandma's farm came to a close. Once again, it was time to move on. The years 1948/49 beckoned with new adventures, new discoveries.

My awareness of wanting to cross dress and my physical attraction to boys were going to become even more apparent in the next chapter of my life.

Darwin & "The Spider Lady"
1948-1949

North of Portland, about 50 miles in Washington State, are Kelso and Longview, two medium size towns in Cowlitz county. Kelso is situated east of the Cowlitz River. Directly west of the Cowlitz River is Longview. In 1948 the major industry for this area were two paper mills located on the banks of the Columbia River.

Mom, Frank, Teresa, Dennis and I finally arrived at Frank's dad's little wooden house, located on the north side of Kelso, where we were to stay temporarily. The car trip from Sherwood had seemed long and arduous in my 10-year-old mind. This was prior to the time of the major freeways such as I-5.

The house into which we eventually moved was east of the highway, part way up a hill. It was a two-bedroom house with a garage. Mom and Frank had the main bedroom, Teresa and Dennis the other bedroom. I slept in the woodshed adjacent to the house with a wooden bed frame and a sleeping bag. We acquired a rust colored dog, named Rusty, who slept with me in the shed.

Frank and I did not get along. Mom wrote Dad saying that I was impossible. At the time, I felt that Frank was mean to Teresa and me. One day he gave her a spanking for using laundry detergent to wash her rubber doll. In the next few years I observed that parents will let their biological kids get away with things that they will reprimand their step-kids for doing. However, other than an occasional spanking, Frank was not abusive to any of us.

Frank landed a job at Longview Fiber Company. Soon after, Grandma and Joe left their rented farm in Sherwood. Joe got a job at Longview Fiber by fibbing about his age. Joe also thought Frank was mean to Teresa and I. Defining the word mean as administering spankings, I thought Joe was far worse than Frank ever was.

As I grew older, my love for the movies increased. Kelso had two theaters. One was the Liberty Theater that changed its bill three times weekly. Like the Blue Mouse in Portland, the Liberty often played films aimed at grade and high school kids. On a Saturday afternoon kids would line up for blocks to get in.

Included on the Liberty's weekend bill was a black and white cliffhanger serial featuring Superman that had 15 weekly 20 -minute episodes. In everyday life, Superman was a reporter for The Daily Planet newspaper named Clark Kent; his news reporter colleagues were Lois Lane and Jimmy Olson. The moment the comic book image of Superman hit the screen, the kids would yell and scream.

The villain in this 1948 piece was a woman, who hid out in a cave, called The Spider Lady. While Superman had X-ray vision eyes, he was unable to see through lead. The walls of the Spider Lady's hideout were made of lead, keeping Superman from finding her. The Spider lady wore a slinky tight black floor length dress, a Lone Ranger type eye mask, and a blonde wig. When she would leave her cave hideout, she removed the wig so as not to be identified. Underneath the drag queen type wig were her natural black tresses.

The Spider Lady's male cohorts would capture their victims and take them to the cave hideout. She had a platform with a big spider web, made with electrical wiring. The victim would be placed on the platform. When The Spider Lady pulled a switch, the wires were activated, and vibrations would cause the victim to fall back on to the electric spider web, resulting in their electrocution.

At the end of one episode the Spider Lady was holding the two Daily Planet reporters captive. Lois Lane was placed on the platform. The segment ended right when Lois was starting to fall back on to the lethal wires. Throughout the week, I could hardly wait for the next Saturday to see what would happen next. At the beginning of the next episode, just as Lois Lane was about to hit the electric spider web, Jimmy Olson broke loose from his bonds and -- just in the nick of time – pulled her off the platform, rescuing her from a fatal fate.

I became fascinated and enamored by The Spider Lady. Although I did not realize it then, this fantasy character was awakening in me desires to don a wig and do show biz drag, even though I did not know that this type of show business existed. It also piqued my curiosity of what it would be like to "capture" someone and have control over them. Although I was not consciously aware of it at the time, erotic drag fantasies were beginning to stir within me.

Mom and Frank saw to it that Teresa and I went to Sunday school. Every Sunday, the bus from the Kelso Assembly of God took us to Sunday school, transporting us back home immediately after. We usually didn't stay for the morning church service. I recall with deep fondness my Sunday school teacher, a buxom elderly mother of Israel we called Sister England. She was very nice to me. Occasionally when I would remain for the church service, I would always sit next to her.

In those days evangelical churches frowned on theater going. In a Sunday school class, Sister England asked us kids: "How do you think I would feel if I saw one of you lined up in front of a theater?" I do not know if she ever saw me in the long line of kids Saturday afternoons at the Liberty. Even after her death, I always wondered if Sister England could see me, when standing in line to get into the movies.

When Sister England passed away unexpectedly, I again lost someone whom I loved, and who had given me love. The replacement Sunday school teacher was a young college guy who did not like me. After that, as long as we lived in Kelso, I no longer looked forward to Sunday school. In fact, I would have stopped going had Mom and Frank not made me go.

My fifth grade started at Kelso Grade School, and was completed across the river at Kessler Grade School in Longview.

Kelso Grade school, was an old single-story brick box. I disliked the teacher, Mrs. Pierce. A younger pretty divorcee, she lived in a two-story brick apartment structure in downtown Kelso. And like Mrs. Nelson and Mrs. Hinshaw before her, she definitely did not like me. Mrs. Pierce was always reprimanding and humiliating me in front of the entire class. I sassed her, and she often sent me to the principal's office.

I liked it when Mrs. Pierce was not there. Our substitute teacher, Mrs. Rakestraw, was a prim and proper older lady who dressed in conservative women's business suits. She was nicer to me than Mrs. Pierce. Carman Miranda movies were in vogue. Mrs. Rakestraw and Carmen Miranda, being exact opposite types, I found it amusing to visualize Mrs. Rakestraw in a Carman Miranda costume, complete with the big fruit headdress. I thought of her as Rumba Dancer Rakestraw. One day, in an unguarded moment, I shared my humorous title with Mrs. Pierce. I can't remember the specifics, but she sure chewed me out!

My favorite subject in the fifth grade was geography. I poured through the Encyclopedia, researching various cities across the United States. I was particularly fascinated with New York City, Times Square, and the numerous movie palaces of the 1940's. The world's largest theater, Radio City Music Hall, particularly intrigued me. The classroom had a pull down map of the United States. As the class was preparing to go to the school cafeteria for lunch one day, I remember running my hand across the map, like traveling from one city to the other, across America. I turned around and the entire class, lined up by the door, was watching me with amusement.

In the 1948 presidential election, the candidates were Republican Thomas Dewey and Democrat Harry Truman, of "the buck stops here" fame. One day Thomas Dewey came through Kelso on a train, speaking from a platform at the railroad station. Our Kelso fifth grade class made a group trip to see him. The perfectly cropped, mustached Dewey was very charming, shaking people's hands and goggling people's children. In spite of this, however, he lost the election to Truman.

My family were all Democrats. I don't know of any relative, over the years (myself included) who ever voted for a Republican candidate. We believed that the Republicans were out to line the pockets of the rich. The Democrats, on the other hand, wanted to help the working people, the elderly, and the indigent. I still believe that.

One day in 1949 as we were getting ready to go to lunch, we suddenly heard an ominous loud rumbling. It was so loud my first thought was that we were being bombed by enemy forces. The windows started shaking violently. The overhead lights, large round glass encasements that hung by long chains from the ceiling, started weaving back and forth and in circles. The building shook intensely. This was the great 1949 Pacific Northwest earthquake. In the school playground, during afternoon recess, my sister Teresa (in the second grade) was not only very frightened, she worried that the quake would hit again.

One of the devastating effects of the earthquake was the cracked wall on the east side of the Liberty Theater. This resulted in the theater's temporary closure. On the playground, the boys taunted me, saying; "You won't be able to find out what happened to The Spider Lady." I was always taking about the Superman serial to classmates. Within a couple of weeks, the theater reopened. Even though I finally did see the final episode with The Spider Lady, I can't remember her fate.

Sitting across the aisle at a desk in the Kelso classroom was a boy classmate named Darwin. Even though I had not reached the age of thinking about having sex, Darwin awakened erotic thoughts within me. Even at the age of 10, Darwin was a sexy little devil. He was my type, sitting there with his legs spread out in sexy Levis. I had always looked at my friend Gertrude at Sherwood Grade School, wishing I could dress like her. But when I looked at Darwin, I wondered what he would look like in jockey shorts. And I fantasized about being able to be The Spider Lady, capturing him, and controlling him. To be sure, my thoughts certainly did not include electrocution!

My feelings toward Cary in Guilds Lake, and Wally in Sherwood, were puppy love crushes, kind of like being in love. With Darwin, on the other hand, my thoughts were strictly on a physical level. I carefully guarded all three fantasies as my secret thoughts. No one, not even the guys themselves, had any idea that I had these kind of thoughts about them. They were suppressed inside me. There was no understanding person I could talk to. No support groups of any kind. I was totally alone with my secrets that, if exposed, would bring me shame. To be sure, I was not ashamed.

Because Frank's paper mill job was in Longview, we soon moved into Huntington Villa, a complex of apartment buildings in Longview, similar to the defense houses in Guilds Lake. Prior to moving to Longview, Frank took our dog Rusty a couple miles north of Kelso and left him there. This made me very sad, and I prayed that Rusty would find a home. Apparently, pets were not allowed in Huntington Villa. I do know we had no animals there.

In those days, Longview was a much prettier town than Kelso. Downtown Longview featured a wide main street, lined with trees. Near downtown was the stately Montecito Hotel, and Lake Sacajewa Park complete with well kept greenery.

Longview also had two theaters. One was a large movie showcase, complete with a huge balcony, named the Columbia Theater. One day I asked the theater manager for a job. He told me to come back when I reached age 18. This was my first introduction to a movie palace. I went to stores all over town, unsuccessfully looking for a photograph of the Columbia's auditorium. Today the Columbia is still used for stage presentations.

Just down the street from the Columbia was the Longview

Theater. Smaller than the Columbia, it also had a balcony. Its counterpart theater in Kelso was also named after the town. Both theaters showcased the entertaining Technicolor MGM musicals such as: The Barkley's of Broadway with Fred Astaire and Ginger Rogers, and A Date With Judy with Jane Powell and Elizabeth Taylor when they were teenagers. The Longview and Kelso theaters also featured the wonderful full-length Walt Disney movies that delighted family audiences.

Walt Disney's So Dear To My Heart with child stars Bobby Driscoll and Luana Patten had a significant impact on me. This was the story of a country boy's love for his pet lamb, which happened to be a black sheep. The "oddball" lamb had to be fed milk with a baby bottle because the mother would not nurse him along with her "normal" white babies. Bobby decided to enter the black sheep into a contest at the County Fair to receive the Blue Ribbon award. The movie had an animated section with a wise old owl, giving Bobby encouragement with the delightful song Stick-to'it-ivity.

In the final reel, the black lamb did not receive the Blue Ribbon award. Instead, the judges honored the lamb that was "different" with a Special Award. This movie was especially an inspiration to me because it was about one of God's creatures, being "born different" from the run-of-the mill, and receiving a special honor. As I had been "born different" myself, even at the age of ten this film gave me much comfort.

Further down Longview's main street was a smaller abandoned theater named the Roxy Theater. From our Huntington Villa apartment, we could see the back of its auditorium. Next door to the old theater was a barbershop. I asked the barber about the theater and found out he had a key to it. At my request, he showed me the auditorium. I told Teresa about it. One day, after school, I took her to be shown the inside of the theater. Mom and Frank were very angry about our going into an empty facility with an older male stranger. It didn't matter that nothing bad happened to us; the fact was that the barber could have been a child molester.

My folks instilled in me the importance of earning money honestly, by working. To pay for movie admissions, I got a job selling the local newspaper. Paper boy "hawkers" were still around. The newspapers sold for a nickel. Each day, after school, I would go to the newspaper office to purchase newspapers two for a nickel, and then go out in the streets and sell them for a nickel each. How many papers I purchased I cannot recall, but I usually pulled down around 50 cents profit each day.

Kessler Grade School in Longview was situated in the heart of beautiful Lake Sacajawea Park. It was a two-story white stucco structure, much nicer than the older Kelso school building. At Kessler, I adored my fifth grade teacher Mrs. Drake, a middle aged kindly type and a loving soul. She and another female teacher lived in a second story apartment situated above a store in downtown Longview. After school, I would often go visit them at their home. This is the only time of my life that I visited a schoolteacher outside of a classroom. In hindsight, knowing what I know today, they could have been lovers. However, I strongly doubt it. They were probably just roommates. Neither one was the stereotypical "butch" type woman.

During recess period at Kessler's playground, I ran into trouble. Some of the older boys bullied, teased, and harassed me. One day, when their persecution was more than I could take, I ran screaming into the classroom, threw myself down on my desk and buried my head in my arms, continuing in that posture even after class resumed. I'll never forget that day, when Mrs. Drake gently defended and supported me to the class. She told them that it was wrong to persecute people-who-are-different. About me, she said: "You know, Larry has a much harder road in life ahead of him than the rest of you. "After that, whenever the playground bullies even came close to me, the guys in Mrs. Drake's class would immediately come to my defense. The bullies left me alone and I finished the fifth grade in peace.

Throughout my life, with all of its troubles, trials, and struggles because I was "different," God has often had someone around who understood me. With all of the prejudice and bigotry rampant in this world, there are still people who are kind, compassionate, and understanding.

My control fantasies, aroused by The Spider Lady, stayed with me. There was a boy my age, who lived a few apartments down from us in the apartment complex string. One summer afternoon, after selling my newspapers, I got him to go underneath a building with me. He went in first, allowing me to block the entrance. I was still not at the age for even thinking about having sex. However, even at 10 years of age, I must have been gay-curious, as a result of my thoughts about Darwin in Kelso. I made him pull his pants down. My mind's eye can still see him there, lying on the dirt ground, crying as he complied. I did not touch him. After a few minutes, I let him pull his pants up and let him go.

Later that day, his dad came knocking on our door. Frank answered. The dad told Frank about what happened. Mom was very upset and embarrassed. I tried to explain to her about The Spider Lady. Mom said: "Well, she certainly did not make someone pull their pants down." Years later, in talking about this incident, Mom said: "We took you to a Doctor to see what made you do that. The Doctor said not to worry, explaining that kids my age often "mess around" in different ways." I never did anything like that again.

Nonetheless, because of the "scandal" Mom called Dad in Portland to come and get me. His mother, my grandmother Fussbudget, had purchased a home in the Rockwood area of SE Portland. Dad had since moved out of the downtown hotel to live with her. Dad drove to Longview, retrieved me, and took me to Portland to live with him and Fussbudget.

The pattern of my going from one side of the family to the other continued. During the next chapter of my life, my innately effeminate interests were to increase.

Early Rockwood Days
1949

Rockwood is a neighborhood in SE Portland, about 10 miles east of downtown, near Gresham. In the summer of 1949 it was a middle class area, inhabited mostly by whites. The two-bedroom home that Grandmother Fussbudget owned was located at 17400 East Burnside, two blocks east of SE 172nd. My remaining three years of grade school, and first three years of high school, were spent here. (In 1955 Dad sold the house and during my final year of high school we lived on SE 130th between Powell and Holgate).

Our East Burnside home was situated several feet off the main thoroughfare, with a driveway. At the end of the driveway, west of the house, stood an old wooden garage with a chicken coop attached to its east wall. Fussbudget raised about two-dozen chickens, egg laying hens, for our own consumption of both eggs and meat. Behind this was a half-acre field extending south to SE Pine Street, then a little dirt road. On the east side of our back yard was an old woodshed. Dad hired a contractor to add a washroom to the back of the house, accommodating a washing machine and clothes dryer.

In the back yard was an apple tree with a two-rope swing attached to one of its branches. I loved to stand in the swing and re-enact the movies I had just seen. In my mind, our woodshed was a theater and I re-enacted movies there also. I had an enormous fascination with the downtown movie palaces, truly the epitome of elegance. Eventually all but one of these magnificent showcases met their fate via the wrecking ball. I dearly loved the elegant Paramount Theater. Today it is the Arlene Schnitzer Concert Hall and is used for special stage events.

When I moved in with her, Fussbudget was 63 years of age. Her ancestry was Scottish and she fulfilled the frugal stereotype through and through. Fussbudget was a very religious woman from a Presbyterian background. Her health was poor. Prior to 1950 her bladder had been surgically removed and she urinated from a catheter that went from her groin into a rubber bag attached to her inner thigh. Her eyesight was dim. One eye had been replaced with a glass eye. Her other eye had a cataract and she needed a strong magnifying glass to read. In spite of the suffering she endured in old age, she possessed a deep and powerful faith.

On the stand next to Fussbudget's bed was a radio. She loved listening to gospel programs. Among her favorites were The Old Fashioned Revival Hour, with Dr. Charles Fuller, an evangelistic program originating in Long Beach, California; The Haven of Rest, with The Crew of the Good Ship Grace hosted by "First Mate Bob"; and The Voice of China, a missionary program featuring Bob Hammond.

Fussbudget always talked about her growing up years in the old country. She loved the Scottish tunes Loch Lomond and In The Gloaming. When the film Mary Queen of Scots played at the Guild Theater, Fussbudget insisted that I see this film. Fussbudget gave me a history lesson about Scottish royalty. By the time I got to the theater, I was very familiar with the characters in the story.

Occasionally Fussbudget took me downtown with her on the bus. She recognized my talent as a singer. One day she took me to the KOIN radio studio, located on the mezzanine of the Heathman Hotel on SW Broadway and Salmon Street, to sing for the host of a radio program. He said I had talent and potential as a performer.

Dad worked the night shift as a longshoreman at Portland's loading docks on the Willamette River. He regularly left home around 6 pm, usually returning in the wee morning hours. He liked his beer and escapades with women he met in taverns. Sometimes, after getting off work he would go to the Liberty Theater, which was open all night, for a late night/early morning movie.

From time to time Fussbudget would have to spend a few days in the hospital. The first time this happened I thought, "Oh boy, when Dad is at work, I'll have the whole house to myself. I will be able to do whatever I like." When this finally happened I experienced my first real dose of loneliness. Being alone in the house was not the great experience I thought it would be. I would storm through the empty house crying out loud, "When is my daddy coming home?" Dad and I often played softball in the front yard.

Located on SW 4th Avenue downtown was a little greasy spoon restaurant called the Sip 'n Bite. Dad was a regular customer. It was there that he met Lanta Mae Ackerman. She moved to Portland from Denver, Colorado, where she had worked as a waitress. In Denver, Lanta Mae had a baby boy, Kenny Wayne, sired from a brief affair. Arriving in Portland, Lanta secured a child day care job with an upper class family in the West Hills of Portland. An older, motherly-type waitress at the Sip 'n Bite, fondly called "Mom" by the customers, befriended Lanta Mae and rented a room to her in her house, located close in SE near Benson High School.

Soon Lanta and Kenny Wayne moved in with Dad, Fussbudget and I. I was so glad to have company when Dad was not there. Fussbudget told Lanta, "Larry has been kind of blue without his Dad." One evening Lanta asked me, "Are you glad you are not alone?" I was delighted that she was there. Lanta Mae was raised as a "hillbilly" in Oklahoma and Arkansas. She told me about the "holy roller" brush arbor meetings in the Arkansas hills, when folk would pick up and handle poisonous snakes, attempting to live out Mark 16:18.

While her housekeeping skills were not the greatest, Lanta was an excellent cook. She said that a typical breakfast during her childhood had been fried squirrel with biscuits and gravy. I loved her southern fried chicken and homemade baked macaroni and cheese. To this day, I have never eaten any better comfort food. Lanta Mae administered my first cooking lessons. She taught me how to make and bake apple pie. I have loved to cook ever since.

Lanta's sloppy housekeeping habits agitated Fussbudget. Often, in moments of anger, Fussbudget would call Lanta a "slap dash rotten woman." One time, when she was really angry, Fussbudget called her "a slut that Alex picked up on the streets of Portland." I am certain that Fussbudget didn't mean the "slut" remark-- However, she did mean her remarks about Lanta's "slap dash" housekeeping.

I first learned about the Second Coming of Christ, as taught in the scriptures, from Lanta Mae. Jesus would come as a "thief in the night" she said. We would often read the Bible together.

After beginning the sixth grade at Rockwood Grade School in 1949, one day I got home from school and Lanta excitedly told me: "Tonight your Dad and I are going to get married." And they did. They got married in Vancouver, Washington. They took me with them to the ceremony. It was in a little home-like chapel. Lanta became my stepmother. She and Dad stayed married for 40 years until her death in 1990.

The early years of their marriage was turbulent. Dad continued to sleep around with other women, following the same pattern he did when he was married to Mom. Lanta Mae would find evidence, such as the proverbial "lipstick on the shirt collar," and other interesting items in the front seat of the car. One time, one of Dad's lady friends called on the telephone to talk to Dad. Lanta told her, "He's married honey."

Dad adopted Kenny Wayne. Lanta Mae became pregnant with Dad's child. When she heard about Lanta's pregnancy, Fussbudget was unhappy about it. Lanta gave birth to a baby girl, naming her Linda Carol. Once the baby arrived, Fussbudget fell in love with Linda, pampering and spoiling her. Holding the newborn child in her arms, Fussbudget would say, "I never dreamed I would love this baby."

Linda was born by caesarean sections and Lanta was unable to have any more children. Lanta was okay with that. "All I wanted," she said, "was to have a boy and a girl." Dad, on the other hand, didn't want a baby girl. When Linda was born, Dad was unhappy that she was not a boy. Apparently, Linda instinctively knew this. As a little girl, she would always insist that she was a boy. When I would tease Linda and tell her that she was a girl, she would cry and get intensely angry, screaming: "I'm a boy!"

Dad loved to booze it up. Yet he was never physically abusive to any of us. Sometimes he would come home late at night highly intoxicated. When in a liquor-induced generous mood, he would whip out his billfold and pass out money to all of us, often five, ten, and twenty-dollar bills. When he sobered up the next morning, he would sometimes want the money back. We did not give it to him!

Compared to those in other parts of the country, most Portland winters were mild. However some years we would have a bad winter. The winter of January 1950 was one such bad winter. We were hit with a blizzard the likes of which I have never seen since. For about three weeks, we were snowed in under six feet of snow, with icicles dripping over the side of the house. The icicles were so large that knocking them down was dangerous. We had a silver thaw, with a crust of ice on top of the six feet of snow.

During the winter storm, Dad stayed at the Gilmore hotel downtown, as driving conditions were treacherous. The schools were often closed because of the treacherous weather. Cooped up together, Lanta, Fussbudget and I did not get along. Although I do not recall the details, I definitely raised hell. A couple of times Fussbudget took over the reins of authority and said, "From now on you are going to obey me." I was so glad to see this winter storm end.

While snow was still on the ground, on my way home from school, I was taunted by a group of boys who smeared my face with snowballs as I screamed and cried out in sheer terror. They stuffed snowballs down the back of my neck. When I got home, Lanta discovered that the snowballs inside my shirt had rocks in them. The memory of this degrading experience has never left me and I have loathed snow ever since.

On one cold blustery winter night Dad was trying to get his car out of the driveway. It wouldn't budge as the tires spun in the snow. He was furious and cussed up a storm! His loud voice boomed so that the neighbors could hear it. Even in the house with the doors and windows closed, when Dad talked on the telephone he could be heard across the street. Dad's loud booming voice was not the only thing I inherited from him. To this day, the "sin that doth so easily beset me" is yelling and swearing in a voice that can be heard several feet away. This sin especially manifests itself at public bus stops when I have just missed a bus. While I have learned to control my anger most of the time, occasionally, in an unguarded moment, the inherited cuss words will flow.

Dad loved animals. We had an adorable little black pet dog named Cookie. I also loved her dearly, and developed a habit of talking as though it was Cookie doing the talking. Cookie would say, "I'm the best dog in the world." One day she was struck by a car, albeit not fatally and a few days later the driver of the car came back to see if Cookie was okay. He said that he would have offered to get me another dog had Cookie not survived. Later, Cookie had a daughter, Queenie. Grandma Hazel adopted Queenie. Queenie also followed the royal tradition of possessing the "best dog in the world" title. When I enter heaven, Cookie and Queenie will greet me at the pearly gates, barking happily, sporting their "best dog in heaven" diamond tiaras!

In the meantime, my drag fantasies were about to resurface, this time as the imaginary hostess of my own radio show....

"The Mary Nielsen Show"
1949-1950

In 1949 I had never heard of female impersonators or drag performers. Nonetheless, even as a sixth grader, I had a desire to cross dress and entertain. Without anyone telling me what to wear, the desire to don apparel intended for women came naturally to me.

In Fussbudget's bedroom closet there was a pair of black 4" high heels that had been worn by Aunt Margie when she was alive. The shoes fit me perfectly. I started wearing them around the house. When going out to the chicken coop to feed the chicks, I stood throwing out the kernels of grain proudly wearing Aunt Margie's shoes. I was careful to be sure, that Dad wasn't looking!

Television had not yet come to Portland. When I lived on Grandma Hazel's farm in Sherwood, I had already thought of having my own radio program. Reading the radio program listings in the newspaper, I visualized the name Larry Nielsen among the radio shows. By the time I was living in Rockwood, I took this one step further. Wearing Aunt Margie's high heels, I would wrap a blanket around me like it was a floor length dress and enact my fantasy radio program. I called it The Mary Nielsen Show. Since I was so young at the time, the family's attitude was: "Larry is just going through a 'phase' and when he gets older, he'll grow out of it."

A famous and popular pinup girl during World War II was Betty Grable, a blonde sex symbol in her famous bathing suit photo. Her "million dollar legs" were insured by Lloyds of London. In 1949 she starred in a technicolor musical western entitled The Beautiful Blonde From Bashful Bend. In the movie poster photo she was dressed in a dance hall girl look, wearing a flashy red tight floor length slinky dress with a slit cut up the side of the left leg from the floor to her upper thigh. Her hair was fabulous.

I fantasized my parents buying me a blond wig with a Betty Grable hairdo, and a red dress such as she wore in the western movie, and high heels to match. In the theater of my mind, I could see myself come Christmas morning, standing by the Christmas tree, entertaining the family dressed in this outfit. This, of course, never happened. Nonetheless, I enjoyed thinking about it.

My sixth grade teacher at Rockwood Grade School, Mrs. McCraw, was a gracious church-ish gray haired lady. She liked me and I liked her. She would lead the class in-group singing, often having me sing the solo part of one of the verses. The song I particularly remember is Winter Wonderland.

One day, at a school open house when Dad and Lanta Mae came to visit, Mrs. McCraw called them aside. About me, she said, "His work is fine. He is very smart and talented. There is just one thing..." and the her facial expression made a mild frown. Later, Lanta told me that her concern was that I sometimes rocked back and forth when sitting or standing and I still do this, today.

One Monday morning, Mrs. McCraw asked the class, "Do you want to know what Mrs. McCraw did this weekend?" She paused and said, "She saw The Wizard of Oz. It was truly beautiful." The popular classic movie debuted in 1939, and often popped up in theatrical engagements over the years. The movie was playing at a neighborhood theater on 28th Avenue & East Burnside Street, the Laurelhurst. A few weeks later, when visiting Mom and Frank in Longview, the Columbia Theater had a special kiddie's matinee showing of The Wizard of Oz. I loved the movie and, just as I had imitated the wicked stepmother in Walt Disney's Cinderella, my emulation of the wicked witch of the west in The Wizard of Oz, particularly her high pitched wicked giggle, was added to my "repertoire." Character actress Margaret Hamilton played the wicked witch. She was renowned for portraying female villains -- the nosy busybody type -- in many MGM films of the 1940's. Lovely Billy Burke, on the other hand, played the "good witch" of the Land of Oz.

Portland's two newspapers, the Oregonian and the Oregon Journal, had all day Saturday activities for kids -- the "Young Oregonians" (YO) and "Journal Juniors". Both papers had Saturday morning radio programs. Occasionally I sang solos on both shows. The Young Oregonians offered free classes in tap dancing, baton twirling, and drama. I also became a "Young Oregonian news reporter" with my articles about YO activities published in the newspaper.

Louise Lawson led the baton twirling classes. Jackie Locke taught tap dancing. Both women had their own dance studios. I fantasized having a dancing school of my own called Larry Nielsen School of Dance (LNSOD). I tap danced at Jackie Locke's recital at Benson High School in a Four Leaf Clover routine. Dad, Lanta Mae, and Fussbudget attended the show. Later Fussbudget told me, "Your dad just beamed with pride when you were on the stage." I also led a group of girls in marching and baton twirling in the annual Junior Rose Festival Parade. Both Jackie Locke and Louise Lawson felt that I had a lot of talent. They encouraged me to pursue a show business career in singing and dancing. I knew that some day I would perform on a stage.

The Young Oregonians had their share of bullies. One Saturday morning in the baton twirling class (mostly girls), I was marching around with the class in a big circle that encompassed the room, marching through a side hallway door, down the hall, and back into the main room. As I went through the doorway, a group of boys were standing there. One of them put out his foot and tripped me and caused me to tumble forward, falling flat on my face. The boys howled with laughter, and as I was got up with tears streaming down my face, and screaming at them, they shouted and jeered, "Beat Sissy up!!" I stormed out of there, shouting, "I'm never coming back here again!!"

Amby Amburn, the YO Director, called Lanta and told her that these boys were expelled from the YO and told not to come back again. I told Fussbudget that if I went back, the kids would say,

"We thought you weren't coming back here." Fussbudget said, "If they do, just say 'my mind is so clean it changes.'" Next Saturday, no one said anything about the previous week's incident.

Another time, in tap dancing class, Clayton, the piano player, asked me: "Are you a morphadite?" I had no idea what the word meant. I asked Jackie Locke what the word meant. She said, "Ask your mother." So, I asked Fussbudget. "A morphadite," she said, "is someone who is half man and half woman." (Using the term "hermaphrodite," Greek for someone possessing characteristics of both sexes -- that's me!!). My knowledge of transsexuality was to come in later years.

While Dad may have beamed with pride when I performed at Jackie Locke's dance recital, as I grew older that changed. Throughout my days in the sixth and seven grades, I looked forward to the weekly Young Oregonian activities. By the time, I reached the eighth grade Dad made me discontinue all Young Oregonian activities. Louise Lawson called Lanta and asked her why I was no longer allowed to participate in the dancing classes. Lanta responded, "His dad wants Larry to grow up to be a man, not a sissy." My tap dancing lessons were the one bright spot in my life. Dad took that away from me, and I hated him for that!

One of the few things I did that Dad approved of was my learning to play the saxophone and participating in the school band. My participation in the band went through grade school and into my first year of high school. As my last two years of grade school approached, my femininity was naturally evolving. I was becoming the exact opposite of what Dad expected of me. By the time I reached high school, he and I grew farther and farther apart. The day was coming when I would stop calling him "Dad".

1959

Finding God in the 50's

My Dad, his mother Fussbudget, Aunt Margie, Aunt Ann, and Uncle Donald

8th Grade of Rockwood Grade School
Class of 1952

High School reunion in 1986 with those students who graduated from Rockwood Grade School in 1952

Saved!

1950

Many times, throughout his life and ministry, the Apostle Paul harkened back to his one-on-one encounter with the ascended Christ on the Damascus road as recorded in Acts 8. Paul's conversion was the pivotal point of his life, ministry, and call to preach. So, it is with me -- my personal encounter with Jesus Christ at Powellhurst Baptist Church became the central sustaining focus of my life. It is because of this experience that I have survived, living to tell my story.

Directly across the street from Rockwood Grade School lived a Christian couple, Ann and Austin Johnson. The Baptist couple were friends of our family. Dad was not a churchgoer. He considered himself a baptized Methodist and a good Democrat. At this particular time, my stepmother, Lanta Mae, was not attending church. The Johnsons attended Powellhurst Baptist Church, then located on SE 122nd between Division & Powell. During the summer of 1950, the Johnsons picked me up every Sunday at the house and took me to church. The pastor was Rev. David Fast. The church was affiliated with the Conservative Baptist denomination. Conservative Baptists believe that every word in the Bible is divinely inspired, "God-breathed," and is to be interpreted literally.

Here is the gospel I heard preached at Powellhurst Baptist Church:

As a result, of Adam & Eve's transgression in the Garden of Eden, every person is born in sin. All have sinned and come short of the glory of God . There is none righteous, no not one." (Romans 3:10,11,23) When Christ died on the Cross-, He took the punishment that we sinners deserved. A Holy God cannot look upon sin. When Jesus became sin for us, God turned His back. This is why Jesus, in his humanity, cried out on the cross: My

God, my God, why hast thou forsaken me? (Matthew 27:46) Today, He is seated at the right hand of God as our Great High Priest, ever living to make intercession for us. (Hebrews 4:14-16)

Every person needs a Savior. We cannot save ourselves. We need pardon. By His vicarious death, Jesus provided that pardon. All that is required for salvation is that one accepts Jesus as their personal Savior. By grace are we saved, through faith, and not of works. It is the gift of God lest anyone should boast. (Ephesians 2:8&9)

Once an individual accepts Christ as his or her personal Savior, that person is "born again." (John 3:3), a "sinner saved by grace." God no longer sees that one' s sin. God looks on the forgiven person through the righteousness of Jesus.

(a) Confession of sin. If we confess our sins, He is faithful and just to forgive us our sin, and to cleanse us from all unrighteousness. (I John 1:9)

(b) Repentance. John the Baptist preached repentance. On the day of Pentecost, Peter preached repentance. To repent is to turn around. In other words, once we confess our sin, we make every effort not to sin.

(c) Water baptism is not necessary for salvation. However, once we are saved, we automatically desire to follow Christ's example and be baptized in water. The form of baptism practiced by Baptists is immersion.

It wasn't long after I started attending this conservative church that I first experienced the convicting power of the Holy Spirit. The Holy Spirit convicts a person of sin. Then, and only then, will an individual want forgiveness of sin. (John 16:44 & 16:7-11

At the conclusion of a Sunday morning worship service, Pastor Fast gave an altar call, inviting those who desired salvation to come forward and publicly acknowledge Christ. The altar call was identical to those given by Dr. Billy Graham in his crusades. Not only was Pastor Fast's message of salvation identical to that preached by Dr. Graham, Powellhurst also used the same invitational hymn, Just As I Am.

There I was -- a twelve year old, innately effeminate boy, without his biological parents present; a dreamer who relished film adventures and the mystique of faraway cities, being drawn by the Holy Spirit to walk down the aisle of a Conservative Baptist church as the congregation sang:

Just as I am, without one plea,
but that Thy blood was shed for me,
And that thou bidst me come to Thee,
oh Lamb of God, I come, I come.

A deacon of the church, in the prayer room, quietly led me in praying the sinner's prayer, acknowledging that I was a sinner. I asked God to forgive my sins. With that sincere prayer, I invited Jesus to come into my heart. It was not an emotional experience, and yet I knew that a transformation had taken place inside of me. I cannot explain this experience intellectually. God's Spirit bore witness with my Spirit that I had passed from death unto life. I knew I was saved. The Holy Spirit instilled that knowledge in my heart; and it has remained with me ever since. I did not become a Baptist. Nor was I converted to the Christian religion. My salvation was the beginning of a one-on-one friendship with Jesus that would remain with me for the rest of my life. From that moment until now, I rejoice and sing:

Saved, by His power Divine,
Saved, to new life sublime,
Life now is sweet, and my joy is complete,
for I'm saved, saved, saved!

On the day of my conversation, on the way home from church, the Johnsons rejoiced that Jesus had come into my heart, and that I was born again. Two months after my conversion, I was baptized (immersed) in water. The Johnsons offered encouragement and support to me as a young Christian. Dad, on the other hand, said I had become a religious crackpot.

Something else that I cannot explain intellectually is the fact that, in that prayer room, along with my salvation, God called me to preach and to do the work of an evangelist. (II Timothy 4:5) To this day, I have never questioned that calling. The gifts and callings of God are without repentance (Romans 11:29) -- they never change. And that call from God is just as real to me today as it was the day God gave it to me. Every evangelical minister in the world can point the finger of judgment at me, and say that, because of my sexuality, I have no right to preach the Gospel. That would not change my evangelistic call one iota. I know to that which God has called me! Nothing will ever change that! Hallelujah for the Cross!

Coming down from the mountain of my salvation experience, I still had to face hassles and bullying as an innately effeminate boy. Only now I did not have to face it alone. Jesus had become my best friend. He walked along beside me.

Coming Down From The Mountain

1950-1951

When Jesus lived on earth He took Peter, James, and John to a high mountain and was transfigured before them. The story is recorded in Matthew 17, Mark 9, and Luke 9. This was indeed a powerful and supernatural experience. Oh yes. Our mountaintop victories, when we are endued with power from on high (Luke 24:49), are truly wonderful. We should pursue these experiences and thank God for them. These supernatural visitations enable us to live victorious Christian lives.

But note this: When reading the Gospel accounts of the transfiguration, one is made keenly aware of the fact that this heavenly brilliance did not last forever; or even a few hours. Immediately following the transfiguration experience, Jesus was confronted with human need in the form of those vexed and controlled by evil spirits. (Luke 9:37-39) Yonder awaited the agony of Gethsemane and the horror of Golgotha.

The day I accepted Christ as my personal Savior, I felt like I could conquer the world. Like most new converts, I believed that now that I was born again, there would be no more problems, and from here on out, life would be one big bed of roses. This feeling was short lived. In any type of marriage, the honeymoon soon ends. Oh yes, my conversion was wonderful. Yet, I had to come down from the mountain and face the hassles, pressures, and frustrations of everyday life.

After my born again experience, I still had heated arguments with Dad, Lanta Mae, and, sometimes, Fussbudget. And I still faced struggles with my weaknesses. For example, I wanted to bring my temper under control, even though at times I didn't. I still battle with controlling my anger and swearing to this very day.

Sometimes when Lanta Mae and I locked horns, and she was angry with me, she would say, "Larry has it [religion] in his head, but not in his heart." Her comments did not deter me from the inner knowledge that I was, in fact, a Christian. In spite of my sins and flaws, Jesus had come into my heart. Like the Apostle Paul, I desired to do what was right, yet I sometimes did the very thing I did not want to do. (Romans 7:18, 19). For example, Paul often quarreled with his colleagues in ministry. One instance of this is recorded in Acts 15:37-40.

After starting His public ministry, Jesus visited Nazareth, where the people knew Him back when. They did not accept Him. This is where He uttered those famous words "A prophet is not without honor except in his own country, among his own relatives, and in his own house." (Mark 6:4)

Once a person "comes out" as a Christian, people often expect him or her to rise above being human. This is especially true of those who live and work with Christians on a day-by-day basis. This does not negate the fact that the professing Christian should make an effort to set a good example in their everyday life.

When a believer knows Jesus on a one-on-one basis, he or she strives to be obedient to His commandments. This is not because they have to; it is because they want to. Yet, when they do falter, it is not intentional. Like the prophets and patriarchs in the Bible, a Christian does possess human traits. Kathryn Kuhlman said: "If perfection were demanded in being a member of Christ's church, there would be no church." People often say, "I am only human." I disagree. Humans consist of body, soul, and spirit. Properly stated, this cliché should say, "I am also human."

It is important that these truths be taught to newly converted Christians. When they do sin, the devil will cause the Christian to doubt his or her salvation. An inner voice will say, "If you were really saved, you would not have done that."

I loved going to movies, and still do. In 1950 Conservative Baptists frowned on Christians patronizing theaters, citing II Corinthians 6:17, Come out from among them, and be ye separate. Yet, it was okay for church young-people to go to roller and ice skating rinks. Why it was okay to skate at roller and ice skating rinks, but not okay to watch films? I could not understand. One day, on the way to church, I asked the Johnsons about this. Mrs. Johnson said that movies exuded bad influence. Mind you, this was before the time of R and X rated movies. Major films of the 50's are considered clean today by comparison. After conversion,

I still enjoyed tap dancing and baton twirling. It is imperative for Christians to live a balanced life. There is no commandment that says, "Thou shalt not have fun."

While an inner change did, in fact, take place once I prayed the sinner's prayer, my feminine actions and interests did not change. God does not change one's personhood. In his book Pentecostal Preaching, Dr. Guy P. Duffield said: "We are divinely anointed personalities, and God never sets aside a [person's] personality. [God] enhances it and sanctifies it and anoints it, but [God] does not vitally change it. [God] uses it."

When the British actor, Sir Alec Guinness was asked why he'd never been open about his homosexuality, he said, "I'm not gay, I'm Alec Guinness." By this, he meant that his sexuality did not define him as a person.

Once regenerated by the Holy Spirit, I developed a strong interest in Bible study. My hunger for spiritual truth was intense. In the Bible, I discovered a new world of spiritual discovery, an inexhaustible gold mine of truth. After over 60 years of studying and preaching God's Word, I still haven't begun to tap the surface of spiritual truth contained in the Bible's Spirit-anointed pages!

I thrill to the old time Gospel chorus that says:

Every promise in the Book is mine,
every chapter, every verse, every line.
I am trusting in His love Divine,
every promise in the Book is mine.

Today I can say as a fact that God's promises have never failed me yet; and they never will! Hallelujah!!

A few months later, I would enter Rockwood Grade School as a 7th grader. (We didn't call it "junior high" back then.) I was about to have new adolescent experiences.

Little Is Much

1950-1951

During the 1950's, men primarily held most professions. Such was not the case with teaching. In the teaching profession, gender did not enter into it. Men and women teachers received the equally low pay. From kindergarten through the sixth grade, my teachers were all women. My first experience with a male teacher was in the 7th grade at Rockwood Grade School. How can I ever forget his name, Mr. Bellerby? (pronounced Beller-bee.) Probably in his late 20's, Mr. Bellerby was an astute man.

One day, Rudy, a mischievous kid in the class, wrote "Bellerbutt" on the blackboard. Our books and supplies were put underneath the top of each student's desk. On another day, Julie, a very pretty, blonde girl in our class, put her hand under the desk cover to retrieve a book when a garter snake slithered across her hand. Rudy was the culprit who put the snake in her desk. Rudy was always getting into trouble with his pranks.

I have an intense fear of snakes. Even a nonpoisonous garter snake and photographs of snakes frighten me. During the 7th grade, I made the mistake of telling someone about my fear of snakes. The word spread quickly. Throughout the 7th and 8th grades, the boys loved to pick up a live garter snake and chase me around while holding the slithering reptile in their hand. Suffice it to say, when moving on from grade school to high school, I kept my feelings about snakes to myself!

To handle kids who got out of line, Mr. Bellerby sported a big wooden paddle with holes in it. Teachers could spank disobedient kids back then. Mr. Bellerby did not like to do this. Only once was I marched into another room to be paddled. I do not recall why. He gave me a light whack with the paddle. There was not any physical pain. My punishment was my fear of pain, and the anticipation of it.

It was in the 7th grade that I met Frank, a classmate who would play a prominent role throughout my lifetime. Frank was also a born again Christian. Frank was not as effeminate as me, yet he was different than your average run of the mill boy. He was the only classmate that I hobnobbed with. The other kids connected the two of us together, much to Frank's discomfort. Frank did like me although he was uncomfortable being identified with me. Two years later, Frank told Lanta Mae that some people said that I was "that way," a "sissy," and that he didn't want them to think that he was "like that" because he ran around with me.

Years later in the late 1960's, Frank came out as a gay man. Frank insisted that he was not gay during his growing up years, though he never had any girlfriends. After high school, Frank attended Northwest Bible College in Seattle. After that, Frank did a stint in the Army. Throughout all of this, in denial, he kept his homosexuality to himself.

Two sisters who were members of Portland's First Assembly of God, Dorothy and Lucille, conducted a neighborhood Bible Club in Dorothy's house in the Rockwood area. Like the lady in Guilds Lake, they also used flannel-graph materials to tell Bible stories. Lucille was a graduate of Northwest Bible College in Seattle, but neither she nor Dorothy were ordained ministers.

Frank and I, along with other kids at Rockwood Grade School, attended the weekly after school Bible Club get together. Within six months, the group outgrew Dorothy's small house. On the property stood an old abandoned chicken coop, which we all fixed up, complete with wooden benches, a platform, and a pulpit. Most of the kids kept going to the Bible Club throughout their high school years.

Dorothy and Lucille each had a car. For over six years, they drove us to the weekly Saturday night Youth For Christ (YFC) rallies, held in the Portland Civic Auditorium. Evangelical churches throughout the metropolitan area cooperated in this outreach to teenagers. Included in the roster of renowned Christian personalities of the 50's, was Stuart Hamblem, author of the famous song It Is No Secret (what God can do). Bob Barber was Director of the large teenage YFC choir. He also directed the choirs at Portland Christian High School and the Portland Foursquare Church. On some Sunday nights Dorothy and Lucille transported carloads of us kids to Portland Foursquare's Sunday night evangelistic services; on other Sunday nights to the evangelistic service at Portland's First Assembly of God. Also, Dorothy and Lucille took us on picnics and outings on the Oregon coast. In the summer, they transported us to the Assemblies of God camp meeting in Brooks, Oregon.

There is a song that says, Little is much when God is in it. Dorothy and Lucille used the little that they had to make a difference in the lives of many grade and high schoolers. Throughout my lifetime, I often recall things that Dorothy taught us during my formative years. Many of us who grew up during the 1950's honor their memory.

Rockwood Grade School's gymnasium and auditorium were in one large room. One afternoon I was on the stage, alone, "performing." I was probably reenacting a movie. Unbeknown to me, Mr. Simon, the school principal, was standing in the wings observing my little show. When I turned around and saw him, he walked up to me and said, "You act more like a girl than girls do." He did not say it in a complimentary tone of voice. Nonetheless, I took it as a compliment. When I told Fussbudget what Mr. Simon said, she was not amused. Her anger was not directed at the school principal; her displeasure was aimed at me. She said, "You did not get that from your Dad -- he is 'all man."

Fussbudget and I shared a bedroom. Her health was slowly waning. She had good days and bad days. Sometimes in the middle of the night, she would cry out in pain. One night in 1951, her suffering was very intense. I can still remember her crying in agony, praying, "Oh, Jesus Christ!" An ambulance was called and she was transported to the hospital. This time she did not return. For the next few days, she was in and out of a coma, did not know where she was, and failed to recognize us when we came to see her. On her hospital deathbed, she would speak in a strong Scottish brogue. Apparently, in her mind, she was conversing with people from her childhood in Scotland.

The last time I saw Fussbudget alive was when Dad, Lanta Mae, and I visited her in the hospital intensive care ward. She showed some improvement and, unlike previous visits, she recognized us, and was able to faintly respond. Dad, with tears streaming down his face, said to his dying mother, "You'll be going home in no time. You're a thousand percent better." Two days later, the phone rang. Lanta Mae took the call. Fussbudget had passed away. She was 65 years old.

Fussbudget's funeral was at a funeral home in Gresham. The service is etched in my memory. This was my first funeral service. Fussbudget's eulogy was conducted by the pastor of a Methodist church in Gresham. Fussbudget had requested that two particular songs be sung at her funeral: the hymn In The Garden and the Negro spiritual Swing Low Sweet Chariot. While sitting in the funeral chapel, I thought back to a time when the Johnsons came by the house to take me to church. Fussbudget was sitting in Dad's recliner, listening to me and Lanta Mae singing The Old Rugged Cross. Mrs. Johnson accompanied us on the piano. Tears flowed down Fussbudget's aging face. The beloved hymns of the church brought her much comfort during her final days on earth.

Fussbudget's body was laid to rest at the cemetery in Gresham, between the graves of her late husband, my grandfather Marcus who died in 1944, and her departed daughter, my beloved Aunt Margie. I am reminded of the beloved hymn by blind composer Fanny Crosby, that says:

Oh, the dear ones in Glory, how they beckon me to come,
and our parting at the river I recall;

To the sweet vales of Eden, they will sing my welcome home,
but I long to see my Savior, first of all.

One year later, when standing over the graves of these beloved family members, I looked up and silently thanked God for the day when their physical remains shall rise in triumphant resurrection power.

The 8th Grade

1951-1952

During the summer between the 7th and 8th grades, I acquired a newspaper delivery route. Boys who delivered newspapers on bicycles were called paperboys. There were two major competitive Portland newspapers, The Oregonian, and The Oregon Journal. My route was with the Journal. I started with a smaller route, usually making about $30 a month. After school started, I moved on to a larger route where I made around $60 a month. In the early 1950's that was big money for a kid my age. Throughout my formative years, I was taught the value of working for a living, based on the Biblical principle, if you don't work, you don't eat. II Thessalonians 3:10.

My 8th grade teacher was also a man. Mr. Jenkins was an ex-Army man, stocky and very masculine. 8th graders were split up into two classes. For years, Mrs. Stoffer was the only 8th grade teacher at Rockwood. Mr. Jenkins was new to the school. Also new on the staff was Mr. Doan, an ex-marine, who served as a physical education coach. Also, a new principal, Mr. Lang, came on board.

Coach Doan did not like me. He was always throwing his weight around. As the day of our 8th grade class graduation neared, Mr. Doan threatened us with not being able to graduate if we didn't stay in line. He claimed that the kids at Rockwood had gotten out of control, and that he was there to whip us into shape. In physical education, he had us stand at attention, and did the military "at ease" command, etc., while he barked at us like a drill sergeant in military basic training. I hated every minute of it.

In physical education class, boys were required to participate in the various sports activities. My interest in any game of sports was, and still is, nil. However, I especially loathed football. The boys used the participation to harass me, "accidentally" bumping hard into me, sometimes kicking me, and all around making my life miserable when on the football field. I tried everything to get out of playing football. I talked to the principal, I talked to Dad, to no avail. Dad's attitude was: "It will make a man out of you." One day, as we were standing at attention, Mr. Doan bellowed loudly at me, "Do you think you are too good to play football with these boys?" I did not respond, or at least I don't recall answering. My status as the "local oddball" was growing. I was like a fish swimming against the current.

Helga, a classmate, predicted, "Larry is going to commit suicide some day." When one of the kids asked her why, she said, "Because nobody will have him." She was wrong. I am a survivor! True, there have been times when I have experienced mild depression, accompanied with self-pity. These feelings have never remained with me very long. There has always been a driving force within me to keep on going, regardless of inner heartache.

Our 8th grade classroom was in a new addition to the grade school building. In the 7th grade, we had desks where we reached underneath to retrieve supplies and books. Our new 8th grade desks had a lid on top that could be raised up to retrieve things. I developed a habit of keeping my desktop lid up and receded into my own little world. I always carried around my tube of Chapstick -- a colorless lipstick balm for chapped lips. Behind the raised lid of my desk, I had a mirror, and applied the Chapstick just like a girl puts on lipstick. Also, I started putting red rouge lightly on my cheeks. A classmate, Marjorie, would tell me if one cheek was redder than the other.

Also, when protected by the raised lid, I started tracing pictures of male pole-vaulters from photos, only my outlines had them naked, and I had them talking dirty. One morning, upon arrival, Mr. Jenkins said that Mr. Lang wanted to see me. Sitting me down in his office, he pulled out some of my drawings, laid them in front of me, and said, "You've got some explaining to do." My face turned red. I was humiliated. I stuttered out, "I don't know." The principal threatened to show the drawings to my parents, although he never did. This is all I remember about that visit to Mr. Lang's office. I never drew any dirty pictures again. Obviously, the contents inside my desk were not as private as I had thought.

It was a tradition at Rockwood Grade School to present an 8th Grade play. Mrs. Stoffer directed. The 1952 play was called Twixteen. I auditioned for the part of "Specks" since I wore glasses. I got the part! Three memorable activities in which I participated that year were playing saxophone in the school band, singing in the Glee Club and being a cast member of the 8th grade play. It was here that I discovered that I had a flare for acting, and I enjoyed every moment of it. The night of the play's performance, Dad and Lanta Mae attended. This was one of the few times that Dad expressed pride in me.

In spite of Mr. Doan's threats in the boys' gym class, we all graduated. The 8th grade graduation ceremonies were held in May of 1952. My most vivid memory of the event was a huge cake that said: "Congratulations to the Class of 1952." Four years of high school loomed ahead of me, which I anticipated with dread, fear, and trepidation. My "hard road in life," as predicted by one of my 5th grade teachers, Mrs. Drake, was just beginning. In 1952, I had no idea where this road would lead. During my turbulent high school years, I would enter into a new dimension of dynamic spiritual power.

Oregon City
1952 - 1953

By 1952, when I graduated from the 8th grade at Rockwood Grade School, Mom and Frank had relocated back to Portland from Longview, Washington, and were living in the suburban SE Portland, Sellwood area.

Frank and Joe (Grandma Hazel's husband) went in together on a logging business. Each day they drove out to the forests, somewhere south east of Oregon City. They chopped down trees, making them into logs, stacking them onto a truck, and delivering the wood to the Oregon City paper mill.

I was still living with Dad and Lanta Mae. During the 8th grade, I often spent the weekend with Mom and Frank. My sister Teresa lived with them, along with my two brothers from Mom's marriage to Frank; Dennis and Steve. I loved city living. Their house was built in Portland's early days, in the Sellwood residential district. Because I liked the area they lived in, I expressed a desire to move back with them. As far as stepparents go, it didn't matter which side of the family I lived with inasmuch as I didn't get along with either stepparent. Frank laid down the ultimatum that if I wanted to move back in with them, I would have to "stop being a sissy."

Dad and Frank conflicted because they were both in love with the same woman. Yet, when it came to me "being a sissy" they were in total agreement, and were determined to "make a man out of me." Yet, no matter how hard I tried to conform to what they expected, I was naturally and innately effeminate. This is a fact that nothing will ever change! The rest of the family never gave me any hassle because I was different. Mom was not overjoyed about having an effeminate son. Yet, she was never loud and outspoken about it. She still gave me the same love that she gave to her other three children.

After graduation from grade school in May of 1952, I went to live with Mom and Frank. Occasionally, Frank would take me with him out into the woods when he went logging. One day, while we were walking down a path through a heavily wooded area, a huge snake darted out across the path in front of me. After that, I was fearful of thickly forested areas.

Toward the end of the summer, Mom and Frank moved into a two-story house in Oregon City, in another suburban neighborhood. Oregon City is located a few miles south of Portland's Sellwood area. Downtown Oregon City is situated on the Willamette River, alongside of the big Crown Zellerbach paper mill. An elevator went from downtown Oregon City to the top of the stone cliff where the upper part of town was located. We were told it was one of the very few municipal elevators in the country, and it operated every day, with a city employee at the controls. It was in this upper part of town where we lived.

Throughout the summer, my sister Teresa and I went berry picking at various commercial berry farms outside of Oregon City. A bus would pick up kids in the early morning hours, and transport us to and from the fields. Teresa and I picked strawberries, raspberries and blackcaps, as well as beans and hops. While I did not enjoy laboring in the hot sun, I did like getting paid at the end of the day. In the cool of the early evening hours, I would spend some of my hard earned money on a nice big cold milkshake from the local Dairy Queen. Mom and Frank insisted that we help purchase clothes and supplies for school in the fall with our earnings. The value of the satisfaction of earning an honest living was being instilled in us.

Our house was located two blocks down the street from Oregon City Junior High School. In the Rockwood/Gresham area, grade school covered kindergarten to the 8th grade. Following that were four years of high school. In the Oregon city area, however, the 7th, 8th, and 9th grades were considered junior high whereas the remaining three grades of high school were senior high. Oregon City Senior High was located about three blocks east of the Junior High school.

One major development during my time in Oregon City was the advent of television. Prior to this, major entertainment was derived from radio programs and theater going. At first, Portland had one television channel, KPTV Channel 27. It was all black and white; color television came in years later. There was a television store located on the hillside part of Oregon City, with a television set in the window. Every night a gaggle of kids would stand outside the window and watch television. It was the era of I Love Lucy, and everyone soon knew of Lucy, Ricky, Fred, and Ethel. Some of the kids called the popular program "I Love Loosely".

In the fall of 1952, I registered for school at Oregon City Junior High. The subject I enjoyed most was Drama, and I got top grades in it. On the other hand, I loathed gym class! After class, the boys all showered together. I refused to do this. The boys made fun of me, taunting me with such remarks as, "He doesn't want anybody to see what he's got." So I would remain sweaty the rest of the day.

A private bus picked kids up in downtown Oregon City and transported us to and from the Saturday night Youth For Christ (YFC) rallies in downtown Portland. A piano was screwed down to the floor in the bus. Someone played the piano while the bus was moving. I loved singing the gospel choruses with the other kids on the bus. I especially remember us singing the popular rousing gospel chorus Do Lord. High schools in the greater Portland metropolitan area had YFC Bible Clubs. The Oregon City Junior High YFC club was held weekly, during lunch hours, at a church about three blocks away. Here I recall singing the gospel chorus Jesus Is A Wonderful Savior.

During this time of my Oregon City tenure, I corresponded with my grade school classmate Frank, who was still living in the Rockwood area. Sometimes I would spend the weekend with Dad and Lanta Mae, and attend Dorothy and Lucille's Bible Club, which I had missed since moving away. I would occasionally spend a weekend with Frank's family. Frank and I would sleep in the same bed. The first time this happened, Frank started talking about sex in general. He said, "Whenever I think about sex my cock gets big and hard." And big it was. (In later years, this would make him very popular in Portland's gay male culture)! Frank rubbed up against me and we dry humped, meaning there was no sexual penetration, just erotic friction and messing around. While I never developed any romantic feelings toward Frank, I thoroughly enjoyed our friendship and physical encounters. Our messing around continued throughout our high school years, and even a few times after that. Years later, Frank told me about some other sexual encounters he had with male classmates. Even so, he was in complete denial about his homosexuality then, definitely not "out." Right up until the time of his death in the 1990's, Frank insisted that he was not gay during his high school days.

When visiting Rockwood, I realized how much I missed Dorothy and Lucille's Bible Club. Dorothy said to Lanta Mae, "Larry is glad to be back with the gang." By the end of the fall quarter at Oregon City Junior High, I moved back in with Dad and Lanta Mae. This ended my bouncing back and forth to different sides of the family. I lived with Dad and Lanta until I graduated from Gresham Union High School (GUHS) in 1956.

Soon after I moved back to Rockwood with Dad and Lanta Mae, a major news story flashed across our television screen.

This story would play a profound role in my life's destiny.

Christine
1952 - 1953

Moving back in with Dad and Lanta Mae meant that I moved into a different school district and became a freshman at GUHS. In 1952, GUHS enveloped a large geographical area, extending from Gresham proper to SE 82nd Avenue in Portland.

My days at GUHS were very turbulent and unhappy. I was a loner and kept to myself. I had no interest whatsoever in school activities. I just did not fit in. In those days, born again Christians did not dance. And even if I had danced, I had no interest in attending high school proms and social functions. Having played the saxophone in grade school, I did join the GUHS Freshman Band. Any social life I had was limited to Church and Bible Club events and activities. With high school subjects, I merely put in my time, doing just enough to get the minimum-passing grade. I lived for the day when I would no longer have to even go near the place!

When I moved back in with Dad and Lanta Mae, they had purchased a television set. One afternoon, when the 5 o'clock news came on, there was a photo of an ex-GI in military attire, alongside the photo of a beautiful woman. Both photos were one and the same person. George Jorgenson was now Christine Jorgenson. Christine was the first publicized person to have male-to-female sex change surgery. George traveled to Denmark and, through surgery, was transformed into a woman. A worldwide celebrity, Christine played a powerful role in determining my destiny.

Shortly thereafter, This Week, a tabloid insert in The Oregonian, published Christine's story in three weekly installments. When I was reading about Christine's childhood and feelings growing up, it was almost like I was reading about myself. This was the first time I had any awareness that there were other people like me -- biologically one gender, while psychologically another.

Early one morning, while I was still in bed, I overheard a discussion between Dad and Lanta Mae about Christine Jorgenson. Lanta said, "Larry thinks he is like that." Dad exploded. "Those kind of people are crazy -- they are fairies!" Up until his death at 84 years of age, his homophobic feelings never changed.

It was during my early days at GUHS that I became aware of strong sexual feelings when looking at some of the boys in the hallways. Some guys wore their pants low, held up with slim belts. T-shirts were the big thing, and the short sleeves were rolled up on to the upper arm which showed their biceps and, to me, made their arms look sexy. Jacket collars were raised up on the back of the neck. Their hair was cut short, complete with sideburns, and combed back into a greasy ducktail. (This was about 15 years before the advent of hippie dudes with long hair).

I had refused to shower with the other boys in gym class at Oregon City Junior High. When I transferred to GUHS, however, as embarrassing as it was for me to undress in front of the other boys, I gritted my teeth and did it. In the shower room, I was never harassed. After showering for the first time, it really felt great not to feel sweaty -- refreshing to feel refreshed. Nevertheless, I never got over feeling self-conscious when naked in front of the others; I merely learned to live with it. Looking at guys in the hallways, or on the basketball floor in shorts, did excite me. Seeing them naked in the shower did not arouse me. To this day, total nudity does nothing for me.

One day, when home alone, I was watching some sailors on a television program, I discovered the art of masturbation as a way to reach a sexual climax.

I never discussed my sexuality or sexual feelings with anyone. There were no support groups for gay, lesbian, bisexual, and trans youth back then. Those who were sexual minorities kept it hidden. Yet, I was so obviously effeminate that everyone knew I was homosexual, even though I never told anyone or said a word about it. The subject was never mentioned in churches. Feeling totally alone, I withdrew into myself. During my high school days, the only comfort I received was from Bible reading, prayer, and reading Christine's story.

One day, while I was walking down the halls of GUHS, someone scotch taped a sign on the back of my jacket with the word FAIRY in big letters. That remained on the back of my coat throughout the entire morning before I discovered it was there. Guys teased me, saying I carried my books like a girl. On the school bus, a guy told me to raise my jacket collar up in the back. I did. The next day, he said, "Never let it be said that Larry is not one of the boys." In hindsight, I wonder exactly what he meant by "one of the boys." Soon, guys started calling me "Christine." Tauntingly, they would call out as I walked by, "Hey Chris!" One afternoon, during lunch break, while I was walking down the street, a car with some teenage boys drove by and yelled, "Hey Larry, let's go out and f---k!"

Barbara, a high school student who lived a few houses down the street, told Lanta Mae that the kids were calling me "Christine." Dad, in a moment of anger, told Mom. She was very upset. As my effeminate tendencies increased, both sets of parents felt that something had to be done. Their efforts "to make a man out of me" were unsuccessful. The irony of it all is the fact that I didn't mind being called "Christine." I idolized this courageous person, and was flattered to be nicknamed after Christine. Of course, I kept this to myself.

Dad and Lanta Mae took me to a psychiatrist. The only thing I recall about the visit was a nurse assistant asking me to draw a picture of a person, and showing me scribbling like drawings, asking what I saw in them. A week later, the psychiatrist sent them a letter, suggesting that I be placed in a boarding school home, located up the Columbia River in White Salmon, Washington, that was advertised as Boys Town of the West. The doctor felt that my being around and under the influence of other boys my own age would result in my developing masculinity, that would result in a decrease of my effeminate mannerisms. Dad, Mom, and Lanta Mae drove me to the school. The conditions there were so deplorable that they decided not to enroll me. This was fine with me.

To this day, I marvel at the ignorance of the psychiatrist. Were I to live in that dormitory environment with those other boys, my homosexual tendencies would have developed and increased much sooner than they actually did. Years later, Ann Shepherd, one of the founders of Parents & Friends of Lesbians and Gays (PFLAG), said that my being there would have been like "a kid in the candy store."

Wanting some kind of acceptance, I showed a couple of the boys in my World History class the letter from the psychiatrist. They doubled over in laughter about my being called "effeminate." They told several of their buddies about it. I was becoming the laughing stock of the entire school. This just made me withdraw even more into myself, shutting out the people and circumstances around me. Having accepted Jesus as my personal Savior, I believed that He was the only person who understood me. Jesus continued to be my best friend.

Another strong personality was about to play a powerful role in my destiny. This time, it would be an independent Pentecostal radio preacher.

Brother Ralph

1953–1954

During the summer of 1953 I discovered a high school, located near SE 117th & Market, called Portland Christian High School (PCHS). Dad agreed to pay the tuition for me to attend PCHS for my sophomore year of high school. Since he considered me to be a "religious crackpot," I don't know what persuaded him to consent to my attending a private religious school.

Lanta Mae filled out the PCHS application. One of the questions asked if my father had accepted Christ as his personal Savior. When Dad read that, he exclaimed, "I've never met Christ!" Two things that Dad liked to call himself were a "registered Democrat" and a "baptized Methodist." He was baptized by way of sprinkling when an infant. When talking about Sunday school, he would say, "I graduated from Sunday school." Lanta Mae told him that one does not "graduate" from Sunday school. Dad insisted that he did. It gave him an "out" when asked to attend church.

It was at PCHS that I learned to type. In 1954 electric typewriters had not yet been developed. I learned typing on a manual typewriter, and I loved to type. Every recess or break of any kind would find me in the typing room. The two brands of typewriters used were Royal and Underwood. Xerox machines were not yet invented. We used carbon paper and mimeograph machines. If one made a typographical error, it would have to be corrected with a gritty rubber eraser, including carbon copies. And you had to be careful to move the carriage so that the rubber crumbs would not drop into the moving parts of the keys and gum up the works. Hence, it was more important to type accurately first, and then build up speed.

I did not use mimeograph machines. They were bulky contraptions that used viscous ink that got everywhere it wasn't supposed to be! First, you had to type your text on to a stencil. If you made a mistake, you had to scrape the erroneous letter off, and then apply a kind of inky goop and wait for it to dry, and then type over it with the correct key. Things like "white out" or "liquid paper" came a few years later.

In the years since the mid-fifties, we evolved to standard electric typewriters, then to IBM selectrics with the little balls inserted for various types of print and correct tape for making corrections. Today, we have multi-faceted computers. Truly a part of the "explosion of knowledge" predicted in Daniel 12:4.

This was also the decade when a Southern Baptist church started in the Rockwood area, with services conducted in the Rockwood Grange Hall at SE 181st Avenue & Stark Street. Lanta Mae and I started attending there. Within a year, the church purchased its own property on 185th Avenue & East Burnside Street, and held its first services in a tent. Soon they built their own church facility. Today, this church is called Burnside Baptist Church; back then, it was named Rockwood Baptist Church.

Sometime during the summer between my freshman and sophomore years of high school, I discovered a radio preacher from Seattle, Washington, Brother Ralph J. Sanders, fondly called "Brother Ralph." He pastored a large independent Pentecostal church called the Seattle Revival Center. His program, The Old Fashioned Camp Meeting Broadcast, aired seven nights a week at 10:00 pm on the Vancouver, Washington station KVAN. I loved Brother Ralph's program, which consisted of a group singing fast gospel choruses while clapping hands with the music.

Through Brother Ralph's ministry I first heard of the Pentecostal experience called the "Baptism [or infilling] with the Holy Spirit," or simply "the Baptism." It was also during this summer that I discontinued attending the Baptist church and started attending Portland's First Assembly of God, at SE 20th Avenue & Madison Street. Dorothy and Lucille, the Bible Club sisters, were members there. I asked Dorothy about this experience. This, she explained, is when a Christian is filled with the Holy Spirit, after they are saved. One will know they are Spirit baptized by the "initial evidence" of speaking in tongues. (Acts 2:4)

When I asked a lady at Rockwood Baptist if they believed in "the Baptism with the Holy Ghost," she said, "God baptizes you with the Holy Ghost when He saves you." Like some other Protestant denominations, Baptists taught that manifestations such as speaking in tongues were only for the original apostolic Church in the book of Acts. I was not knowledgeable enough on Bible doctrine to dispute her. At that time, two facts were clear to me; First, I knew I was saved. Second, I knew that God had something more for me.

Back at PCHS, the teachers did not directly teach against Pentecostalism. They were from basic Baptist theologies. The school itself was non-denominational, and the student body represented both Pentecostals and mainline Protestants. One particular student was upset when a renowned healing evangelist came to town with large ads and promotions on the religion page of newspapers. She said, "I think these healings are of the devil." Pentecostals taught that sickness was of the devil, and that God healed. It seemed to me like this classmate's theology was just the reverse -- sickness was of God and one was healed by the devil. Jesus warned that attributing the works of the Holy Spirit to be of satanic origin was blaspheming the Holy Spirit, which is called "the unpardonable sin."

Throughout the 1950's, traveling tent revivalists conducted "Salvation/Healing" revivals, complete with healing lines where people would fill out a card, and when their number was called, would go forward to have the evangelist lay hands on them. The most prominent evangelist of this type was Oral Roberts. When Brother Roberts brought his tent revival to Portland, I attended every one of his services, and even served as an usher. Pentecostal doctrine proclaimed that healing for the physical body is included in Christ's atonement, as much as salvation from sin. Hence, Pentecostals were also called "Full Gospel."

There was an association with headquarters in Dallas, Texas that published a magazine called The Voice of Healing, reporting on the success of church and tent revivals held by different evangelists who were associated with them. The magazine's editor, Gordon Lindsay, wrote many books on divine healing. Lindsay was also a prolific author and speaker on Bible prophecy. He often traveled with a healing evangelist, Alton Hayes, conducting Salvation/Healing campaigns in local churches. Sometime in 1953 or 1954, the team held a two-week revival at Portland's First Assembly of God. Alton Hayes sang the popular gospel song Victory In Jesus, and it is still one of my favorites.

Another traveling evangelist, associated with Voice of Healing, held a revival at First Assembly. Her name was Louise Nankivell. She preached in a robe made of sackcloth, which is similar to coarse burlap. The garment was simply put together; there was nothing glamorous about it. Also, she had what was then called the spiritual gift of "discernment," where she called people out of the audience to come forward for laying on of hands and prayer, naming their illness. I was fearful that she would call me out of the audience and reveal to the congregation that I was homosexual. She never did.

I am not sure if it was because of my being effeminate, or because of my being outspoken about my Pentecostal beliefs, or a combination of both, that at the end of 1953 Mr. Martin, the PCHS principal, called Lanta Mae and told her that they did not want me to return after the Christmas holidays. When I heard this, I was broken hearted. I went into my bedroom, closed the door, threw myself across the bed, and wept. Aloneness overpowered me. It seemed like no one understood me. My Bible was on the bed, and without thinking, I opened up its pages at random. Suddenly, a scripture verse stood out to me, literally leaping right off the sacred pages. It contained the words of Jesus:

"In the world ye shall have tribulation, but be of good cheer -- I have overcome the world." (John 16:33)

In that moment of deep sadness, I felt God's peaceful and comforting presence surround me. It was as though Jesus Himself were in that room with me, speaking those words of comfort. When no one else wanted me, Jesus was still my best friend.

Mr. Martin met with me, Dad and Lanta Mae in his office,

and suggested to them that they send me to an Assembly of God high school in Canyonville, a small Southern Oregon town. They felt I would be happier with Pentecostal kids. The details now allude me. The result was that I did not go to the school in Canyonville, and that PCHS changed its mind and decided I could return for the next semester in January 1954. In spring of 1954, however, Mr. Martin reversed course again and told me I could not return to PCHS for my junior year of high school in the fall of 1954. This time I did not cry.

Nearly every Sunday night at First Assembly of God, there I was at the altar, or in a prayer room, at the conclusion of the evangelistic service, crying out to God and seeking the Baptism with the Holy Spirit. Even though I had not prayed through to The Baptism yet, my awareness of Jesus being my personal friend grew even more powerful.

Grandma Hazel and Joe had moved back to Portland. After a few months, Joe passed on, leaving Grandma alone in a little rented house. I invited her to attend First Assembly of God with me on a Sunday morning. Normally the Sunday morning service was formal, leaning towards that of a Baptist church. The Sunday evening evangelistic service, on the other hand was more Pentecostal in style. Back on the farm in Sherwood, Grandma would sometimes talk about the Foursquare Church in the nearby town of Hillsboro, and how noisy they were. Not knowing how she would react to a service where everybody praised God loudly at one time, I figured it would be safe to take her to First Assembly on a Sunday morning, when they were usually quiet.

As fate would have it, this particular Sunday morning just happened to be the exception! The service started out formal as usual. Then, midway through the service, a lady, sitting toward the front of the sanctuary, shot up out of her seat, put both hands in the air, and started giving a loud "message in tongues," exercising a spiritual gift listed in I Corinthians 12. Soon, a brother stood up and gave the interpretation (not "translation") of what she was saying, a practice outlined for public worship services in I Corinthians 12. The power of the Holy Ghost was poured out from heaven on the congregation, filling the place with the Glory of God (called "The Shekinah" in the scriptures). Everyone continued to praise God out loud. A sister in the front row of the Choir started "dancing in the Spirit," just like David danced before the Ark in Old Testament times. This went on for the remainder of the service. The pastor never got a chance to preach.

There was a particular lady who was always very demonstrative in this type of worship. She just happened to be sitting in the seat directly behind Grandma Hazel. Back home, a few days later, Grandma described the service in detail to Dad and Lanta Mae, emulating the choir member dancing in the Spirit, among other things. "And then," she said, "While all this was going on this woman in back of me would let out a war whoop. They were crazy." Grandma was not putting down this style of worship -- she simply did not understand it, and it genuinely frightened her.

A couple of years later, when I was attending the Wings of Healing Temple, once again Grandma Hazel went to church with me. This church was far more noisy and demonstrative than First Assembly ever thought of being. However, she actually enjoyed their services and started attending both the Sunday school and church on a regular basis. She especially enjoyed the preaching of Dr. Thomas Wyatt, Wings of Healing's founder and pastor.

When Dad heard about First Assembly, he felt like it was making me more of a "crackpot" than ever. Now, instead of grounding me from the movies as punishment he would not let me go to church or allow me to listen to Brother Ralph on the radio. He even forbade me from receiving my subscription to the Voice of Healing Magazine. A friend let me have the magazines mailed to his address. I would then hide the magazines underneath the mattress on my bed.

When I was saved at the Baptist church, Dad often spoke

about how his friend, Austin, who took me to Powellhurst Baptist, "believed all that shit at the church." Once I switched over to the Pentecostal church, he then insisted that I go back to attending a Baptist church. Lanta Mae, by this time, had switched over to attending Lynch Conservative Baptist Church. Against my will, I attended there for a short time. The formal Baptist worship no longer did anything for me.

Whenever Dad grounded me from going to First Assembly of God, Lanta Mae - who had grown up in the brush arbor meetings of the south - sided with him. One day Dad, Lanta Mae, and I had a heated dispute about me being so "fanatical." Lanta Mae triumphantly marched into my bedroom, pulled the mattress back, revealing my collection of the healing magazines that I was not supposed to have. I was so angry and upset, I slapped her. This was the only time in my life that I ever did anything like that when angry.

Dad called the police and said, "We've got this Assembly of God kid here who is out of control." A police officer came. After listening to both sides of the argument, he said to Dad and Lanta Mae, "He is an intellectual genius. He believes that what he is doing is right." However, the officer did side with them, and told me that if he were called again, they would have to take me to a juvenile facility. The officer added that he did not want to do that. This never happened.

This experience, coupled with Dad constantly calling me a "goddamn big sissy" and a "religious crackpot", and voicing his disapproval of everything I did, evolved into my intense dislike of him. It was at this juncture that I stopped calling him "Dad". For the rest of my life, I referred to him as Alex. As time went on, I found it difficult, if not impossible, to forgive him. My feelings for him, over the years that followed, were neither good nor bad -- just nothing.

It took me many years to learn a powerful lesson about forgiveness. You forgive for yourself, and not the other person. I never totally forgave my father until I visited his grave in 2006. The last time I saw him alive was back in 1960. After that, he and I went our separate ways. He just couldn't accept me for who I was, and am. After I changed my identity to Paula in 1963, he denied my existence completely.

As I was thinking about writing this book, I thought that when I got to this part of the story, I was going to hereinafter refer to him as "Alex". However, I changed my mind. As an act of forgiveness, I will continue to call him "Dad" throughout the rest of my story.

At this part of my life, I was about to enter into what I fondly call "The Summer of '54." With all of my struggles and personal heartache, I was about to be baptized with the Holy Ghost.

Baptized With The Holy Ghost!

1954

The 20th Century commenced with a powerful religious revival called "The Pentecostal movement," a dynamic restoration of supernatural Holy Ghost power that was experienced 2,000 years ago in the original apostolic church, as recorded in the Acts of the Apostles. While there had been manifestations of this power down through the centuries, for the most part the charismatic gifts of the Holy Spirit were lost to later generations of the Church. The Old Testament prophet Joel prophesied about this promised restoration of power.

In 1901 at Bethel Bible School in Topeka, Kansas; and in 1906 at a mission hall on Azusa Street in Los Angeles, scores of people discovered the truth that:

> Pentecost can be repeated, for the Lord is just the same yesterday, today, forever -- Glory to His precious Name!

Saints of God can be victorious, over sin and death and hell,
have a full and free salvation, and the blessed story tell!

My first contact with Pentecostalism came through Brother Ralph's radio ministry, aired from the Seattle Revival Center. I continued to listen to Brother Ralph nightly, and discontinued attending the Baptist churches. I moved my church membership to Portland's First Assembly of God. From time to time all night prayer meetings were held there. My hunger for the Pentecostal experience intensified.

In the summer of 1954 I attended the Oregon District Assemblies of God camp meeting. My classmate Frank and I shared a tent on the campground, at Bethel Gospel Park in Brooks, Oregon, just north of Salem. I washed pots and pans in the kitchen to pay for my meals. There was a smile on my face and a song in my heart while I was scrubbing those big pans. I was glad to be serving God. Deep within my soul surged an inner hunger for all that God had for me. The experience called "The Baptism" would enable me to fulfill my call to do the work of an evangelist.

Pentecostal worship consists people praising God loudly in unison with upraised hands. At the conclusion of the sermon, the preacher invites people seeking salvation and/or the infilling of the Holy Spirit, to come to the altar. During the post-worship altar services, many are "slain in the Spirit," entering a trance like state, buckling to the floor, lying flat on their back under the power of God. This was experienced by the Apostle Paul on the Damascus Road, and is also mentioned by John in the book of Revelation. While everyone who receives The Baptism will speak in tongues, not everyone will be "slain in the Spirit," and not everyone will receive the "gift of tongues." In I Corinthians 12 & 14, the Apostle Paul clearly makes this distinction.

Situated in the middle of the camp was an enormous barn-like structure, seating over 1,000 people, complete with wooden benches and a sawdust floor. It was at about 1am, during a camp meeting altar service, that God baptized me with the Holy Ghost. As I lay flat on my back on the sawdust floor of that great big old-fashioned glory barn, waves of power and ecstasy literally flowed through me. In years to come, Kathryn Kuhlman would call this “the slaying power of the Holy Spirit.” From my innermost being flowed the heavenly prayer language, rivers of living water just as Jesus had promised.

The Baptism with the Holy Spirit made my relationship with Jesus even more real and personal than ever before. It gave me courage to witness in the face of opposition. This was an experience that would remain with me throughout the difficult years that followed. The Baptism not only enabled me to pursue my calling in life but it made my relationship with Jesus even more like a personal one-on-one relationship. Since 1954 I have learned that the infilling of the Holy Spirit is an ongoing daily experience. I have also discovered that while God does operate through contemporary Pentecostalism, the Infinite Personage is not limited to that particular realm. And yet, I would not trade my experience in that *holy roller* meeting for all the money in the world.

Just around the corner lay the Fall of 1954, when I would return to GUHS for my remaining two years of high school. Now it became easier to tune out ridicule that surrounded me as an innately effeminate boy. I could now cope with anything the devil (or anyone else) threw in my path.

From Glory To Glory

1954-1955

My “personal Pentecost” opened up an entirely new dimension of faith and power in my life. The Apostle Paul wrote that we go from faith to faith, and from glory to glory. (II Cor. 3:18) The Baptism with the Holy Spirit is not a “goal” -- rather it is a gateway into further avenues of faith and spirituality.

After any spiritual "mountaintop experience," one has to return to the pressures and problems of everyday living. I experienced harassment at home and at school after being saved in 1950 at Powellhurst Baptist Church. In 1954, after being filled with the Holy Spirit at the Assemblies of God camp meeting, again I had to "come down from the mountain." As I developed spiritually, Dad's disapproval of me as a "religious crackpot" grew even stronger. Yet, as a Spirit filled Christian, I was no longer bothered by his remarks. It became increasingly easier to tune him out.

It no longer bothered me when high school classmates made fun of me. The Baptism made my personal friendship with Jesus increasingly real. The reality of this ongoing spiritual experience has remained with me throughout my lifetime. This is a Divine reality that God has placed in my heart, and no one will ever be able to take it away from me. Hallelujah!

Lanta Mae enjoyed listening to Revivaltime, the Assemblies of God worldwide radio broadcast. The program featured the dynamic preaching of Dr. C.M. Ward, who was a brilliant Bible scholar with an ability to make intellectual truths spiritually real. Dr. Ward often spoke at Assemblies of God camp meetings. At the 1954 Oregon District camp meeting he spoke in one service. Dorothy and Lucille drove Lanta Mae to this particular service because she wanted to hear Dr. Ward preach. He was in rare form that night, even referring to himself as a "holy roller." The altar service, following the sermon, saw scores of people laid out in the sawdust under the power. Upon returning home, Lanta Mae told Dad all about it. He was not amused!

On the final day of the camp meeting, Dad and Lanta Mae drove to the campground to fetch me and take me home. This was right in the middle of a Sunday afternoon service. From the platform a loud speaker system could be heard throughout the campground. When Dad got out of the car, he could hear the sounds of preaching, and loud shouts of "Praise the Lord!" and "Hallelujah!"

On the way home in the car, Dad started mouthing strange sounds. "What is wrong with you?" Lanta Mae asked. Dad replied, "I'm having a spell." He was making fun of the camp meeting sounds. Being clothed with Holy Ghost power, I was not fazed one iota by his mocking of Pentecostal worship. Right then and there, sitting in the back seat of the car, I knew that I could now rise above and overcome just about anything.

This does not mean that life became easy. God does not deliver us from wilderness experiences. God walks alongside the Christian, and gives him or her a divine ability to go through hard times, and come out spiritually stronger as a result of the valley experience. This is why Jesus called the Holy Spirit the "Paraclete," the "Comforter," meaning "one called alongside to help." (John 14:26) My fifth grade teacher's prediction of a hard life for me suddenly became more bearable and endurable.

The time spent during my two final years at Gresham Union High School (GUHS), commencing in the Fall of 1954 and ending in the Spring of 1956, hold few, if any, precious memories for me. During my Junior year of high school I had a nasty and unpleasant experience. It happened during gym class. One day a group of boys locked me into a small, narrow dark closet where the gymnasium's stage curtains were housed. I screamed in terror, tears streaming down my face, begging them to let me out. They laughed in derision. I recall one boy saying, "If I let you out, will you suck my cock?" (This type of sexual activity was entirely foreign to me).

After about 15 minutes of the boys taunting me, while I pounded and kicked at the wall, they finally let me out. I ran from the stage, across the gymnasium floor, and out into the hall. I have never shared this harrowing nightmare experience with anyone until this very moment as I sit here at the computer, writing about my life experiences. I will say this: throughout the rest of my junior year, and all of my senior year, I was never harassed like this again. Yet, because of this experience, I still suffer from claustrophobia.

I only halfheartedly applied myself to my high school studies, just enough to get the minimum passing grade required for graduation. Even though many people tell me that I am a prolific writer, my senior year grammar teacher told me, "You don't understand grammar, and I don't think you ever will." I loathed high school, and lived for the day when I would no longer have to return to GUHS. Socially, I did not participate in any high school extra-curricular activities. Sports events and proms held no interest for me. At GUHS I was just putting in my time, anxiously anticipating graduation day as a gateway into better times.

Throughout my senior year of high school at GUHS, I attended Wings of Healing nightly in spite of Dad's threats to call the police if I did. He was dead set against my attending any Pentecostal church. He still felt that I was a "religious crackpot." He was displeased because I had refused to get involved in high school sports activities. I challenged him by saying, "Most people would be delighted their child was attending church instead of getting into trouble with the law. I am sure the police have better things to do than to pull someone out of a church!" Dad finally gave up and did not stop me from going to church after that.

The time spent from the Fall of 1954 through the Spring of 1956, apart from GUHS, do contain precious memories. I was about to enter another gateway in my spiritual journey, from glory to glory.

Wings Of Healing
1955-1956

During the late 1940s an outpouring of the Holy Spirit commenced in North Battleford, Saskatchewan, Canada, moving to Vancouver, BC, Canada -- and on to large cities throughout the United States. It was called the Latter Rain, an Old Testament term referring to the harvesting of crops in Jewish history, and interpreted by Pentecostals as a type and shadow of contemporary Holy Ghost revival.

Often called "this revival", Latter Rain was an offshoot of 20th century Pentecostalism. It was considered to be a visitation from heaven. Two distinctive manifestations accompanied the revival. One was the heavenly choir, the congregation singing in perfect unison "in the Spirit" as a beautiful form of worship. Another was the impartation of spiritual gifts by the laying on of hands and prophesying over believers, usually done by a minister. (I Timothy 4:14)

Throughout the 1950's this movement sprang up in independent revival centers such as The Wings of Healing Temple. My last two years of high school are filled with memories of this large church, then situated on the corner of SW 3rd and Mill in downtown Portland. A former Methodist minister named Dr. Thomas Wyatt founded and built this church in 1942.

At the Wings of Healing Temple, revival services were held every night of the week, with three services on Sunday -- morning, afternoon, and evening. Visiting evangelists were called in to conduct revival meetings. Bethesda Bible Institute, owned and operated by Wings of Healing, provided Bible college courses, and trained people for the mission field in other countries. Students of Bethesda were required to attend all of the services at the Wings of Healing Temple.

Throughout the 1950's Dr. Wyatt preached on his worldwide Wings of Healing international radio broadcast on two major radio networks. It was advertised in the March of Faith magazine as "the world's largest religious broadcast." In addition to the weekly international broadcast, Wings of Healing had a local radio program-airing weekday mornings and Sunday afternoons on radio station KWJJ.

One evangelist, named George Popoff, possessed a gift of laying on of hands and prophecy. At a youth prayer meeting,

Brother Popoff prophesied over me, saying:

"God shows me that you are not going to be like the other young people. Many times you will be called on to make a sacrifice. Yet, to you, it will not be a sacrifice. You will know the Will of God and do it gladly."

The teenagers at Wings of Healing were nicer to me than were the GUHS kids. The church kids tolerated me, albeit in a friendly way. Most of the time I was a loner, although many of the church grandmas at Wings of Healing were motherly to me.

During the summer months of 1955, in between my junior and senior years of high school, I took a summer semester course at Bethesda Bible Institute. The two story brick facility, at 2828 SW Front Avenue in Portland housed dormitories for both men and women, a large gymnasium, a kitchen and dining room facility, a chapel, classrooms, and a living room with a fireplace. Upstairs apartments housed some of the office staff and Bible school teachers. Dr. Wyatt and his wife Evelyn resided in the building.

During my tenure at Bethesda, I thought about fasting. My hunger for the things of God was intense. A Bible school classmate, Elzora McEwen, approached me one day in the Bible school lobby, and said, "God told me to tell you to fast." I took this as a confirmation and decided to commence fasting the next day.

A typical weekday went like this: Bible school classes from early morning to mid-afternoon. In the afternoon I often did volunteer office work at the church, working on worldwide mailings of letters and the March of Faith magazine. In the late afternoon Bible school students and others met in one of the basement chapels to pray individually over hundreds of prayer requests that poured in daily in the mail from all over the world. Dr. Wyatt prayed over them collectively. The day culminated with the evening church service.

I went through an entire day without anything to eat. Rejoicing over the fact that I hadn't even thought about food all day, giving priority to things of the Spirit rather than the needs of the flesh, I took the bus home. As I entered the kitchen, there on the stove sat a big casserole of Lanta Mae's homemade baked macaroni and cheese. I couldn't stand it another second! I dived into that comfort food like it was the only thing worth living for. My career in fasting ended right then and there. I made a couple more feeble attempts at fasting and then decided that it just wasn't for me. I have never fasted since.

Nonetheless, my hunger for spiritual truth in God's word was powerful, and my desire to preach was intense. During this time I passed out gospel tracts, and preached in a couple of storefront missions. I also participated in street meetings on SW 3rd Avenue & Burnside Street, the heart of Portland's skid row. It was obvious that the bums didn't care anything about my testimony. It didn't matter. This was the only venue where preaching opportunities were open for me. While I was preaching in an afternoon street meeting, a bum from a skid row hotel stuck his head out of the second story window and yelled at me, "Aw, shut up!" That just fueled me to preach all the louder. In one storefront mission the bums had to sit through the sermon in order to be fed afterward. As a zealous, yet inexperienced preacher, I preached to the bums and winos about heaven with vivid Bible descriptions of the heavenly city's pearly gates and streets of gold. During a service when Sister Boatright was preaching, and I sat in the back of the room, I observed the winos. Two were reading paperback books, one was snoozing. Another man said under his breath, "Aw shut up, you old bitch".

Evelyn Wyatt was one person at Wings of Healing who had a strong influence on my life. Although I didn't realize it as a teenager, she was everything I wanted to be. For years I dreamed of becoming a preacher's wife. In later years, Kathleen, her granddaughter, called Mrs. Wyatt a "grand woman," and that she was. She dressed smartly and impeccably in business suits, and conducted herself as a lady. She was gifted to preach and possessed a remarkable ability to deliver spontaneous exhortations from the pulpit.

Evelyn Wyatt also had a strong ministry of intercessory prayer, coupled with a heart of compassion. One time in Portland she interceded from behind the pulpit, beseeching God to "send the rain." "Send us the rain, Lord." she repeatedly implored while praying in the Spirit. She was, of course, praying for a fresh outpouring of the Holy Spirit, the spiritual rain from heaven. Nonetheless, for three days afterward the weather poured down literal rain in the city of Portland!

At last the day came! In the spring of 1956 I graduated from high school. It was like the title of a popular gospel song Oh Happy Day! I was about to embark on my journey into the workaday world, taking yet another step in my search for identity and acceptance.

Free At Last!
1956

Out of high school at last! Though I was contemplating the furtherance of my Bible education at Bethesda Bible Institute, I was uncertain as to what would happen to me next. The question that raced through my mind was "Where will I be ten years from now?" Little did I suspect then that I was beginning a seven-year countdown to ending my identity as Larry.

First things first -- I had to find a job. A phone call from Mom started me out in that direction. "There is a job listing for a delivery boy in today's Oregonian," Mom said. I responded to the ad. The man said that he was taking names and phone numbers and would be calling applicants back to schedule interviews.

One of our neighbors, the Boatrights, attended Wings of Healing, and often gave me a ride to and from church. That weekend, on the way to church, I told the Boatrights I had called a newspaper ad about a delivery boy job, and was waiting for a call back for an interview. Mr. Boatright encouraged me to call the employer back and not wait for him to get in touch with me. First thing Monday morning I was on the phone. The man said, "Friday a young man came in for an interview and I hired him". Trying to hide my disappointment, I thanked him and hung up. Two days later, he called me back and said that they did not want to hire someone who had plans on going to college in the fall, and that the young man he had hired admitted that he was already enrolled in college. I said nary a word about my thoughts of maybe going to Bible college sometime in the future. The prospective employer set up a job interview for me the next day.

I excitedly called Mom about the job interview. Mom advised me, "When you go to see about the job, keep your hands in your pockets." She did not want my effeminate mannerisms to show through at the interview. And so, wanting to get a job, I put forth my best effort to appear masculine, and walked into the office with my hands in my pockets and kept them there for most of the interview. I got the job.

Soon after starting work, I found out that when the boss, a Presbyterian business man named Mr. Borkman, had placed an ad for a delivery boy in the newspaper, he had several responses. The only reason he called me back for an interview, after the other boy didn't work out, was the fact that I was the only one who called him back. I learned the valuable lesson that persistence pays off.

The company was named Miller-Bryant-Pierce (MBP), a national company headquartered in Illinois, and a subsidiary of a typewriter manufacturer, Smith Corona Marchant. MBP manufactured typewriter ribbons and carbon paper. The delivery boy job paid $1.00 an hour (minimum wage at the time) to start. The job consisted of delivering office supplies to businesses and, in many instances, installing the typewriter ribbons on site. IBM standard electric typewriters had just come out and were the hottest new technology to hit the business world since the typewriter first appeared nearly 100 years earlier.

When I got my first paycheck, I wasted no time in freeing myself from Dad and Lanta Mae. I rented a small room downtown, near Portland State University. Free at last I said to myself. I loved the job, and the freedom it entailed. While many office supply delivery boys delivered on bicycles, I made my downtown deliveries by foot. There were a couple of good looking delivery boys, just my type, who worked for one of the office supply retailers who purchased typewriter ribbons and carbon paper wholesale from MBP.

Ron, the stock clerk at MBP, rented a room from the a family in the Montavilla superb of SE Portland. They had previously attended Wings of Healing, and when I met them, they were attending a little independent Pentecostal church on SE 80th Avenue & Washington Street called the Montavilla Tabernacle. (Over the years, this small congregation evolved into a mega church, known today as City Bible Church). One of their sons in his teens, Raymond, had been gloriously converted a year before at Wings of Healing. "Heaven came down and filled his soul," said Roberta, one of the secretaries at Wings of Healing. I fell in love with Raymond. Within a few months I rented a room in their home. Raymond's mother treated me and Ron as her own sons.

Raymond and I slept in the same bed. He was not homosexual. For me, this went beyond a mere physical attraction. My secret inner spiritual feelings for Raymond were powerful. Raymond felt a call into the ministry. This started my first fantasy of being a preacher's wife. There will always be a fond memory and warm spot in my heart for Raymond. I have no idea what happened to him over the years. In 1974 I called his older brother William, who was listed in the telephone directory. William told me that Raymond had married, and was the Pastor of an Assembly of God church somewhere in the State of Washington.

Summer turned into fall. Having experienced a taste of freedom in the workaday world, I disregarded any ideas of attending Bible college. In fact, by then I stopped attending church. Rarely did I contact Dad and Lanta Mae. I was entering a lifestyle that did not include them.

As I grew older, my innate feminine tendencies increased. I didn't grow out of them like family members had hoped would happen. Now that I was independent, I was about to discover that an entire homosexual community existed. The word "gay" was about to be added to my everyday vocabulary.

"Fairy" Tales

1956–1959

When I asked a friend whether or not I should include in this book my sexual escapades as a young fairy after graduating from high school, he said, "Just tell the truth."

I worked for MBP from 1956 to 1959. Three years of delivering supplies to offices in downtown, Portland was indeed an education for me. By July 1959 when I reached my 21st birthday, I realized how naive I had been in high school when I lived in my little cocoon. Urban Portland was a far cry from the more simple community of rural Gresham.

It was during this time of my life that I discovered the term "gay" to describe homosexuals. This term was applied to both women and men, although gay women were also called "lesbian." During the 1950's there were many gay couples, both women and men, who lived quiet suburban closeted lives, keeping to themselves and rarely frequenting gay bars. In these relationships, usually one partner leaned toward masculine, and the other feminine. Masculine gay women were called "butches" or "butch," and "dykes." Effeminate gay men were called "queens."

In the mid 1950's, there were none of the numerous local or national gay support organizations that exist today. In Portland, there was a notorious bar, the Harbor Club on SW 2nd Avenue & Yamhill Street. The Harbor Club housed a street level restaurant and bar which catered to straights and gays, while upstairs was a bar frequented exclusively by gays at nighttime. Nearby was a tavern, at SW Ist Avenue & Morrison Street, The Half Moon. The Harbor Club was off limits to soldiers and sailors. I heard there was a steam bath over on SW 4th called the Olympic which was frequented by gay men for sexual purposes. I was not interested in finding out about this establishment, and have never patronized the baths. To my knowledge, there were no other places in Portland where one could be openly gay. I was soon to learn that an "underground" homosexual community did indeed exist!

I first learned about this from my boss at MBP, Mr. Borkman. "A bunch of queers who like to play with boys hang out at the Blue Mouse Theater," he said. He was not gay. He was a family man, and was very active in a Presbyterian church.

In 1956 the Blue Mouse was still located on SW 11th & Washington. This was the very same theater that my cousins and I attended every Saturday afternoon in 1946, when the auditorium would be jam packed with screaming kids. It had become a third-run grind house. One could see three movies for 30 cents. The upstairs balcony had become a heavy cruising spot for homosexual men. There were three other sleazy theaters downtown, the Circle, the Capitol, and the Roundup, where homosexuals sought out brief clandestine sexual encounters. The three theaters were situated in a three block radius. Men gave and received oral sex in the theater balconies and restrooms. Some heterosexual high school and college age guys offered sexual favors for money. They were called "hustlers" (male prostitutes). Young attractive masculine heterosexual men would let gay men "blow" them for $5 or $10.

I will never forget the first time a gay man hit on me in a theater. It was on a Saturday night at the first run Broadway Theater. The theater was packed, and I sat in the balcony. During a sneak preview of The First Traveling Saleslady with Carol Channing, a middle-age man sat next to me and placed his hand on my knee. When I did not object to this, slowly his hand moved up a little higher to my thigh, and eventually found its way inside my pants. Throughout my grade and high school years, even though I attended movies frequently, I had no idea that this kind of activity took place in the darkened showplaces. This marked the beginning of my entrance into the gay world of secretive sexual encounters.

During my days at MBP I would often stay downtown for dinner and a movie. I loved the downtown Portland movie palaces. I would sit next to attractive young guys in theaters and start by placing my hand on their knee just like the gay man at the Broadway Theater had done with me. If the guy said nothing and slid down further in his seat, this usually meant it was okay for me to proceed further. Slowly my hand would slide up his leg. Sometimes a guy would just get up and move to another seat. I recall a couple of times when a guy would yell at me and call me a queer.

Yep! My activities as a young fairy were coming into fruition! Since I had suppressed my sexual urges throughout my high school days, keeping my homosexual feelings to myself, the pendulum of my sexual activities now swung to the other extreme. I believe this is why there has been so much promiscuity amongst gay men who had to hide and suppress their sexual urges during their growing up years. Inwardly I felt that God understood, even though my church friends would disagree. And I still believe that.

I was not sexually interested in homosexual men. I preferred straight guys. It wasn't long before I discovered that straight guys liked receiving blow jobs. At first I was repelled by the idea of performing oral sex by bringing a man to climax until he ejaculated or found release. In order to sexually satisfy the type of guys I preferred, it was necessary for me to learn to do this, and so I adjusted. However, I only gave pleasure to the jock type guys who were my type. To this day, I find guys in sexy attire more attractive than with total nudity.

Years later, in the early 1980's, the dark cloud of AIDS, then called the "gay cancer" loomed heavily over the homosexual community. Once this happened, I stopped giving blow jobs altogether. Like many in the community, I learned many alternate ways of giving and receiving sexual pleasure that did not involve either penetration or the transmission of bodily fluids. "Dry" sexual activity, which I had preferred for years, became popular.

I lived for the day when I would turn 21 and be able to frequent bars. When the day arrived it didn't take me long to discover that picking up men in bars wasn't as easy as I thought it would be. Most of the homosexual men in the bars were looking for the same type of guys I liked, and so competition was fierce. Finding sexual activities in theaters was much easier. I also cruised public restrooms, and had good luck "scoring" in both the Greyhound and Trailways Bus Depots.

It was also during this time that I discovered that not all gay men are effeminate in appearance and mannerisms. I discovered that many masculine men, such as police officers, mechanics, construction workers, etc., are totally homosexual in their private life. Many marry women, sire children, and live a straight life with secret homosexual encounters on the side.

After turning 21 and going to the Harbor Club, I ran into some guys who could pass as straight, whom I had known in high school. I was surprised to see them in a gay bar, but they were not surprised to see me there. One of them told me about activities that went on in private places on the campus of Gresham High school, back when I was a student there, that I had no idea even existed. "Oh," I thought to myself, "If only I had known then what I know now."

In addition to frequenting theaters and bars during my time working at MBP, I discovered a wonderful community theater, the Portland Civic Theatre. There I met many open-minded people, in my quest for acceptance. This was a major step toward me moving completely away from church involvement.

Even though my church friends considered me "back slidden," my faith in God remained intact. Not once, since I walked down the aisle of Powellhurst Baptist Church in 1950, have I ever doubted that Jesus is my best friend and that He understands me when people do not. Yet, my faith in the church people waned, and I found meaningful friendships elsewhere. I discovered that true Christian principles of love and acceptance were practiced among folk whom my church friends considered "sinners". My priorities took on a major shift.

Bible Gene
1956-1959

Soon after graduating from high school, not only did I learn that a gay community existed, it wasn't long before I became friends with many lesbian and gay people. My first friendship with a (then closeted) gay man actually had started before I completed high school.

During my final year of high school, while still attending the Wings of Healing Temple, a young man named Gene came into my life. Eventually he was to play a significant part of my blossoming as a young fairy.

I first met Gene on a Sunday afternoon at Wings of Healing, in between the Sunday morning and afternoon services. He was wearing a suit and a tie and carrying his Bible. Gene was the same age and height as I. We immediately became friends. He had just relocated to Portland from Montana, being drawn to the City of

Roses through the Wings of Healing international radio broadcast. He was studying for the ministry. At the time we met, Gene was a student at Cascade College. For a time he was caught up by literature circulated by a hierarchy of self-appointed "apostles", situated in North Battleford, Canada, where the Latter Rain movement began in the late 1940's.

Soon, Gene became involved with the United Pentecostal Church (UPC). The UPC taught the "Oneness" doctrine, also called the "Jesus only" teaching. Consequently, Gene left Cascade College to enroll at UPC's Conquerors Bible College in North Portland. The "Jesus only" theology rejects the traditional Christian doctrine of "The Trinity" -- one God manifested as three persons, Father, Son, and Holy Ghost. "Oneness" preaching declares that Jesus is the one true God, manifested as the Father in Old Testament times, the Son when here on earth, and today, after Jesus' ascension, as the Holy Ghost. .

After I graduated from high school Gene and I remained friends and ran around together. One evening we met for coffee at a restaurant called The Cupboard, situated next door to the Broadway Theater. There was a coffee shop in the front, and a bar in the back room where female strippers performed. The Cupboard was not a gay restaurant, although many gay men hung out in the coffee shop and visited. Up to this time, the subject of homosexuality was never discussed between Gene and I. That evening, however, Gene came out to me. He was happy with his self identification as a homosexual. He said that he didn't care if I told it all over town. "I have been going to gay parties," he said, "and I am having the time of my life." Soon his church activities discontinued. A few times Gene and I rented a room for the night at the downtown YMCA to have sex.

Gene was a talented piano player, and was hired to play piano for ballet classes at a dance studio above the Bohemian Restaurant on SW Washington. Through him, I met Cleo, one of the male ballet students, with whom I had a brief sexual liaison. Soon I was running around with a group of young fairies my age. Years later I learned that the ballet dancers called him Bible Gene. After moving to California in 1960, I lost track of Gene. The last I heard he went into the Army, and was stationed somewhere in Germany.

Ten Cents A Dance
1956-1959

Shortly after starting to deliver typewriter ribbons and carbon paper to offices throughout the downtown Portland area, I discovered the world of 33rpm vinyl record albums, or LPs. One day I wandered into a music store that sold record albums. It was here I discovered that one could purchase sound tracks of popular movie musicals and Broadway stage productions. Stores such as these had glass booths where customers could listen to record albums, free of charge, with a time limit.

During my lunch hour, I started listening to albums in the booths of two different stores. The first album I really got into featured the songs of movie star Doris Day from the movie soundtrack of Love Me or Leave Me, a film biography of the 1920's singer Ruth Etting. I especially loved her rendition of Shaking The Blues Away.

When they hold a revival way down south,
everybody with care and trouble that day,
tries to shake it away...

Since I grew up as a moviegoer who attended Pentecostal churches, I liked this song.Another Ruth Etting song from this movie touched upon my desire to be an entertainer:

Ten cents a dance, that's what they pay me,
gosh how they weigh me down,
Ten cents a dance - dandies and rough guys,

tough guys who tear my gown....
And the song concludes:
Sometimes I think I've found my hero,
but it's a queer romance....

These songs were starting to bring to the surface my inner desire for a romantic involvement that entailed more than sex. I was trying to find emotional fulfillment by seeking out clandestine sexual encounters in theaters and bus depots. I found sex, and yet after a one-time physical encounter was over, there still remained a deep inner emotional emptiness. My new found freedom of sexual expression did not satisfy me within.

Soon I developed an enormous fascination with the lives of vaudeville and nightclub entertainers of the 1920's and 30's. I did extensive research through old newspapers at the public library, along with reading through books and encyclopedias. I discovered Helen Morgan, another popular blues cabaret singer from the 1920's and 30's, who died a tragic death from alcoholism. When listening to a 33rpm album, recorded from old 78rpm records of the torch singer's renditions of The Man I Love, Bill (from Showboat), Body & Soul and others, I would feel a strong emotion of nostalgia sweep over me. When I shared this with a friend, he said, "No, you feel sentimental." I responded, "No, I feel nostalgic." Sentimentality can be past, present, or future, whereas nostalgia is a fond memory of what one has experienced in the past. I began to think that if the teaching of reincarnation is, indeed, true, then I must have lived during the days of burlesque and vaudeville in a decade called The Roaring Twenties. Whether or not my being reincarnated is a fact, I do not know. The Christian teachings I had been taught take issue with this idea.

More than anything else, the blues songs ignited within me the emotion of unrequited love, which was to play a strong role throughout my lifetime. The lyrics of songs sung by Helen Morgan say:

I used to dream that I would discover, a perfect lover, someday.
I knew I'd recognize him, if ever, he came round my way.
I always used to picture him, he'd be one of those Godlike kind of men,
with a giant brain, and a noble head,
like the heroes in the books I've read.
Then along came Bill, whose not the type at all...
And:
Someday he'll come along, the man I love,
and he'll be big and strong, the man I love...
And:
Once I built castles in the air, happiness was there,
then a certain party ceased to care,
The castles fell, and broke the spell...
And:
What lies before me? The future is stormy,
a winter that's gray and cold.
Unless there's magic, the end will be tragic,
an echo of a tale that's been told so often...

These, and others, were songs that would give me solace and comfort over the years in my desperate search for a romantic involvement.

The tragic stories of blues singers were not the only discoveries I made in the world of LP records. While the blues singers could make me cry, I also discovered the magic of laughter. I came in contact with those beloved comedy burlesque, vaudeville, and cabaret entertainers from days gone by, wonderful gifted people who could make audiences laugh, helping people to rise above sorrow and heartache.

Yes, in those glass encased booths of the music stores, I was about to discover the grand lady of show business -- the queen of comedy songs -- whom I grew to idolize, a gal who would become a part of me throughout the years, and still does. Meet Sophie Tucker, billed in theaters and nightclubs throughout six decades as The Last of the Red Hot Mamas.

The Spice Of Life
1956-1959

One day when I was browsing through the record albums, I stumbled across an album that featured a recording of a cabaret show at a night club in the North Beach section of San Francisco, called Goman's Gay Nineties. Included in the performance were risqué comedy songs, performed by Bea Goman, talking with accompanying live music. Songs such as Be Careful Whom You Pick for a Picnic, Those Old Overnight Boats, and The Good Ones Can Be Just as Bad as the Bad Ones, delighted me. For example, from the picnic routine:

When he starts in searching, for a spot that's nice and dry,
and he has that 'hungry look,' and a gleam is in his eye
He wants more than just a 'piece' of mother's pumpkin pie!
And:
So girls eat your lunch, with the rest of the bunch
and not some hidden spot a man has found.
For you can get in danger,
with a boyfriend or a stranger,
If you're not careful where you put your 'basket' down!

One day when I was visiting Mom and Frank, I played the Goman's Gay Nineties record album for them. Mom said, "This reminds me of Sophie Tucker." So, the next time I visited the record stores, I looked for a Sophie Tucker record, and found one entitled The Spice of Life. As time went on I discovered other albums containing Sophie's night club material. The albums featured such songs as I'm Living Alone and I Like It and You Can't Deep Freeze a Red Hot Mama. In her routine, No One Woman Can Satisfy Any One Man All The Time, she said:

Men are only grown up boys, and boys like playing hookie,
and you know how a kid enjoys a 'piece' of stolen cookie.

The Spice of Life album also contained a vaudeville comedy song Sophie introduced in the 1920's, Mama Goes Where Poppa Goes sung in both English and Yiddish. I learned Sophie was a full-figured, heavy set Jewish gal whose long show business career started in the early 1900's. She became a spangled burlesque queen, and later a vaudeville star. When vaudeville died she migrated to night clubs. In 1954 she celebrated her Golden Jubilee, fifty years in show business. She poked good natured fun at her weight, and, as she grew older, her age. As she said:

I know that I'm no glamor gal, no motion picture beauty;
I've had 40 years of service, and I'm still on active duty!
And:
The more candles on my birthday cake, the hotter I become!
And:
When I go truckin' on down,
swinging my tailgate,
the way those wolves keep prowlin' around,
you'd think I was jailbait

I developed an enormous fascination for the cabaret entertainer, billed on theater marquees in vaudeville days as The Last Of The Red Hot Mommas. Two songs that became Sophie's trademarks were My Yiddisha Mama, and Some of These Days, the latter being the title of her autobiography.

I learned Sophie's material on the albums by listening to them over and over. Throughout my lifetime, I would entertain friends at parties by reciting Sophie Tucker's wonderful nightclub material. Years later, in the 1980s, I performed as an entertainer at Darcelle XV in Portland, Oregon, billed as Portland's Own Red Hot Mama. I do not imitate Sophie, rather I emulate her. The Red Hot Mama persona is a part of who I am.

Sophie's material is risqué but not vulgar. Her songs contain things that all people -- gay or straight -- can relate to in the arena of life's experiences. In addition to her risqué material, she had serious philosophical songs that digressed from the frivolous, such as Be As Big As The World You Live In, and Take A Look at Yourself. During the 1950's and 1960's, she often appeared on the nationally syndicated Sunday night television show hosted by Ed Sullivan.

In 1957, Sophie made her last night club appearance in Portland, Oregon at Amato's Supper Club in downtown Portland. Because of liquor laws, one had to be 21 to get into bars and night clubs, therefore I was not able to see her perform. However, one afternoon, Sophie, along with Ted Shapiro, her long-time piano player, made a charity fund raising appearance in the daytime at Director's Furniture Store. While doing my deliveries, I stopped in and saw her. I did not introduce myself to her. In hindsight, I wish I had. Sophie continued working the night club circuit, drawing large salaries in places like Las Vegas, right up until the day she died in 1966.

Sophie Tucker is one of the women who had a profound influence on my life's experiences. I treasure her memory. My sense of humor has gotten me through many rough spots in my life's journey and I most certainly have Sophie Tucker to thank for it.

In the 1960's, another popular night club entertainer, Rusty Warren, billed as the Knockers Up Girl said, "If you can't learn to laugh at sex, you have a problem with it." I totally agree.

And now that I am in my life's golden years, along with Sophie I say, "Don't give me that old rocking chair, and something to knit on; what this old gal has got, is still too damn good to sit on!"

Oh yes I was evolving as a "young fairy."

Portland Civic Theater 1958-1960

I was working for MBP when my eye caught a newspaper article announcing a new season of plays at the Portland Civic Theater (PCT) for the 1957-1959 season. The article also gave a day, date, and time for auditions for the first show of the season. Ever since I was the 8th grade play at Rockwood Grade School, I had had a desire to act.

PCT was a community theater in downtown Portland, where local personalities volunteered to appear in shows as well as work behind the scenes with props, sound effects, and whatnot. This was an avocation with participants maintaining their daytime jobs. PCT had two theaters -- the main stage and The Blue Room, a theater in the round.

I auditioned for the part of a young boy in Anniversary Waltz, later made into a movie called Happy Anniversary. I did not get the part, so I decided to attend a meeting for stagehands. I loved the smell of greasepaint and the atmosphere of the theater. My first PCT project was doing sound effects for the Main Stage production of Anniversary Waltz and as time went on, I also ran the sound and light booth for many of the plays presented in the Blue Room.

PCT drew a diversity of people from all walks of life. I soon became involved with an entirely new circle of friends. Consequently, I moved away from my church friends. Once I was involved with PCT, my after working hours activities shifted from church to theater projects. I moved into a large rooming house in Northwest Portland where some PCT guys lived, managed by a buxom motherly woman fondly called Hattiebell. I rented a small room there for $15 a month. Dick Jones, a gay man who was Director for The Blue Room, rented the attic apartment. Hattiebell was a mother figure to both straight and gay people. Everyone respected her. The residents of the large house on NW Kearney Street were her kids. She affectionately called me "Pipsqueak."

Some well-known colorful Portland personalities appeared in the stage plays. Mary Marsh, a brilliant actress, played Blanche in PCT's production of A Streetcar Named Desire. In my opinion, Mary's characterization topped Vivien Leigh's performance in the film version of the renowned Tennessee Williams play. When Witness For the Prosecution hit the PCT stage, a local actress named Margretta Ramsey played the role portrayed by Marlene Dietrich in the movie version. In later years Margretta landed an occasional role in Hollywood "B" movies. Margretta encouraged me to take a creative dancing class. She was very flamboyant and theatrical, and soon I started emulating her in my speech -- an exaggerated blending of Ethel Barrymore and Tallulah Bankhead -- using such phrases as "how are things at the theatuh dahling," saying "closses" instead of "classes," and "doncing" instead of "dancing." Using a deep throaty affected voice, I would say, "We in the theatuh do it this way..." I even went so far as to nickname myself Tallulah. Oh yes, I had arrived at being a flamboyant fairy.

Another local personality involved with PCT was a tall slender woman, with long black hair, who hosted late night scary movies on local television. There she was called Tarantula Ghoul. Amongst her circle of friends, she was credited as saying: "I can't STAND that word *fuck*!," although she did not say that on air.

A beautiful and colorful local personality, Ollie Nodel gave weekly night drama classes at PCT. I signed up. At that time, she was married to Rabbi Nodel of Temple Beth Israel, a prestigious Reformed Jewish synagogue in Northwest Portland. When the Rabbi divorced her, she moved to Los Angeles, and landed a job as a medical secretary at CBS.

When auditions for the Main Stage production of The Diary of Anne Frank were announced, I told Ollie Nodel that I would like to play the part of Peter in the renowned story of two Jewish families hiding out from the Nazis in Holland during World War II. She told Chuck Morrison, the director, "I think Larry would be good in that part." It was the male romantic lead in the story. As fate had it, I got the part. I was ecstatic. My photo was on the theater page in the Sunday Oregonian.

In The Diary of Anne Frank, Mark Allen, a popular local radio DJ, played the role of my father, Mr. Van Daan. He had gone to Pasadena Playhouse with Jack Webb. Mark told Jack Webb, "You'll never make it in this business. Your voice is too flat." "And now," said Mark Allen, "I am a local radio DJ, and Jack Webb became the star of Dragnet." This was Mark Allen's first role in the Portland local theater scene. He appeared in many other plays for PCT, and eventually organized his own dinner theater group called The Mark Allen Players, performing popular plays in prestigious hotel restaurants.

Renee Marx, wife of the man who owned and operated Marx Jewelers in downtown Portland, played my mother, Mrs. Van Daan. She was Jewish, and she shared with us that she had lived in Germany when Hitler came to power. In referring to her role in this powerful drama, she said: "I lived this story. Every time there was a knock on our door, we froze in fear, thinking it could be the gestapo. Our family escaped on the last train out of Berlin to Switzerland. Had we not been on that train, we would have been sent to a concentration camp, which was the fate of some of my relatives." After the war, she said, they were unable to find many of their family members, who had undoubtedly died in the Nazi death camps.

For me, re-enacting the experience of being a Jew in hiding from the Nazis was a powerful and emotional experience. In real life, Peter -- the person I portrayed in the play -- along with many others, died in a concentration camp. Otto Frank, Anne's father, was the only one who returned after the war. He found his daughter's diary in the attic where they had been in hiding. In her diary, Anne Frank said: "I want to go on living after my death." Through the printed page, Anne still lives today to share her story. Like Anne Frank, my prayer is that, through this book, my story will also live on years after my departure from this earthly scene.

To this day, I have a very warm spot in my heart for the Jewish people. Over the years, I have grown to dearly love and appreciate these wonderful, kind, and generous people. They are the apple of God's eye.

My circle of friends were all theater people during this time. Soon I started smoking cigarettes. "It's light up time for Larry," I would jokingly say. At the end of a play's run, someone always gave a party for the cast and crew of the production in their home. It was at one of these parties that I got drunk for the first time. This was on a Saturday night. The next morning, Sunday, I had to be in the Blue Room for a technical meeting. I went to that meeting with my first hangover -- a far cry from my days of going to church on Sunday mornings.

My boss at MBP, Mr. Borkman, said that I was "a nice Christian boy, gone to the dogs." One Saturday afternoon, I answered the front door at Hattiebell's, and there stood Elzora, Evelyn, and Robert -- classmates from my days at Bethesda Bible Institute in 1955 -- expressing concern about my salvation. They had seen my photo in the Sunday newspaper from my appearance in The Diary of Anne Frank. How they found out where I was living, I do not recall. They undoubtedly heard that I no longer attended church. We had a friendly visit; it was good to see them again. They invited me to attend services at a church they were frequenting. They prayed with me. I could not tell them that I was happy in my new environment, where I did not have to hide my homosexuality. I also did not tell them that I was gay. However, like others from my church life, they probably knew, or at least had a good idea. After that visit, I never saw them again.

I was keeping very long hours, working 40 hours a week in the daytime and spending another 4 - 5 hours a night and all weekends at the PCT. My eating habits were erratic, and although I had not yet turned 21, I was drinking a lot.

I liked my job at MBP. However, the only promotion possible would entail becoming a salesman. So I started looking for a other job. Sometime in 1959, I was hired as a typist for the Southern Pacific Railroad. Shortly after I turned 21, my boss said to me, "Your eyes are yellow." At another glance, he said, "In fact your skin is yellow. You are sick." He sent me to the company doctor. I was diagnosed with infectious hepatitis and was hospitalized. While in the hospital, I read in the newspaper about Judy Garland's bout with the same strand of hepatitis

Though I wasn't going to church, I listened to the Portland Foursquare Church broadcasts of their Sunday morning worship services over the radio. Dr. Harold Jefferies was the pastor, and he announced an upcoming revival campaign with an evangelist named Jean Darnall. One Sunday morning, while I was in the hospital, I heard her preach on the Sunday morning broadcast. Little did I know what a profound role Jean Darnall would play in my life four years later.

Up to this point, Mom did not know for a fact that I was gay. Soon, this would change.

Three Months as Paula, taken for the Glad Tidings Assembly of God church directory in San Francisco.
1963

Cataclysmic Changes of the 60's

HARRY BENJAMIN, M. D.
NEW YORK AND SAN FRANCISCO

July 1963

2232 450 Sutter st.
San Francisco 8

TO WHOM IT MAY CONCERN:

This is to certify that the bearer, Paula (Larry) Nielsen, of 1265 Pine Street, San Francisco, is under my professional care and observation.

This patient belongs to the rather rare group of (male) transsexuals, also referred to in medical literature as psychic hermaphrodites. Psychologically they are female, and anatomically they are male. They feel completely as women, and if they live and dress as such they do so out of an irrepressible inner urge, and not in order to commit a crime, to "masquerade," or to impersonate illegally. To dress in female attire is good for their mental health and emotional balance.

It is my considered opinion, based on many years' experience, that transsexuals are mostly introverted and non-aggressive, and therefore no threat to society. In their feminine role, they can live happier lives and they are usually less neurotic than if they were forced to live as men. I do not think that society is endangered when it assumes a permissive attitude and grants these people the right to their particular pursuit of happiness.

Like all patients of this type, Paula (Larry) Nielsen has been advised to behave well and inconspicuously at all times, and to avoid undesirable people and objectionable places.

Harry Benjamin, M. D.

The letter from Dr Benjamin I had to carry in case I was stopped by the police.

1965

On my way to church
1965

Outed!
1960

"What's too painful to remember, we try so hard to forget."

This chapter is the most difficult part of my story to write. What I am about to share with you I have never told anyone. All these years, I have kept the inner hurt and pain to myself. And now, as I recall these events for the first time since 1960, I am unfolding to you the scene with the heartache buried inside.

I had arrived as a young and practicing flamboyant fairy. My family suspected as much, even though I had not told them. My innate feminine mannerisms made it very apparent that I was homosexual. Mom did not want it to be true.

When Dad had let it be known that my high school classmates were calling me "Christine," Mom cried over this. After my graduation from high school, one day at the dinner table, the topic of homosexuality came up. In front of everyone, including Mom, Frank said, "If you are that way, don't ever tell your mother -- it will break her heart." I did not tell her. It would have been far better had I told her, rather than the way she found out.

It happened in 1960, after I had been out of high school for about four years. I was working as a freight bill typist at the Southern Pacific Railroad Park Street Freight Station. I had my first automobile, an old Studebaker. Just as I had discovered how to cruise men in theaters and bus depots, now that I had a car, it didn't take long for me to discover the world of hitchhikers. Many of them seemed interested in sexual encounters. Also, I would pull up to bus stops and offer a ride to good looking guys. I was soon to discover pitfalls in the world of clandestine sexual encounters, where set ups and traps lurk in the shadows.

By this time Grandma Hazel and I were sharing a two bedroom duplex apartment, close to where Mom and Frank lived. Grandma worked as a live-in housekeeper/cook, taking care of a working woman's four children. The apartment gave her a place to go on her days off. Five days a week, I had the apartment all to myself and this gave me smooth sailing for bringing men home with me.

I remember the fateful night as if it were yesterday. It was a Sunday evening, and I was cruising in the downtown area. Driving by the Trailways bus depot, I spotted an attractive guy walking down SW Salmon Street. I pulled over and asked him if he would like a ride. Without hesitation, he said "yes" and got into the car. I ascertained that he was 19 years old. I invited him to my apartment to have a beer, and spend the night. He readily accepted the invitation. He was a college jock type, and was very friendly and cordial. On the way home, I stopped at a convenience store and purchased a quart of beer. I knew that he was under the legal drinking age. Yet, during my high school days, many of my classmates drank beer, and he was certainly old enough to make his own choices. Little did I realize that a trap was being set, and that I was about to walk into it.

Together we consumed the quart of beer. He was very friendly, and gave every indication that he was open minded about different kinds of people. After we drank the beer, we got undressed and ready for bed. He definitely gave me the impression that he was in the mood for sex. It was obvious that he was in a state of arousal, as he laid down next to me on the bed. As I reached over to touch him, he said he felt the need to step outside for some fresh air. After he went outside, I could hear him knocking on the duplex neighbor's door. Suddenly I knew something was awry, and I got dressed and went out to my car. As I was turning the ignition to start the engine, he came running out and said, "The police are on their way."

In a state of sheer panic, I took off and drove over to Mom's house. I do not recall what I said when I came in. I only recall lying down on her couch, trying to sleep, and hiding out until morning. It was very late at night, and everyone else was in bed. It suddenly flashed into my mind that I had left something on my dining room table that had Mom's address on it.

Sure enough, within a half hour, a police car drove up and shined its spotlight into the living room window. I crawled across the living room floor to avoid being seen. It felt like I was being hunted down like a criminal. Never before, or since, was I so frightened and filled with fear. Nightmarish thoughts of being locked up in jail flashed through my mind. A suicidal thought even pushed its way into my mind. (This was the only time in my entire life that I entertained even a brief thought of suicide).

The police officer knocked on the door, and Mom got up, wearing her baby doll pajamas, and answered. The policeman told Mom that this guy had called in a complaint that I tried to have sex with him, and tried to kiss him. He also told Mom that the Trailways Bus Depot was a "hangout for queers." "What is your relationship to him?" he asked Mom. "I am his mother," she replied, not expressing any emotion. The officer said that it was up to the young man if he wanted to file a complaint with the District Attorney. With that, the policeman left, with the young man in his car.

Mom said, "You had better hope that this guy does not press charges." While she was unhappy about this troubling situation, she displayed no anger. I was too frightened to express any emotion myself. After she returned to her bedroom, I could hear Frank say to Mom that I had picked up the wrong person. Later, Mom told me that the morning following the visit from the police, the neighbor lady from across the street came over to chat for no apparent reason. She was probably wondering why the police were there the night before. "I didn't say a thing," Mom said. "I don't want people to know that I have a son who is like that."

This did upset me, and I wished I could have changed from gay to straight. This, of course, was impossible. Besides, I did not want to change. My homosexuality was something that has always been a part of me, and I knew that any effort on my part to become straight and/or masculine would be an exercise in futility. Mom disapproved of homosexuality and yet she never disowned me. Whether she told Dad about this situation, I do not know. I regretted that this was an embarrassment to the family. In 1960, there were no support groups of any kind for parents whose children were gay.

Not understanding that some people are innately homosexual, Mom sometimes expressed the feeling that my being gay was her fault. After this incident, I wished that she and I would have had open dialogue about why some people are innately homosexual. This did not happen until years later.

The next two days, I worried that the police were going to book and arrest me. I had to talk to someone, and so I visited my friend Judy, a Pentecostal woman who I trusted, and told her about the incident. She was very loving and kind about my predicament. She felt that the young man set me up. She also said, "The Lord told me that you have an effeminate spirit." She prayed with me and asked the Lord to stop this young man dead in his tracks from taking any legal action against me. She invited me to her home prayer group the next day.

I went to Judy's home prayer meeting, and sat in a chair while the group held hands and formed a circle around me. Whether she had told them about the homosexual incident, I do not know. They prayed for my deliverance. As I sat there, I could feel their love and compassion sweep over me. Later, a friend who was part of the group said to me, "I could feel the demons leaving." Whether he meant "homosexual demons," or "effeminate demons," I do not know. The fact remained that I was still gay. I continued on in my desperate search for a love relationship.

Within two days, an investigator from the Oregon Liquor Control Commission (OLCC) called on me. The reason they were brought in on this was because I was 21, and the guy with whom I had shared the quart of beer was 19. The investigator said, "I was not impressed with the young man, when we met at the District Attorney's office." He went on to explain that the DA asked him if he knew I was gay when he got into the car with me. "Oh yes," the guy said, "I knew what he was the minute he pulled over and offered me a ride." Next, the DA asked him why he got into the car with me. He replied, "I hate queers, and I was playing detective." The DA threw the sex complaint out. Although I did pick him up, nonetheless it was he who lured me into a sex scenario and not the other way around. However, I was charged with giving beer to a minor, and had to appear before a Judge. The OLCC investigator picked me up at work and went to court with me.

When the Judge heard the circumstances surrounding the charge of me giving an alcoholic beverage to a minor, he picked up on the gay issue right away. Whether or not the elderly Judge was gay, I do not know. He was very kind and sympathetic toward me. He said, " I can see that you are a fine young man. If I thought you belonged in jail, I would put you there." He then went on to say, "I know the younger ones are more attractive, but you need to focus on men who are older, and especially stay away from guys under 21." He fined me $20, and let me go, and urged me to stay out of trouble. I stood there before the Judge, with my head bowed low, and quietly said "thank you." There were no words adequate to express my gratitude for the mercy this kind man extended to me. When driving me back to my job, the OLCC investigator said, "That Judge gave you one helluva break."

Now that this was over, I breathed a sigh of relief, and felt grateful for God's protection. It could have been worse. Homophobia takes on different manifestations. Often gay men are victimized and lured into sexual situations, and are brutally beaten and sometimes murdered. Did this young man have homoerotic desires and fantasies, suffering guilt because of it? Was he exploring when he allowed me to pick him up and then hit with a surge of guilt that resulted in his going to my neighbor and calling the police? Only God knows.

It was at this time of my life that I became friends with many lesbian and gay people. It wouldn't be long before I moved to the San Francisco Bay area.

Jacki & Esther

1960-1963

In the late 1950's, I hung out at the Harbor Club and the Half Moon Tavern. The Harbor Club was off limits to servicemen and military personnel. During the city's annual Rose Festival celebration, several Navy ships docked at Portland's waterfront. The Half Moon would be jam packed with Canadian sailors. Sometimes military men would patronize the Harbor Club in civilian clothes. Most of the military men went to gay bars to find sexual encounters. However, a few would lure gay men away from the bar, their buddies waiting outside to rob them and sometimes beat them up.

In those days, there was a strong bond between masculine women and effeminate men. Many of them hung out at the Harbor Club, forming strong friendship bonds. It was there that I met a lesbian couple, Jacki and Esther. Jacki (the "e" was intentionally left off the end of her name) was the butch (masculine) partner in their relationship. Jacki's given name was Betty. She changed her first name from Betty to Jacki when she and Esther became lovers. Jacki did assembly line work in a factory and sported a haircut like a man. Her wardrobe was all male except for the fact that she was forced to wear a bra because of her large breasts. Her partner, Esther, was femme, and could pass herself off as straight. Esther was previously married to a man and had a son. They both loved to hang out in bars and get the older men to buy them beer.

When I met Jacki and Esther for the first time, they had already moved from Portland to Oakland, California. They were back visiting Portland. We became good friends right away.

Jacki's prior lover, Trudy, was a hardcore alcoholic.. Trudy had a very butch sister, Louise, who was also an alcoholic. They, along with other lesbians, worked for a bag factory in Northwest Portland. I often partied with them. Sometimes I spent the night at Trudy's apartment, the two of us sleeping together in a large double bed. One night, I woke up to Trudy coming on to me sexually, breathing heavy. I got up from the bed and spent the rest of the night sleeping in her large easy chair. Having sex with a woman has never interested me and never will.

When preparing to return to Oakland, Jacki and Esther told me to be sure and look them up should I ever come to California. This was while I was working for the Southern Pacific Railroad at their Park Street freight station in NW Portland. When the Park Street station was demolished in 1961, I moved to Oakland. Jacki and Esther were living in a small cheap room in an old house situated on Grove Street, just around the corner from the Greyhound Bus Depot. They let me sleep on their couch while I looked for a job. Once I landed a job at the Colonial Cafeteria in downtown Oakland, I rented a small sleeping room of my own. The cafeteria job consisted mainly of taking dishes, pots and pans and trays off of a large conveyor belt.

Every Friday, I would cash my weekly paycheck from the Colonial Cafeteria and take the bus across the Bay Bridge to San Francisco where I would sit through all four of the shows at Finocchio's, the famous nightclub that featured female impersonators. While I idolized all of the performers, I was especially enamored by LaVerne Cummings, a strong feature attraction. Unlike the other performers, LaVerne did not wear a wig. His blonde hair was done up in high fashion and he sang in a falsetto voice. (Men were not sporting long hair at that time.) LaVerne was so convincing that some of the tourists in the audience insisted that he was actually a woman, and not a female impersonator. LaVerne's home phone number was listed in the telephone book -- and I often called him. We became friends over the telephone.

Soon I let my own hair grow long. I went to a beauty shop for a permanent and to have my hair tinted red. Eventually I lost my job at the Colonial Cafeteria because of it. When the boss presented me with my walking papers, he pointed out that many of their older conservative customers were offended by my effeminate appearance. He said, "We need these customers for our business. You are a good worker, Larry, but you just can't seem to do things our way."

When I visited Mom and Frank in Portland during the 1961 Christmas holidays with my bright red curly hair, they were shocked and appalled. I also visited Hattiebell and she, too, was not amused with my long flashy hair. She said, "You have the nerve to walk down the streets of Portland looking like that?!"

Frank, my classmate from grade and high school days, was stationed at an Army base in California. While on leave, he stopped by to visit me in Oakland. He didn't like my hair like that either. Years later, when reminiscing about visiting me in Oakland, he said, "I was going to spend a few days with you, but changed my mind when I saw what you did with your hair. I did not like what I saw."

In 1962 I moved back to Portland and got a job selling subscriptions to Life and Time magazines over the telephone. Here I discovered that I had a sales ability as well as a strong telephone personality. During this period I also worked for a construction company as a telephone solicitor, procuring sales leads for home improvement, mainly roofing and siding. I was very successful in this job as well.

A few months after I began this job, I got my greetings letter from Uncle Sam, informing me that I had to report for a military pre-induction physical examination. I was frightened. I feared the persecution in the Army would be far worse than what I experienced in my high school gym classes. Dad was elated. He said, "The Army will make a man out of you."

Jacki said to me on the telephone, "Don't worry, they aren't going to take you into the Army. You just go down there and be yourself and you won't have any trouble." In those days, homosexuals were not wanted in the military. The induction center was downtown, near SW 4th Avenue & Taylor Street. Jacki was right. I got through the pre-induction physical without a problem, and was given a 4-F classification, meaning that I was excused from my military obligation due to a medical condition.

"Homosexual tendencies" were listed on the medical form right along with physical ailments and disabilities. When reviewing my completed form, an Army psychiatrist asked me, "You say you are suffering from homosexual tendencies?" I responded that I had them, but that I was not "suffering." I was thoroughly questioned by two different psychiatrists, and answered all of their questions as honestly as I could. I was asked if I would be uncomfortable living in the barracks with the young men with whom I took the physical examination. My response was, "I don't know. I do find a couple of them very attractive." When we were all standing in a big circle totally naked, we had to bend over. A military doctor went around looking up the butt holes with a flashlight. "I'm looking for squares," he explained.

One of the psychiatrists told me that at least two men every week claimed to be homosexual to avoid the draft. This was one time in my life when I was delighted to be discriminated against. In the military, the other men would have made my life hell -- far worse than the guys in my high school gym class.

I moved back to Oakland in late 1962 where I would complete my final days under the identity of Larry. I sold newspaper subscriptions over the phone for the Berkeley Gazette, and then landed anther telephone solicitor job in Oakland for a company named East Bay Rentals. After they discontinued telephone soliciting and started getting their leads through radio advertising, they kept me on their staff to do general office work and check the credit references of potential customers. Eventually, they laid me off because business was slow, and I got my final job as Larry working for a painting contractor as a telephone solicitor.

In early 1963 I met Laura, a male to female trans-person. A complete change in my identity was soon to transpire.

Good-Bye Larry -- Hello Paula

1962-1963

A large military base was located in close-by Alameda. Horny sailors poured into Oakland. Picking them up in theaters, and at the bus depot, was easy. If a guy was in between buses, waiting at the Greyhound Bus Depot, I would invite him to my room just around the corner.

As a boy, I was obviously effeminate, even from a distance. One day when I was walking down San Pablo Boulevard, a car with teenage boys called out to me. I thought they said, "Hey Larry." I turned right around and responded. I realized that they were actually saying "Hey Fairy." They laughed and drove on.

During this time, men going out in female attire were arrested if detected in public. The exception was on Halloween when people went to costume parties. And so, effeminate gay men who liked dressing up as women planned all year for Halloween, when they could be "legal." Gay bars hosted costume parties and contests on Halloween.

When I relocated to Oakland from Portland the second time, Jacki and Esther had become managers of the rooming house in which they lived. They moved out of their small rented room on the first floor to the one-bedroom basement apartment, with a separate entrance. I rented a room in the same house on the second floor for $35 a month. Two other gay men resided on the second floor, and we all shared the same bathroom. One was a flamboyant fairy with bleached blonde hair, named Schlitz. Living across the hall from me was an elderly effeminate gay man whose given name was Marshall. Everyone called him "Lady Diane."

Lady Diane barely survived on a government retirement income of $48 a month. He paid $25 a month for his rented room. Lady Diane had a wealthy brother who refused to help him because he was homosexual. Jacki and Esther were very nice to Lady Diane and often invited him to their apartment for dinner.

Effeminate gay men were often addressed by the female pronoun. Jacki would say, "Don't underestimate Lady Diane. There are some good looking men who go to her apartment for blow jobs." . Apparently, some men considered Lady Diane to be an expert in the art of oral sex. One time, a gentleman caller stole her false teeth.

By the time I lived in Oakland, I had changed my feminine nickname from Talullah to Lola Mae. I derived Lola from a song in the Broadway play Damn Yankees: Whatever Lola Wants, Lola Gets. The Mae part came from my stepmother Lanta Mae.

One evening Jacki, Esther, Schlitz and I went out to a gay bar. Schlitz pointed out a person who appeared to be a sophisticated and attractive middle age woman. "That's Lori, he said. "She often goes out in drag." Upon talking to Lori, I ascertained that she was a hairdresser. She also said that she was friends with Stormy Lee, a female impersonator who performed as a stripper at Finocchio's. Little did I know then what a profound role Lori would play in my life.

When I visited Lori at her apartment, she shared her transsexuality. She was still working under her male identity, and planned on visiting Dr. Harry Benjamin, a renowned sexologist who coined the word transsexual. Dr. Benjamin had two offices, one in New York City and the other in San Francisco. An elderly man, he spent summers in San Francisco in order to avoid the summer heat waves in New York. Lori talked about transitioning her identity from Lloyd to Lori. This resurrected a spark in me that was first ignited when I read Christine Jorgenson's story in 1952.

And so, I started buying attire made for women. Jacki and Esther said they would buy me a panty girdle for Christmas, and so off we went to get one. When the saleslady was showing us the various girdle models, Jacki picked up one and I promptly pointed to another girdle, and said, "That's the one I want!" Jacki was furious and stormed out of the store. She did not want the sales lady to know that the panty girdle was for me. Later, Lady Diane came to my room and said, "You embarrassed Jacki in the clothing store and she does not ever want to see you again." In an effort to get back into Jacki's good graces, I went to a nearby barber and got a man's crew cut. When I was talking to Esther on the phone, she said, "She is pissed off at you. Just give her time, she'll get over it." And, within a couple of weeks, Jacki's anger cooled and we were friends again.

At this time hat-wigs were in vogue. They were inexpensive, and while they were worn as hats, they could be combed into a feminine hairstyle. My wardrobe of female clothing was building. One evening I called Lori and told her that I was going out as a woman. "If you need some place to go," she said, "you can come to my place." Lori's roommate, Rodger, often went out dressed as "Connie Rogers."

And so I donned my black hat-wig, put on some makeup and a dress, and out into public I ventured. This was my first time to go out in public as a woman. I got on a bus and went over to Lori's house. Later, on my way home on the bus, I sat toward the back.

A man got on the bus and said something to the driver, and they turned and looked at me. Fear shot through me like a bullet. I pulled the cord asking for the next stop, got off the bus, and took a cab the rest of the way home.

The next time I ventured out as a woman, wearing my hat wig, it was a stormy rainy day. I took the bus to San Francisco and went browsing through department stores. At one store, a man was demonstrating some product, and he called me "ma'am." This was the first time I had been called that. It made me feel like I was passing. When I got home, Schlitz said, "It is easier to go out in drag when it is raining as people don't notice others so much."

Soon I purchased a blonde wig. Come Halloween I went to a costume party in drag, held at a popular Oakland Gay bar called The Back Yard. The popular east bay drag queens were there in full regalia. The contest would be judged by two renowned drag queens from the area. Lori and Connie were there. When it came for the contestants to line up, Lori and Connie said they were not entering. The bar manager said to them: "All drags must enter." Lori turned to Connie and said, "Let's get out of here." The manager reneged and they were allowed to remain without entering the contest. Later, Schlitz said, "It is ridiculous, Lori and Connie sitting there thinking they are girls" Well, as fate had it, I won first prize in the contest.

My coworkers, Gene and Pauline came to the party that night. Gene was a salesman for East Bay Rentals, and his wife Pauline was office manager. At work, Pauline said to me: "You'd be a strange looking girl." However, that night at The Back Yard, when Pauline saw me in drag for the first time, she changed her mind and said: "By God you can pass as a woman."

By this time I was going out as a woman more and more. When visiting Lori and Connie I wore my blonde wig. Lori and I started discussing changing our identities in order to live as women full time. Lori said to me: "Now we've got to come up with a name for you. 'Lola Mae' sounds too much like a street walker." The words of a popular song, hey, hey, Paula.... emanated from the radio. I said to Lori: "How about the name Paula?" Lori responded: "You look like a Paula."

A month passed. Laura tinted my wig a bright red combined with dark auburn. She also gave me makeup tips. I started going out as Paula more and more. Jacki was not amused. Exactly why my cross dressing angered her, I do not know, particularly when she wore male attire. When talking about living as Paula full-time, Jacki said: "You'll never get away with that shit!" Some elderly straight tenants living on the first floor, who knew who I was, complained about me going up and down the halls dressed in women's clothes. Consequently, I moved to a rooming house in East Oakland, where it was easier to sneak in and out as a woman without being noticed.

One Sunday morning I decided to try my wings and go to church as Paula. I picked the First Assembly of God in Oakland. Like women did in those days, I wore matching shoes, purse, and gloves, very smartly dressed like a good Christian girl. I was made to feel welcome the moment I walked through the door.

A lady invited me to her home for dinner after church with her husband, mother, and children I was beginning to realize that Paula was gaining acceptance that Larry never enjoyed. When we arrived at her home, she invited me to come with her to the bedroom and visit while she changed clothes. Like she would do with a girl friend, she undressed in front of me. This was the first time a woman had ever undressed in my presence. Since this had never happened before, at first I was a tad bit aghast; however, after a couple of minutes it just seemed right and natural.

Being so happy to receive this kind of acceptance from a heterosexual church family, I called Jacki and Esther while sitting at their dining room table. Jacki answered the phone. I had already told them I was going to church that Sunday as Paula. With my voice softened and raised, I told her how much I enjoyed the church service and was visiting with some folk from church who had invited me to their home for dinner. Jacki was furious. She said: "I don't like this shit you are pulling, Larry, and I would appreciate it if you would not call me up and tell me about it!" And with that she angrily hung up on me, slamming down the receiver. I faked the end of the conversation by saying: "Okay. I'll see you later. Bye."

The following April of 1963, Lori and I decided it was time for us to assume a female identity full time. We talked about getting new Social Security numbers. Lori decided to change her girl's name to Laura. Lloyd Lawrence became Laura Leigh. Standing in Lori's kitchen discussing what name I would have on my new Social Security card, Lori said: "Paula Nielsen". It fit. In that moment, an embryo was formed in my soul: Larry Nielsen being reborn as Paula Nielsen. I could see no reason to change my last name. A few days later I went to the Social Security office, and filled out an application. In those days, ID was not required to get a Social Security number. Within a week, I got my new Social Security card as Paula Nielsen in the mail.

By this time I was doing telephone canvassing for the painting firm and was making good money, enough to make it possible for me to relocate in San Francisco and start my new life as Paula. On the evening of May 1, 1963, Laura helped me move my belongings into her apartment. I had developed both a male and female wardrobe. When moving, I took only the female wardrobe, and left all of the boys clothes behind. That night, Larry died and Paula was born.

Two things happened which propelled Laura and me to relocate in San Francisco. Laura got a job as a woman, working for a hair salon in Walnut Park. Some fairy dropped a dime on Laura, called the salon and told them that Laura was a man. They let her go. Rodger dropped the name of "Connie Rogers" and discontinued cross dressing altogether.

Next, the neighbors who lived across the hall from Laura caught on that Lloyd and Laura were one and the same. The man was a strong redneck. One day when I came home, he saw me in the hallway and said, "Are you one of those guys who wears the wig, like Lawrence?" "I don't know what you mean," I replied. Gruffly, he said, "I think you do." Also, one day while Laura was walking up the stairs, this same neighbor said about her, "Isn't that disgusting?" A friend had sent a card addressed to "Connie and Laura" and someone had written on the envelope Queers! Obviously it was time to relocate.

A well-known San Francisco transvestite, Louise Lawrence, who had lived under that identity for 20 years, told Laura, "You cannot change identity without changing residence." Louise managed an apartment building, named Dolphin Square in the Nob Hill section of San Francisco. Laura and Rodger rented separate apartments in Dolphin Square. I moved into the Julia Hotel, a cheap hotel about a block down the street. About two months later, when Louise had another vacancy in Dolphin Square, I moved in.

So, here we were: Two transsexuals, just starting out. Our next step was to find a job under our new identities. I was about to pound the pavement of the streets of San Francisco, looking for work, wearing 4 inch spike high heels with pointed toes!

Years As Paula

Pounding The Pavement
1963

After being laid off at East Bay Rentals in Oakland, I remained good friends with most of the people I had met there. To help me get started living in my new identity, Pauline the office manager agreed to give me a job reference as Paula. She explained to me that many employers require that their employees be bonded, and that there are two different kinds of bonds. One is a blanket bond when a newly hired employee's name is routinely added to a list of insured employees with no detailed background investigation. When one is bonded individually and personally, Pauline explained, the insurance company providing the bond does an extensive investigation into the prospective employee's background.

And so, armed with the job reference from Pauline, I started looking for a job in San Francisco as Paula. The 4" spike high heeled shoes, with pointed toes, were obviously not made for comfort. After spending a day of walking up and down hills, filling out employment applications at various employment agencies, and all that goes with job hunting, I was exhausted. Blisters formed on the heels of my aching feet, my toes hurt and my legs felt like rubber. In spite of this, I was very happy in my new, and true, identity as Paula.

Laura, on the other hand, lucked out and was spared having to endure pounding the pavements in high heels. Right away she landed a job as a teacher/office manager for a business school on Market Street in downtown San Francisco, where people learned typing and shorthand. Her boss was an ex-police officer.

A private employment agency sent me to interview as a statistical typist for a steamship company. As soon as I took their typing test, they hired me. While stat typing is not my favorite kind of work, the job paid well. When I reported for work the first day, the supervisor said, "We require a physical examination by our company doctor." He had already made an appointment for me to see their doctor later that week. He also gave me an application for a personal bond. On my coffee break, I called Pauline, and she said, "You are going to have to quit. Being a man impersonating a woman would be a reason to decline your bond." I finished the day, and never went back. For about a week I went out on other interviews set up by employment agencies. After interviewing me, many prospective employers said, "We have other people coming in, and expect to make our decision next week." It was the old polite don't call us, we'll call you routine.

One day, I had an interview with a large insurance company at 4pm. After walking the streets all day, I was exhausted. While filling out the application, the personnel director said to me, "Been looking for work huh?" I snapped back, "Yes, and I am a sick and tired of it!" Job hunting has always been very stressful to me, both as Larry and as Paula. When I finished filling out the lengthy forms, he said that a Mr. so-and-so has to review the application, and "unfortunately he is out of town."

Next, I responded to a newspaper ad for a dictaphone typist job. It was for the claims department of a small insurance company. After I took their typing test, they were so impressed that they hired me on the spot. I managed to learn that their employees were placed under a blanket bond, and that no physical examination was required. Later, Pauline told me that they had called her to check my job reference. She said, "You are going to have to make this job last. Mr. Lewis [her boss] does not want me doing this anymore."

My official job title was claims secretary. The morning hours were spent typing drafts [checks] for claimants; the afternoon was spent transcribing form letters, such as letters to doctors requesting information, rejection letters to claimants, etc. I also transcribed correspondence for the claims manager and two claims adjusters off a dictaphone. After I had been there two months, the claims manager told me that my work production was more than double than that of my predecessors.

When going on coffee breaks with female co-workers, it was easy for me to adjust to being Paula. At first, however, it seemed strange to hear women discussing personal things, such as their periods and other "female" things that women only talk about with other women. One of the gals asked me if I would come in early one morning to show her how I applied makeup!

Once established in an apartment and gainfully employed, I felt the need to go to church. I visited Glad Tidings Assembly of God in San Francisco, which was located near the Fillmore District. That first Sunday morning at Glad Tidings in the summer of 1963 remains forever etched on the magic screen of my mind. During the preaching part of the service, I felt the inner voice of the Holy Spirit say to me, Can I have Paula? My thoughts harkened back to my days as a 12 year old boy at Powellhurst Baptist Church in Portland, where God saved me and called me to preach, and do the work of an evangelist. Powerful emotions surged through me with the realization that my transition in identity to Paula did not change my call to preach. Truly, the gifts and callings of God are without repentance. (Romans 11:29). I returned that evening for the Sunday night evangelistic service. At the conclusion of the service, I went forward to the altar and joined others in the prayer room, where I re-consecrated my life to God, as Paula.

Soon I joined the church choir, singing the alto part. I would have preferred to sing bass. My deep and strong voice is what God gave me. It is not a male or female voice; it is Paula's voice! Obviously, however, these evangelical Christians would not have understood this. And so I muddled along with the ladies in the alto section. For the Christmas cantata that year we presented Handel's Messiah. I literally thrilled to being part of the stirring anthem of The Hallelujah Chorus. Laura came to the cantata. Afterward, she said to me, "You are doing the things as Paula that you tried to do as Larry." There was no doubt about it: I was enjoying acceptance as Paula that Larry never received.

Soon after joining the choir, I became friends with the choir director and his wife. They invited me to go out and eat with them every Sunday following the worship service. The restaurant we patronized was a sidewalk cafe in the North Beach section of San Francisco, situated directly below Finocchio's!

There was no way I would ever consider going back to being tolerated as an effeminate boy.

A Pill A Day Keeps The Falsies Away
1963

Before I proceed any further in my story, some enlightenment on the misunderstood subject of transsexualism is necessary. At the very least, it may clarify this topic, which seems confusing to someone who has not faced or studied, human sexuality.

I have often been asked, "What is the difference between a tranvestite and a transsexual?

"Tranvestites are happy with their biological sex (the genitals they were born with), even though they may cross dress occasionally or full-time. They do not feel like they are trapped in the wrong body. Some enjoy public role-playing as the opposite sex; others only cross dress in private.

Transsexuals, on the other hand, are unhappy with their biological sex, whether they cross dress occasionally, full-time, or not at all. They do feel that they are, in fact, trapped in the wrong body. This is not a matter of sexual preference; it has to do with gender identity.

Another question I am frequently asked is, "What is the difference between transsexual and transgender?" To accommodate transsexuals who cannot have surgery for a number of reasons, i.e., financial inability to have it done, some who cannot be operated on for health reasons, and others who do not want surgery, and yet who prefer to live full time in what they believe to be their true psychological identity, the word transgender was coined in 1980. In his book The Transsexual Phenomenon, first published in 1966, Dr. Harry Benjamin, a prominent medical doctor and a leader in transsexual treatment, states:

"According to the dictionary, sex is synonymous with gender. But, in actuality, this is not true...'Sex' is more applicable where there is the implication of sexuality, of libido, and of sexual activity. 'Gender' is the non-sexual side of sex. As someone once expressed it: Gender is located above, and sex below the belt. This differentiation, however, cannot always be very sharp or constant and therefore, to avoid pedantry, sex and gender must, here and there, be used interchangeably."

He further elaborates:

"Sex is a matter of anatomy and physiology. 'male' and 'female' are sexual terms. 'Gender', however, can be considered a mixture of inborn and acquired, that is, learned characteristics. 'Masculine' and 'feminine' are therefore expressions belonging to the gender concept....The dominant status of the genital organs for the determination of one's sex has been shaken, at least in the world of science. Genitals receive an over emphasis in our minds compared to their importance in the full scheme of one's sexual identity and activity; indeed, they comprise a relatively small part of one's sexual identity. "

Dr. Benjamin continues:

"For the uneducated, there are only two sexes: a person is either male or female -- Adam or Eve. The educated and enlightened realize that every Adam contains elements of Eve and every Eve harbors traces of Adam, physically as well as psychologically."

Everyone is androgynous to some degree.

In his book Dr. Benjamin elaborates in minute detail the varying degrees of transvestism and transsexualism in individuals. Dr. Benjamin coined the word transsexual to describe an individual who feels that he or she is trapped in the wrong body. Transsexuals have an intense desire to live full time in the identity opposite of their biological sex whether or not they have, or pursue, sex reassignment surgery.

Now that I was established in my new identity as Paula, it was time to consider moving toward sex change surgery. The first step was to make an appointment with Dr. Benjamin. While Dr. Benjamin was impressed that I was holding down a job as Paula, he strongly admonished me to not even consider sex change surgery until I had functioned full time in society as a woman for at least one year. This is wise advice. Some male to female trans-persons go through estrogen therapy and, in some cases, sex change surgery prior to living as women. Laura and I believed in doing just the opposite.

Dr. Benjamin started both of us on estrogen therapy immediately. This consisted of high potency weekly estrogen injections, plus a strong pill daily. Over time, while I was on the medication, I experienced many overall physical changes, including breast development. Laura and I would joke, A pill a day keeps the falsies away.

In reminiscing about the 1920's, Sophie Tucker said:

The men were not concerned about,
what a girl wore underneath
They didn't have to guess
what was inside a dress,
In those days, falsies were teeth.

It didn't take long for me to discover that a change in physical characteristics was not the only side effect of strong estrogen medication. I had emotional, menopausal side effects similar to a woman going through the change in life. I had strong emotional mood swings, coupled with an intense desire to have a romantic relationship with a man. About three years later when I discontinued estrogen therapy, these emotional side effects went away.

In 1970, a doctor in Beverly Hills told me that about 35% of his transsexual patients had these emotional side effects. Laura did not have them. This doctor put me on a different type of estrogen, and the strong emotional side effects returned, so I discontinued the hormone treatments altogether. Even though I have not been on estrogen therapy since 1970, over the years I have maintained a passable amount of breast development. And my breasts did not become saggy later on in my senior years.

In 1990 the Gresham Outlook did a feature article about me. In describing me to his readers, the writer said that I wore a padded bra. I wrote a letter to the editor correcting this statement immediately. I said, "I've got good news for some of your male readers. I do not own a bra, padded or otherwise." The letter was published. I told a friend, "If the writer assumed that I was wearing a padded bra, then my boobs must look pretty darn good!" Like Sophie Tucker would say:

I believe in giving tit for tat
that's the way I live,
And I'm entitled to a helluva lot of tat,
for what I've got to give!

Family Ties
1963

Often I am asked, "How did your relatives react when you transitioned your identity from Larry to Paula?" or "Does your family accept you as Paula?"

After transitioning my identity to Paula, I was working a full time job and attending church, where they did not know I had the former identity as Larry. With experience, I learned never to assume who would, or who would not, accept my transsexuality if they knew my entire story. There have been times when someone whom I thought would surely understand did not approve upon finding out. On the other hand, some folks who I thought would never accept me as a transperson, did accept me.

Once living full time in the identity of Paula, I wrote Mom a letter and told her about it. Initially, she did not approve. She said, "You may feel that Larry is dead, but to me you will always be my son." She also said, "You could put all of that energy into being a man." This brought to mind a letter she had sent me when I was living in Oakland. In anger, she said, "If you're going to be a queer all your life..." However, in another letter she apologized for that remark. She just did not understand that I had no choice about my sexuality. I explained to her that it is impossible for me to be someone that I am not. While I was discussing this with Dr. Benjamin he said, "A woman does not have a son for 25 years and then, overnight, say she has a daughter." I wrote to Mom and quoted what Dr. Benjamin said to Laura's mother: "Would you rather have an unhappy homosexual son, or a happy heterosexual daughter?" Over the years, Mom has adjusted to me being Paula. She never disowned me.

Of course, Mom had to address mail to me as "Paula Nielsen." In her first few letters, however, the salutation said "Dear Larry." Eventually, the salutation was changed to "Hi dear." I still remember the day when I opened up a letter from her that said "Dear Paula." She was adjusting.

I thought for sure that my sister Teresa would accept my change in identity. Today, she totally accepts me as her sister. Back in 1963, Mom told me over the telephone, "I wouldn't expect to hear from her if I were you. She isn't too happy about it." Other than an occasional card, for the next ten years, Teresa and I were not in touch.

Dad never did accept me as Paula. When Mom first told him he refused to believe it. This came as no surprise to me, inasmuch as he and I had gone our separate ways back in 1960, the last time I ever saw him. He and I had no contact of any kind until my stepmother, Lanta Mae, died in 1990. I sent flowers to her funeral, and he sent me a note thanking me for them. I sent Dad a letter which went out to my television mailing list, asking for help in purchasing a car. In hindsight, I wish I had never done that.

He sent me back a scathing letter which said, "I don't know anyone named Sister Paula. I used to have a nice boy named Larry but I don't know whatever happened to him." He also said, "You could have been a longshoreman..." I responded with an angry letter that said, "You didn't treat me like I was a nice boy. You humiliated me in front of people, calling me a 'goddamn big sissy'. You never approved of anything I did, even calling me a 'religious crackpot' and forbidding me to go to the Assembly of God church." And I told him if he could not let go of his prejudicial feelings, he and I could continue going our separate ways. He did not write back. And when he died, I did not send flowers to his funeral. I had no feelings, good or bad, for him whatsoever.

His rejection of me as Paula had not changed over the years. I was hoping that he and I could reunite. Mom thought it was deplorable that anyone could disown their own child. Today, Dad and Lanta Mae are buried together in the same grave. Every year I put flowers on their grave as an act of forgiveness.

The rest of my relatives all came around to accepting me as Paula. Dad was the only one in the family who was adamantly against it. There are many trans-people whose entire families totally disown them, so I consider myself fortunate to have the acceptance of most of my relatives.

Finocchio's

1960-1964

When I originally moved to the San Francisco Bay area, my big dream was to be a performer at Finocchio's. However, after starting to live and work full time as Paula, that dream was put on the back burner. By the time I started living full time as Paula, I became friends with some of the performers at the world famous nightclub.

Finocchio's was a major San Francisco tourist attraction from the 1930s to the 1990s. Because of a major rent increase and declining attendance as cross-dressing became less unusual, the club would eventually close on November 27, 1999.

When I first hit the Bay area In the early 1960's, everyone of prominence -- movie stars, celebrities, etc. -- included a night out at Finocchio's when visiting the city by the Bay. Seven nights a week, from 8 pm until 2 am, four shows a night, a cast of capable performers were entertaining.

All of the acts were performed live. A three-piece combo, consisting of piano, saxophone, and drums, provided the music. After a rousing musical intro, the voice of one of the performers said over a loud speaker:

"Good evening ladies and gentlemen. Welcome to the world famous Finocchio's, the home of mirth, laughter and gayety, and featuring the world's most glamorous and talented female impersonators. And now, meet the producer of our show, and your master of merriment, Mr. Lester LaMonte, the fabulous Paper Fashion Plate. Let's hear it..."

In addition to being the show's emcee, Lester choreographed the nightclub's production numbers. Lester, a man in his 60's, looking somewhat like Sophie Tucker, was quick to explain his title to the audience:

"Let me explain why I am called the 'Paper Fashion Plate.' "All of the gowns you see me wear, throughout the entire course of the revue, are made entirely of Dennison's crepe paper."

One night a heckler called out from the audience "Light a match!" to which Lester calmly replied:

"I'm not that hot to burn, honey. Besides, your match is too small."

Lester introduced each act in the show individually, and each time he would come out sporting a different paper dress. He made the costumes himself. During the heyday of Vaudeville, in the 1920's and 30's, Lester had a theatrical production in New York called Paper Creations. He was backed up by a group of chorus girl dancers, all wearing the paper costumes created by LaMonte. He worked with big name stars such as Gypsy Rose Lee.

Nearly every female type and caricature was emulated in the world famous show. Included in the cast was: Flamenco dancer, Tonya Damolina; 50's comedy sweater gal, Jackie Phillips; that long tall gal Elton Paris (who shifted his singing voice from high female soprano to a deep male voice in one breath); Francis & Blair, the two old bags from Oakland; Kara Montez, dancer; Stormy Lee, stripper; Lucien, the original male Sophie Tucker; J.J. Van Dyke, excelling in comedy caricatures (granny, the drunk, Phyllis Diller); the young and beautiful Marilyn Monroe of the show, Lee Shaw; and the ultra-glamorous, incomparable LaVerne Cummings.

Lucien Phelps, the legendary and original male Sophie

Tucker appeared at Finocchio's for 27 years. Sophie Tucker herself often visited Finocchio's. The first night Sophie heard Lucien sing the songs that made her famous, she was so intrigued that she gave him her Russian ermine coat.

Most of the audience at Finocchio's were heterosexual tourists, out for a good time and a night on the town. The Greyline tourist bus offered their clientele a tour of San Francisco night clubs and Finocchio's was on the list. Lucien did banter with the audience, asking folk where they were from, etc. One night, while J.J. Van Dyke was doing his Phyllis Diller routine, a male heckler in the audience asked, "Are you 'one of them'?" J.J. responded, "Well, it takes one to know one, so we'll let you make the decision."

During my first year living as Paula in 1963-1964, I became close friends with stripper Stormy Lee, whom I met through Laura. Having worked as an entertainer at a club in New Orleans prior to moving to San Francisco, Stormy was introduced as The Girl From Bourbon Street. How well I recall Stormy's banter the first time I attended Finocchio's:

They say I'm in the big time
here at Finocchio's,
Let's dim the lights,
and shed the clothes.

Two stripper gimmicks that Stormy used effectively were: (1) working with a black light with hands glowing on the breasts and buttocks and (2) light bulbs highlighting the breasts, and saying the end on his buttocks as he exited the stage.

Stormy was also a patient of Dr. Harry Benjamin, taking estrogen pills and injections, and had developed very real female breasts. Mr. Finocchio insisted that the performers arrive and leave the club in male attire. He did not consider transsexuals to be female impersonators. When initially hired by Finocchio's,

Stormy had not yet started estrogen therapy. Stormy was strictly forbidden to show his female breasts to the audience. In his strip act, when he was down to bra and g-string, with the erotic sound of the drum beat to Temptation, Stormy would say, "Don't get nervous boys, I've got the same thing you've got!" In 1964, Stormy traveled to Casablanca where he had sex change surgery. On his very last night at Finocchio's, Stormy got drunk during his strip routine and took off his bra, revealing his female breasts to the audience.

While performing at Finocchio's, Stormy Lee had a daytime female identity as 'Kathy.' Kathy used her own hair in the daytime and looked entirely different than her nighttime stage persona. In fact, she was legally married to Bob, a handsome man who was part owner of a beauty salon. She proudly wore their wedding ring. Kathy and Bob's heterosexual friends had no idea that Kathy performed at Finocchio's. One night, while in the middle of her routine, Stormy spotted one of her and Bob's straight couple friends in the front row. She was wearing her wedding ring. Fearful that the couple would see, and recognize, the ring, Stormy quickly pulled the ring off her finger, keeping it clutched in her hand, out of sight, while doing her strip routine.

On Saturday mornings, Kathy would call me and invite me over to spend the day at her apartment, and have me pick up something from a bakery en route. During my year in San Francisco we were close friends. I do not recall how the conversation came about, when I asked her why she wanted me to come over on a given day. Her response: "To keep me company, bitch!"

Yes, I had arrived: Living and working full time as Paula; enjoying acceptance at an Assembly of Church; receiving estrogen therapy and well on my way toward sex change surgery.

Everything was great -- until I fell in love!

I Left My Heart In San Francisco
1964

Every Christian has at least one question they are going to ask God once they have passed over into the realm of the Infinite. The late Kathryn Kuhlman, a leading charismatic healing evangelist of the 20th Century, said that she is going to ask God why everyone was not healed in her miracle services. Often, many who were unbelievers would walk away healed. Yet, others who were believers left the meetings with the same physical malady they came in with.

I am no exception. I will present God with two questions: First, Why was I born a transsexual? And second, Why do people fall in love with someone who is not in love with them? I believe that two of the deepest forms of emotional pain are: (1) The pain of a mother when losing a child and (2) the pain of unrequited love. It seems that over the years the cross I bore was the deep emotional pain of unrequited love. When this happened, the object of my affection genuinely loved me as a best friend. However, he was not in love with me. I have never enjoyed a two-sided romance.

There is not a human emotion that Jesus did not experience when he lived and walked among us in His humanity as the Son of Man. Jesus wept because the people whom He loved the most rejected that love. He came unto His own and "His own received Him not." (John 1:11) Jesus certainly felt the inner pain of unrequited love when he wept over the city of Jerusalem, saying, "Oh Jerusalem, Jerusalem, which killeth the prophets, and stonest them that are sent unto thee; how often would I have gathered thy children together, as a hen doth gather her brood under her wings, and ye would not!" (Luke 13:34 & Matthew 23:37) And, interestingly enough, Jesus speaks of Himself using the female imagery of a mother hen as He experiences the inner pain of unrequited love.

A close friend told me that much of what I experienced over the years was not love, but rather, obsession. When in an obsessive place about another person, I could not think of anything or anyone else. Consequently other areas of my life suffered because of it. The good news is the fact that this did not happen very often. However, when it did, it took me about six months to recover. Also, once I did get over someone, I never went back into that deep romantic emotional place with that person again. In fact, with the passage of time, usually the person and I became good friends.

Being in love did not make me happy. Rather, it made me very unhappy. Rather than looking within myself, and to God, for emotional fulfillment, I was expecting a particular person to make me happy. I grew up with Walt Disney classics such as Cinderella and Snow White. I truly believed that my Prince charming would come along and sweep me off my feet, and that he and I would live happily ever after.

I can easily handle close platonic friendships, close working relationships; and even casual sexual encounters. So long as I do not fall in love with the person(s) close to me, everything is fine. Yet, the casual sexual encounters leave me with a feeling of emptiness. Not only is promiscuous behavior unfulfilling, it is far below God's standards and ideals. I yearned for a two-sided monogamous life-time experience with another person. I wanted to marry a preacher.

Many gay, lesbian, bisexual, and trans-people have the desire to raise children. Not me. Never have I had any inclination to raise a family. As the Sophie Tucker classic I'm Living Alone & I Like It says

I'm a single bed one-pillow mama...

Yes, I am a loner. An old-time gospel song says:
"It is Jesus and me, for each tomorrow,
for every heartache, and every sorrow...

My one-on-one friendship with Jesus helped get me through the loneliness of my high school days. And when I suffered the pain of rejection in a one-sided love relationship, Jesus was always there for me. Because of that I have always survived these experiences, and have been able to move on with my life, even when it meant relocating to another city.

And this is exactly why I moved from San Francisco to Los Angeles in the summer of 1964. While living in Dolphin Square, I fell in love with a handsome young man named Len. Interestingly enough, this was not a sexual relationship, per se. Len was Paula's first love. Dr. Benjamin encouraged his pre-op male-to-female trans patients, while living as women, not to pick up men. Len genuinely liked and respected me. However, he was not in love with me on a romantic level. During this time I was on intense estrogen treatment of weekly injections and strong daily oral medication, creating deep emotions. I needed to be in new surroundings that did not remind me of my relationship with Len.

So, there I was -- on a plane to Los Angeles, with tears streaming down my face, while the Tony Bennett song I Left My Heart in San Francisco filled my innermost being. To this day, whenever I hear this song, or sing it as an entertainer, I think of Len. After I relocated to Southern California, I never saw or heard from Len again.

Alone In Huntington Park

1964

As the airplane approached the Los Angeles airport at nighttime, I saw miles and miles of lights stretching out over the vast metropolitan area. I didn't know that the loneliest moments of my life would be spent in Huntington Park, a SE suburb of Los Angeles, located on the outskirts of a large industrial area. Four years later, Troy Perry would start Metropolitan Community Church, the first Christian ministry to gays, in a small house in Huntington Park with twelve people in attendance at the first service.

Since I needed new surroundings, where there was nothing to remind me of Len, I left San Francisco. Kathy had said, "Why don't you move to Los Angeles and stay with Aleisha?" When performing at Finocchio's, Aleisha's stage name was Lee Shaw. After relocating in Southern California, Aleisha had sex change surgery performed by Dr. Elmer Belt, and legally became Aleisha Crenshaw. She resided in a studio apartment in Huntington Park. She was employed as a receptionist in a beauty salon, where she met and befriended Steve, a gay hairdresser who worked there. Steve and I would become good friends for many years to come.

It was time to hit the pavement and look for a job in my new town. When I left my position in San Francisco, the Claims Manager said, "Paula, you are going to be hard to replace on that desk." I had diligently worked to improve my typing skills, feeling that I had to be better than most because of my trans-sexuality. This paid off, inasmuch as fast and accurate typists were in great demand in the job market.

An employment agency sent me to a company in Vernon, a large industrial area near Huntington Park. On my first day of employment, I was informed that the company required a birth certificate. I managed to stall them, stating I had to send off for the legal document. As soon as I got a paycheck, I abandoned the job.

Next, I answered a newspaper ad for dictaphone typists placed by a major insurance company in downtown LA. As soon as I took their typing test, they hired me on the spot, telling me to report the next morning to the Personnel Department to fill out tax forms. When I did this, they informed me that a physical examination by their company doctor was required, and I was handed an appointment slip to see their doctor that morning, about three blocks away. I took the appointment slip and did not return.

After leaving the insurance company I picked up a newspaper, and over a cup of coffee at a corner drug store fountain, I scanned the want ads. I noticed an ad for a stenographer, that stated 'insurance experience helpful.' The ad only gave a street address, which was one-half block away. It was located on the 12th floor of an office building. Alighting from the elevator, and walking down the hall to the designated room number, I saw a sign that read Law Offices. Not having any legal experience, I turned and walked back toward the elevator.

Then the thought occurred to me that the ad said nothing about legal secretarial experience. So, I turned around and walked in, took their steno typing test, and was offered a position at a salary larger than the other two jobs I was unable to keep. It was a small law firm with six lawyers, whose specialty was defending insurance companies in workers compensation claims. The lawyers dictated correspondence and legal documents on a tape machine called a Stenorette. The steno pool consisted of three girls.

Since nothing was said about a birth certificate or a physical examination, I got to keep this job, and stayed there for a little over two years.

It wasn't long before Kathy and Bob came to visit from San Francisco, on their way to a holiday in Las Vegas. Aleisha decided to go with them, and then move back to San Francisco. This left me alone in an apartment that was not rented to me. When the landlady discovered that Aleisha was gone, she told me I would have to move. I found an apartment close by.

Aleisha did not have a phone in her apartment. After she left, I tried to call Len in San Francisco from a phone booth. His roommate informed me that as soon as I had left San Francisco, Len moved in with Val, a drag queen whom we met through Kathy, and they became lovers. While I was crushed by this, I also knew that there was nothing I could do about it. With entirely new surroundings, and the passage of time, my wound healed.

As I walked back from the phone booth to Aleisha's empty apartment, I felt totally and completely alone. There has never been a time in my life, before or since, when I felt so lonely. I had hoped desperately that, after I moved to LA, Len would follow me there. I also felt a sense of betrayal, because Aleisha had left right at a time that I needed her companionship.

It was while I was sitting in that empty room that my thoughts flashed back to my teenage days at the Wings of Healing Temple in Portland. A longing to go back to those days overwhelmed me. I suddenly remembered that Wings of Healing had relocated from Portland to Los Angeles in 1959.

Wings Of Healing Revisited

1964-1965

I was at a very low moment in my life, very much alone and broken hearted. Yet, Jesus, the healer of broken hearts was there for me. (Luke 4:18) I am reminded of the beloved song:

Jesus is near, to comfort and cheer,
just when I need Him most.

I looked up Wings of Healing in the telephone directory and got their downtown Los Angeles street location. They had purchased the Embassy Hotel and conducted their services in the auditorium. Their international radio ministry continued.

The first time I entered the lobby of the Embassy Auditorium, I was greeted by one of the staff ministers who told me that Dr. Wyatt had recently passed away. I soon learned that Dr. Wyatt had bequeathed the Wings of Healing ministry to his wife Evelyn.

Within a few weeks I became part of the Wings of Healing

choir. The first choir rehearsal that I attended in the Spring of 1964 remains etched in my memory. One of the songs we sang was I Must Tell Jesus. Through this song I experienced a deep and powerful comfort as the Holy Spirit became the One called alongside to help. (John 14:26)

I must tell Jesus, I must tell Jesus,
I cannot bear these burdens alone
I must tell Jesus, I must tell Jesus,
Jesus can help me, Jesus alone.

Evelyn Wyatt was also experiencing the pain of a broken heart, passing through a time of bereavement over the loss of her beloved husband, Dr. Thomas Wyatt. Dr. Wyatt had served his generation well as a powerful global radio preacher. I recall two different occasions when Evelyn Wyatt shared her sorrow with the Los Angeles congregation. Both times she fought back tears. "We have said that we are going to talk about Wings of Healing, and not Dr. Wyatt. It is hard to talk about the one without talking about the other. He represented Wings of Healing to us."

And on another occasion she said, "When Dr. Wyatt passed away, I felt so alone. Who is going to keep the radio ministry going? I was praying for guidance in choosing someone to preach on the broadcast; when I realized that God wanted me to do it."

This was in 1964. Evelyn Wyatt stepped into her husband's shoes, and became a powerful radio minister to thousands worldwide. The spot on the program -- It's testimony time on Wings of Healing – previously held by Evelyn Wyatt, was turned over to Roberta Tuthill, a long time faithful and devoted follower of the Wyatts.

When Wings of Healing relocated to Los Angeles in 1959, most of Dr. Wyatt's staff had moved to Southern California as well. And so, there I was, living under the identity of Paula, associating with people who had known me as Larry. While transitioning in identity, I retained my original family last name, which led to some awkward situations.

In choir rehearsal, I had become friendly with Delores Collins, wife of Dale Collins, a staff minister. In Portland, I had never really gotten to know Delores. Sitting there at that first choir rehearsal, Roberta Tuthill walked in and sat next to us. Immediately, upon hearing the name 'Nielsen,' Roberta said, "Larry Nielsen?" Delores responded to Roberta, "She [me] doesn't know him." This could indicate that there had been some discussion about my identity. I sat there, not expressing any emotion, and said nothing.

Later, in the hallway, Roberta said to me, "You may not know it, but you have a twin brother in Portland." They only knew I had just moved to LA from San Francisco. When Dorothy Long, also a staff member from Portland, first saw me, she turned to someone and said, "Doesn't she remind you of a boy in Portland?" Later, Dorothy said, "I still think Paula is connected to Larry." Roberta responded, "I do too." Here again, I said nothing.

The teenagers at Wings of Healing treated Paula much nicer than the young people in the Portland church had treated Larry. Teenagers, who would never accept me as Larry, did accept me as Paula. I became good friends with Deena and Bonnie, then teenagers, who were little kids when I was still living in Portland. One Sunday, after church in a nearby restaurant, Deena told me that rumor had it Paula and Larry were one and the same. I denied it. I was fearful of losing Deena and Bonnie's friendship.

Today, I wish I could have told them that Paula and Larry were, in fact, one and the same. Instead, I used the ploy of disguising the truth by drawing attention to it. I complained to Delores Collins about what Deena had told me in the restaurant. Delores hugged me and apologized that my feelings were hurt. She defended me and said to others, "Someone can be psychologically damaged for life by this kind of a story." Years later, when I wrote to Wings of Healing and told them the truth in a letter, I apologized to Delores.

After it had been made known that I was upset about finding out that comments had been made about Paula and Larry being one and the same, Roberta said to me, "Larry was very effeminate, and so that really isn't as bad of a remark as you might think." She also said, "You are much more intelligent and capable than he was." This brought to mind what Laura had said to me in San Francisco, when I participated in the Assembly of God church choir cantata, "You are doing the things as Paula that you tried to do as Larry."

To this day, I carry a letter from Evelyn Wyatt in my purse that I cherish. It is dated October 8, 2003. Knowing then that Paula was formerly Larry, it says in part:

"In addition to Roberta, several others on the staff remember you....Everyone sends their greetings and best wishes...

It always gives me joy to hear from friends who remember the wonderful days in Portland, and meetings in the Embassy Auditorium [in LA]...I will always think of those times with great affection and many warm memories, and your recollection of 'rain in the time of the latter rain..."

In a letter dated June 16, 2004, Roberta Tuthill, wrote me, saying, in part:

"With deep sorrow for our loss, but profound gratitude for the extraordinary life of a 'good and faithful servant,' this is to let you know that Evelyn Wyatt went to her Heavenly reward June 11, 2004...

...Just know that Evelyn Wyatt deeply appreciated you, prayed for you, and went to her reward with the Wings of Healing family on her heart, of which you are such a vital part, Paula."

It was Evelyn Wyatt's wish that, after her passing, her grandson, Dr. Thomas R. Wyatt, would take over the ongoing Wings of Healing ministry. The broadcast still airs worldwide, with wonderful gospel messages being preached by Dr. Wyatt. His wife Sharon reads the scriptures. The program continues to add new radio stations worldwide. What a grand and glorious legacy!

May it be said that history will say of Thomas and Evelyn Wyatt:

"Blessed are they who die in the Lord, yea saith the Holy Spirit, that they may rest from their labors, and their works do follow them." (Revelation 14:13).

When I was a lonely teenager, Wings of Healing was there for me. In my early days living as Paula, suffering heartache from an unrequited love affair, again Wings of Healing was there for me. And today, every Sunday morning I start out my day with a radio sermon from Dr. Thomas R. Wyatt.

In 1964, I faithfully attended Wings of Healing in Los Angeles for about eight months. In time, I felt strongly led by the Holy Spirit to Angelus Temple, the famous historic church situated on Glendale Boulevard, across the street from Echo Park, west of downtown LA. It was the headquarter church for the International Church of the Foursquare Gospel. Its doors were opened in 1923. This wonderful edifice, founded by Aimee Semple McPherson, was to become my church home for the next two years.

Angelus Temple
1964-1966

While conducting a revival campaign in Oakland, California in 1924, pioneer evangelist Aimee Semple McPherson preached a sermon based on the Old Testament prophet Ezekiel's vision of a four faced man. (Ezekiel 1:10) In a moment of Divine inspiration, while preaching on this text, Sister McPherson received the revelation of The Foursquare Gospel, proclaiming the ministry of Jesus Christ as the Saviour, Healer, Baptizer with the Holy Ghost, and Coming King. A "complete gospel, meeting the needs of body, soul, and spirit -- both in this world and the life to come." Hence the organization she founded, previously nondenominational, was named The International Church of the Foursquare Gospel.

After 15 years of barnstorming all over America with a gospel tent, preacher McPherson purchased a pie-shaped lot across the street from Echo Park in Los Angeles, California. At a time when Pentecostal congregations were still meeting in tents and store-front mission halls, Sister Aimee pioneered the mega-church concept.

In her autobiography The Story of My Life (1951), she used the phrase:

"Angelus Temple, from its crystal doors to its radio tower, I love her."

Angelus Temple's crystal doors were opened in 1923. It boasted of having the world's largest dome at the time it was built. The 5,300 seat structure, with two layers of balconies, was surrounded by beautiful stained glass windows depicting the life of Christ.

Eventually, other structures were built adjacent to Angelus Temple: LIFE Bible College (Lighthouse of International Foursquare Evangelism), a parsonage, and dormitories for Bible college students. Angelus Auditorium was housed on the street level of LIFE Bible College. When radio first came in, Sister Aimee founded a radio station, KFSG (Kall Foursquare Gospel). All of the Temple services were broadcast live and could be heard as far north as Idaho.

Sister McPherson was greeted by thunderous applause when she made her entrance at a service, wearing flowing robes, carrying large bouquets of flowers, walking down one of the side aisles extending from the lower balcony. Newspapers called her Sister Aimee while her followers fondly referred to her as Sister. She composed and produced sacred operas, illustrated sermons, and numerous songs and hymns.

In spite of several media magnified sensationalized episodes in her life, her flock remained loyal until her death in 1944. During the time I worshiped at Angelus Temple, twenty years after her passing, her memory was still honored there.

On a Sunday evening in the summer of 1964 I walked into Angelus Temple for the first time. Little did I realize that I was walking into another chapter of my life story that would evolve into two of the happiest and most meaningful years of my life. No one at the Temple knew that I was a trans-person. I was totally accepted as Paula, the person God created me to be. The God who saved me and called me to preach, in 1950, looked beyond the outward appearance and perceived my true inner identity.

It wasn't long before I became very active in the life of Angelus Temple. For a while I was attending both Angelus Temple and Wings of Healing. Soon, however, all of my evening and weekend time was taken up with Temple activities.

First, as I had done at Glad Tidings Assembly of God in San Francisco, and Wings of Healing in Los Angeles, I joined the choir. I sang the alto part. The choir made its entrance on Sunday mornings down the same ramp which Sister McPherson had made her dramatic entrances in days gone by. One Sunday, after the morning service, a man walked up to me and said, "When I saw you up there in the choir, I thought, 'That lady looks so much like Sister McPherson.'"

Soon, Eileen Hummel, the choir director, asked me to join a women's singing group called The Ladies' Choralette. Shortly after that, she approached me about being part of a Tall Girls' Trio. The three of us totaled over 18' in height. When we sang over the radio in a weeknight service, the pastor said that our theme song could be I'm Going Higher Some Day.

One Sunday, following the morning worship service, Eileen Hummel called me aside and said, "I am going to talk to you as if you were my own daughter. I was raised in a church where Christian women were told not to wear makeup. I resented that. I am not against wearing makeup." She continued, "Paula, I wish I had the beautiful skin that you have. By wearing such heavy makeup, you are hiding your natural beauty. I know why you do it. You wear makeup to hide the fact that you shave your chin and upper lip. Instead of shaving, I suggest you use wax on your chin and upper lip." I am certain the real reason why I shaved never entered her mind.

A fond memory of Eileen Hummel remains with me. At a youth gathering following a Sunday evening evangelistic service, she said to those young people, "I am happy. I know my place." At that moment, I also knew my place. Living full-time as Paula, both in my professional life and in my church life, I knew my true identity. I too was happy. The words of a hymn composed by Sister McPherson rang true to my innermost being:

I have found a charmed circle, tis the center of God's will;
there's a wall of fire around it, and its glory lingers still...

In 1964 the Temple pastoral staff included: Dr. Guy P. Duffield, a brilliant preacher, teacher, and Bible scholar; Rev. Jean

Darnall, Associate Pastor; and Rev. Milton Ellithorpe, Staff Evangelist. Mike Mansfield, a retired police officer who had served as a bodyguard to Sister McPherson during her time, conducted the Saturday afternoon service in the 500 Room, a smaller edifice. Services were held every weekday afternoon in the 500 Room. Also, Rev. Mable Tisdale led Friday evening all-night prayer meetings in the 500 Room.

Sister McPherson's son, Dr. Rolf McPherson, served as President of the denomination. Dr. McPherson was married to a lovely lady named Lorna Dee, who often shared memories of Sister McPherson. She told of a time when she preached a sermon, and Sister McPherson's critique was: "It was fine Lorna Dee, only there was no humor in it." Aimee Semple McPherson, like most successful evangelists, was also gifted as an entertainer.

Mike Mansfield told me about an amusing incident during his tenure as a bodyguard to Sister McPherson. Sister resided in the parsonage adjacent to the Temple and LIFE Bible College structures. A man approached Mike and said, "The Lord told me that I am going to marry Sister." Mike went into the parsonage and delivered the message to Sister Aimee. Her response, "Well, the Lord played a dirty trick on me; He didn't tell me a thing about it."

Mike Mansfield asked me to lead singing in his Saturday afternoon 500 Room service. Occasionally he had me preach. One dress I wore slid up about two inches above the knee when I sat down. Some of the elderly ladies complained about me wearing a short dress on the platform. During a time of sharing, an elderly lady, stood up and said: "I'll tell you why we are not having a revival. It's these women with their short dresses!!" The remark was obviously intended for me. Darryl, a young man who had a crush on me, was in the group. He countered with a prophetic utterance, stating that people should not be judged by how they dress or what they look like. However, I accepted the ladies' criticism. After that, I made sure that my dresses and skirts were two inches below the knee when I sat down. Inasmuch as I was not raised as a female, during my early years of living full time in a female identity, these were lessons I had to learn.

Once during an altar service, staff pastor Jean Darnall corrected me when I started to pray with a young man who had responded to the altar call. While I was standing behind the young man, praying with my hand on his shoulder. Sister Darnall walked up to me said, “We have a rule here that men only pray with men, and women only pray with women.”

Another such incident occurred when I visited my friend Darryl at his room in a house located in the same block as LIFE Bible College. A woman from the church saw me going into the house with Darryl. She said to him, “It looks terrible, Paula going up to your room.” When Darryl replied that it was innocent, she said, “WE know that. But others don’t. Christians need to be careful to not give out a wrong impression when in public.”

Darryl was in his 20’s, and was called to preach. He and I became friends and hung out together. While he did not ‘know’ I was trans, one time he hinted at it and said, “It doesn’t make any difference.” Out of fear I quickly changed the subject. Darryl fell in love with me, and believed that God had put me in this life as his “helpmate.” The fact remained that I was not in love with him.

This was one unrequited love experience in my life where the other person was in love with me, rather than the other way around. I was honest with Darryl about the fact that I liked him only as a good friend. As is the case with a one-sided romance, the one in love hears what they want to hear from the object of their affection. I know because I have been in that position myself. Darryl bought me gifts, and Sister Darnall felt that I should not accept them under these circumstances. Sister Darnall said to me, “The Lord has somebody special for you, Paula.”

Unfortunately, the relationship with Darryl ended with a shouting match between us on Lemoyne Street, a few doors down from the Bible college. I kept trying to tell Darryl that, while I enjoyed his friendship, I was not in love with him. He insisted that I did, in fact, have deep feelings for him, and that I was resisting those feelings. I told him on the telephone that we needed to stop running around together. Too many people were thinking of me as Darryl's girl. In spite of the fact that I asked him not to, he kept calling me. Finally, I gave him an ultimatum to not call me anymore. He responded, "Oh you'll be hearing from me." So, I marched over to the rooming house where Darryl resided, and right there on the sidewalk we had the shouting match. The next day, Sister Darnall told Darryl, "Any chance of you having a relationship with Paula is ruined." Eventually, he did get over me.

One-sided love relationships are painful for both parties involved. The one who is in love suffers hurt over rejected feelings. The one who is not in love feels guilt for not having those feelings for the other person.

And so, here I was, nearly three years after changing my identity to Paula. Working in a law firm, active in a church, living totally in the straight life. At both my job, and at church, I got acceptance as Paula that I never had when living as Larry. Now I knew what my life would have been like had I been born biologically female, and I loved it.

One thing I could not do as Paula was attend LIFE Bible College. In 1955, I took a summer semester at Bethesda Bible Institute in Portland, prior to my final year of high school. My plans on going to Bible college after graduating from high school never came to fruition. Now that I was active in Angelus Temple, with LIFE Bible College adjacent, my desire to complete a formal Biblical education rose to the surface, and so I decided to take on the task of attending LIFE Bible College classes at night while keeping my daytime job. While we were discussing my decision to enroll as a student at LIFE, one of the students said, "When you apply, you will need your high school transcript." This was tantamount to throwing a bucket of water on a fire.

If I gave them my high school transcript, under the name of Larry, they would know I was trans. There is no way that either the church or the Bible school would have accepted that. Inasmuch as I was a strong evangelical, it did not enter my mind to apply for admission at a liberal university. And so, over the years, I took correspondence courses, with no college credits, where a high school transcript was not required. I studied diligently, and was constantly writing sermons and giving them to friends at the Temple. Some of the Bible school students fondly nick named me The Apostle Paula.

Throughout my lifetime, my training for the Sister Paula evangelistic outreach would be in the School of the Holy Ghost. While I did not realize it then, my ultimate purpose in life was to show the world that God does, in fact, accept trans-people. In those days, my big dream was to have sex change surgery and become a preacher's wife, assisting my husband with his ministry and preach on occasion, where no one knew of my original male identity.

The happiest moments of my life began when I became secretary to Rev. Jean Darnall, Associate Pastor of Angelus Temple. This part of my story is a chapter in and of itself.

Finding My Place In Life 1964-1966

"This is the girl God gave me," exclaimed Rev. Jean Darnall, as she had me stand up before the congregation in a Sunday afternoon service in Angelus Auditorium in 1964. She went on to explain that the secretarial work I did for her was an answer to prayer. Because of my office support, much of her time was freed up to spend with her family. This endeared me to her husband, Elmer, and her daughter LaDonna.

From the pulpit in a weeknight service, Sister Darnall said, "Paula, the first time I saw you in the audience [a Saturday night youth rally in the main sanctuary], you stood out to me. It was not because of your height, or your bright red hair. I saw someone who was searching desperately to find her place in life." She went on, "I don't see that now. What happened?" I proceeded to stand up and give the assembly a brief testimony of how God led me to Angelus Temple, the powerful spiritual experiences I had received there, how God had opened up many doors of opportunity to serve, and how happy I was to have found my place.

The first time I saw Sister Darnall, I thought, "That name sounds familiar." On my way home that night, I suddenly flashed on my time in a Portland hospital, about four years prior, listening to her preach over the radio from the Portland Foursquare Church Sunday morning worship service.

I continued working weekdays, 9 to 5 at the downtown workers' comp law firm, as a stenographer. After attending Angelus Temple for about two months, and visiting with Sister Darnall in her office, I noticed she had a dictaphone. I offered to give her part time secretarial help on some evenings, and on Saturdays. A student at LIFE Bible College had been helping her, however Sister Darnall could not always count on this person to show up. Since all of the services at the Temple were broadcast live, she received a volume of mail from listeners. A stack of unanswered letters sat on her desk.

And so, one evening I came to her office and transcribed a bunch of letters. When she came in the next morning and saw them all answered, she was delighted. My lifelong ministry of assisting ministers commenced, and continues to this very day. As time went on, she stopped dictating many of the letters from radio listeners and would write a brief note on the envelopes as to what she wanted to say, and I would compose the actual letter from that. Eventually, with much of the mail, she would merely write "Paula, answer this for me."

One day when I came into to type the letters, there was a note from Sister Darnall on the desk in which she expressed her gratitude for my help. She said, "Really, I believe the Lord has anointed you to answer these letters just as I would, if I had to time to think them through." Occasionally, she would rewrite a letter, but not often. Soon, she asked Dr. McPherson to put me on the payroll for eight hours a week, minimum wage. I continued to be her secretary for the duration of her time as a Staff Minister of Angelus Temple.

Sister Darnall's family, her husband Elmer and two children, John and LaDonna, were delighted that I was doing her dictation. This enabled her to spend more time with them. Often Elmer and LaDonna, then in her early teens, would visit with me in the office. Elmer often shared memories of Angelus Temple during Sister McPherson's time. Elmer had met Jean in the late 1930's when they were students at LIFE Bible College. He said, "People reminisce about the good old days when Sister was alive. We had our inner struggles and problems then, just like we do now."

Although the Foursquare denomination was founded by a woman evangelist, there were some within the organization who disapproved of women preachers. A Foursquare pastor once booked Sister Darnall to conduct a revival campaign in his church. He had to cancel her meetings because his Board of Directors disapproved of women preachers.

Even at Angelus Temple, some people taught against women being ministers. One Sunday morning, while entering the 500 Room where a Sunday School class was in progress, Sister Darnall walked in to hear a male teacher expounding against women preachers.

In the mid-60's a move of the Spirit swept into non-Pentecostal churches, as people of all Christian churches, including many Roman Catholic priests and nuns, experienced glossolalia, speaking in tongues. This became known as the charismatic renewal, also called neo-Pentecostalism. Jean Darnall hosted occasional all-day Saturday services in the main sanctuary of Angelus Temple, which drew folk from churches throughout Southern California -- a day to "honor the ministry of the Holy Spirit." Not only was Jean Darnall a pastor, she was also an evangelist. As an evangelist, she was not content preaching to the same group of people all of the time. She had a strong need to see people converted to Christianity, healed of physical ailments, and filled with the Holy Spirit through her ministry.

During her ministry at Angelus Temple, Jean Darnall also held Saturday night Voice of Youth rallies in the main sanctuary, drawing large groups of teenagers from all over Los Angeles -- a "Pentecostal Youth for Christ." Famous singers like Andre Crouch and Audrey Meier often conducted services for Voice of Youth.

During the time of prayer at the altar, at the conclusion of a weeknight service in Angelus Auditorium, Sister Darnall was slain in the Spirit, like St. John in the book of Revelation. During this euphoric experience, she kept saying, "There is nothing too hard for God." Later, in a Sunday afternoon service she shared with the congregation a vision she had when under the power at that weeknight service. She saw thousands of young people, rising up out of the slime, forming a spiritual Army, cleansed by the blood of the Lamb, proclaiming Jesus. This vision came to fulfillment in 1968 with a revival among the flower children; when thousands of hippies, delivered from drug addiction, became the Jesus' Movement. Later, at a Voice of Youth staff meeting, she also predicted worldwide Christian television.

When Sister Darnall resigned her position at Angelus Temple in late 1966, I felt that my purpose in being there was over. She and Elmer eventually settled in London, England, where they worked for many years with the charismatic renewal in the Church of England.

In 1978, twelve years after Jean Darnall left Angelus Temple,

I attended a General Conference of the Universal Fellowship of Metropolitan Community Churches (UFMCC) in Los Angeles. Rev. Elder Jean White -- the lesbian pastor of Metropolitan Community Church (MCC) in London -- told of a woman who prophesied over her, accurately predicting that Rev. Elder White would travel all over the world as a missionary. Later I learned that the woman Jean White made reference to was Jean Darnall. Whether or not Sister Darnall knew of Jean White's sexuality at the time, I do not know.

In 1980 I wrote a coming-out letter to Elmer and Jean Darnall in London, telling them about my transsexuality. I also told them about my involvement with MCC and that I knew Jean White. Elmer called Jean White, and she in turn called me. Elmer shared with Rev. White what a blessing I was to their family when I assisted Jean Darnall during their Angelus Temple days. "We had no idea Paula was TS," he said. Elmer also told Jean White that Sister Darnall had a breakdown from overwork, and that this would not have been a good time to tell her of my transsexuality. "Jean will be coming to America next year," Elmer said. "Paula can tell her then." Unfortunately, this never happened.

It was through Jean Darnall that God confirmed my purpose in life. She faithfully honored the ministry of the Holy Spirit. As I tell my life story, I am now pleased and proud to honor her. There will always be a special place in my heart for her. She played a powerful role in helping me find my place in life.

After Jean Darnall left Angelus Temple, I stopped attending church on a weekly basis. In upcoming years, I went through both church- and non-church-going periods. Nevertheless, my one-on-one relationship with God remained intact. For years, my day began with the wonderful radio teaching ministry of Kathryn Kuhlman. I had initially started listening to Miss Kuhlman every weekday back in the mid 1950's. Every Sunday morning I listened to Evelyn Wyatt on the Wings of Healing radio program. Also, on Sunday afternoons, I listened to Dr. C.M. Ward, Revivaltime speaker on the international radio broadcast of the Assemblies of God. Whether or not I was attending church, there was always some kind of a spiritual contact.

During the second half of the 1960's, revolutionary social changes started to evolve that would play a powerful and profound role in my ongoing search for self fulfillment.

The Sexual Revolution
1966-1970

During the first half of the 1960's, I went through the cataclysmic change of transitioning my identity from Larry to Paula. By the second half of this turbulent decade, I was well established as Paula.

Throughout the decade of the 1960's many cultural and cataclysmic changes were transpiring. President John F. Kennedy, civic rights activist Martin Luther King, Jr. and Senator Robert Kennedy were assassinated. The grizzly and horrific crimes of the Charles Manson family became a major news story. Ramon Novarro, movie star of the silent screen era, was murdered.

During this turbulent decade, a new culture suddenly came on the scene. As the era of the hippie culture exploded, men started growing their hair long,. Marijuana and psychedelic drugs became popular. Youth chanted, turn on and drop out. The new sexual morality decreed, do your own thing.

Pornography came out of the underground into commercial theaters. The Pussycat Theater, on Santa Monica Boulevard, featured the infamous Deep Throat, with Linda Lovelace. The Park Theater, in the Westlake District of LA was the first to show all-male gay sex films.

Another powerful ideological explosion that took place

was the birth of gay liberation. In 1969 a group gays and many drag queens rioted on Christopher Street in New York City. This was a major revolt that came about because of the police harassment of gay bars. Within a few years, Gay Pride parades started in major cities all over the country. The movement continues to grow to this very day.

It was during this time that a group of twelve gay Christians met in a home in Huntington Park, California. The group was started by Troy Perry, a gay Pentecostal preacher, who had been excommunicated from The Church of God of Prophecy. This was the first worship service of the Metropolitan Community Church (MCC). Troy Perry pioneered the first Christian ministry that openly welcomed and accepted homosexuals as part of the Body of Christ. This small group grew rapidly and soon became a major worldwide denomination called The Universal Fellowship of Metropolitan Community Churches (UFMCC). The Rev. Elder Nancy Wilson has said that Troy is probably not the first person that God called to start this much-needed ministry to people who have been ostracized from their churches. Troy, she said, was the first one who had the courage to do it.

By 1969 MCC-Los Angeles was holding weekly Sunday services in the Encore Theatre on Melrose Avenue in Hollywood. My gay friend Steve urged me to become involved in MCC. At that time I was still working on jobs and attending churches where they did not know I was transgender. I said to Steve, "I know that what Troy Perry is doing is of God. I just cannot become openly involved with a gay group."

At Steve's prodding, I decided to attend a Sunday morning service of MCC at the Encore Theatre. The room was jam packed with people lined up against the walls. When I entered the auditorium, a young man got up and offered me his seat. God's presence was definitely there.

When Troy got up and joyfully said, "If you love the Lord, say

Amen!" I felt right at home. I was delighted that God anointed a Pentecostal to start a ministry to gay people. At the conclusion of the service, I walked up to receive the sacrament of Holy Communion from Troy. Without even thinking about it, my hands automatically went up in the air and I started speaking in tongues.

Years later, when Troy appeared on my television program as a guest, he recalled this incident. He said, "When your hands went up in the air, I thought to myself, 'Oh my God, another Pentecostal!'" I attended MCC one more time, when they had relocated to their own building on Union Street. This was shortly before the building was destroyed by arsonists.

With the backdrop of all of these societal and social upheavals, my work situation was also fluid. I remained on my transcribing job at the workers compensation law firm for about two years. My stenographic skills had improved -- I worked my way up to a typing speed of 100 wpm, testing with no errors. At this juncture, I took night classes at a downtown L.A. business school and learned Greg shorthand. While the law firm paid more than the insurance companies, their salaries for stenos had a ceiling. Raises were sparse. With my secretarial skills, coupled with my female identity, finding work was easy. Fast typists were in great demand.

While still working at the workers comp law firm, I put in applications at some employment agencies. It was at the Atlas Employment Agency where I met Elizabeth, a job counselor. My relationship with her evolved into a lifetime friendship. Job placement counselors in employment agencies usually used a desk name. Elizabeth's desk name was Elizabeth Hilton. She chose the name Hilton because it denoted success. By this time I knew what type of companies did extensive background checks, and those who did not. Also, I knew who required a pre-employment physical examination, and who did not. When in between jobs, I worked through temporary agencies. This gave me an opportunity to check out different industries. I even tried my wings as a job placement counselor for a couple of employment agencies.

In early 1967, I landed a job as secretary to Lou Goldberg, the comptroller at the William Morris Agency in Beverly Hills. William Morris is the oldest and largest theatrical agency in the business, with offices in Beverly Hills, New York, and London. The Beverly Hills office was on El Camino Drive, off of Wilshire Boulevard, a few doors behind the Beverly Wilshire Hotel.

During the heyday of vaudeville in the early years of the 20th century, Sophie Tucker was a client of William Morris. Abe Lastfogel, president of the agency in the 1960's, was an office boy back when Sophie first became their client. Sophie Tucker had died about one year prior to my being hired at William Morris.

Big name movie stars came in and out of the office. George Hamilton was very friendly to me. Elvis Presley's extravagant wedding bills came through our office. Elvis' manager, Colonel Tom Parker, was in and out of the office constantly. Warren Beatty, who lived in a penthouse suite at the Beverly Wilshire Hotel, was directing and starring in Bonnie & Clyde at that time. I thought he was the hottest and sexiest man on earth. I cannot recall the name of a wonderful black man who was Abe Lastfogel's personal chauffeur. He knew Warren Beatty well, and even got me an autographed photo from the set of Bonnie & Clyde that said "To Paula, love, Warren." At the end of one day, he came to me and said, "Warren is in Mr. Lastfogel's office right now, if you would like to meet him." I chickened out, acting like a school girl blushing from her first crush.

Nancy, the girl sitting next to me at the transportation desk quit her job when she became pregnant. Mr. Goldberg, who was notoriously difficult to please, was delighted with my work. My typing skills were so fast that I wound up taking over Nancy's desk as well. This involved making hotel reservations, booking car rentals, etc., for big name clients. Walter Matthau called me regularly. Most of the clients were easy to please. On the other hand, some of the theatrical agents were very temperamental. They would insist on a certain hotel, with a particular view, demanding that the room of their choice be vacated if already occupied. With car rentals they often insisted on a certain car, and even sometimes demanded that the car be a certain color.

Hotel reservation clerks and car rental agencies courted me, taking me to lunch. Budget Car Rental gave me a complimentary car rental when I flew up to the Bay area to visit my lesbian friends, Jacki and Esther. By this time, Jacki had accepted me as Paula. This visit was the last time I saw them.

A large percentage of the personnel at William Morris were Jewish. The most generous employers I ever had were Jewish. God has given me a deep love for the chosen people, who are the apple of God's eye. One of the secretaries at William Morris said, "We Jews are called 'the chosen people.' Many of us wish that God would choose someone else."

Leaving the William Morris Agency in late 1968 was one of many stupid decisions I have made during my lifetime. In a moment of anger, I stormed out of the office in the middle of the day. Throughout my lifetime, whenever I have made changes in my life while angry, I regretted it later.

While working at William Morris, one Sunday afternoon, I turned on the radio prior to the Revivaltime time slot. I discovered a broadcast that was aired from the Full Gospel Assembly of God in Bell Gardens. Bell Gardens is situated in the southeastern industrial section of the greater Los Angeles area, a few miles from Huntington Park. Many of the residents in this area were industrial workers who had migrated to California from the Bible Belt portion of America, which included Arkansas and Oklahoma.

One Sunday night, I drove from my apartment in Hollywood to attend the Sunday night evangelistic service at the Full Gospel Assembly of God in Bell Gardens. I loved it. They had two outstanding choirs, the adult choir, and the youth choir. When I walked into this church the youth choir was singing and clapping "give me that old time religion like we used to have." The service opened with an old-time favorite song from my youth, There's Going To Be A Meeting In The Air. This was the old-time Pentecostal style of worship and preaching. For the next two years, I attended this church every Sunday night. So here I was, working for a theatrical agency, a theater circuit, and a film distributor, living in Hollywood, and driving out to Bell Gardens on Sunday nights to a Pentecostal church.

In 1969, I became Secretary to Orville Crouch, President of Loew's California Theatres, with thirty movie theatres in the Southern California area. A year later, I quit this job. Next, I went to work as secretary to the General Sales Manager of Crown International Pictures, a film distributor that marketed grade-B movies to the drive-in theater circuit.

It was also in 1969 that I discovered an inter-church, charismatic Monday night prayer meeting at the North Hollywood Assembly of God. People from non-Pentecostal churches, Catholic and Protestant, who were part of the charismatic renewal attended. Here I became friends with Sylvia Pennington. Sylvia had been my co-worker for a short period of time when I was a job placement counselor at the Hollywood office of the Nancy Nolan employment agency. Sylvia, a heterosexual Pentecostal woman, eventually became a licensed minister in the gay Christian denomination, the Universal Fellowship of Metropolitan Community Churches. Later, she authored two books: But Lord, They're Gay and Ex Gays? There Are None.

In 1969, I did not know that for 10 years Sylvia had been searching the scriptures to back up the fact that she had seen Jesus enter into the lives of many gay people. She strongly suspected that when it came to one's homosexuality, that sin was not the issue. At that time, Sylvia had no idea that I was transgender. Her search for truth soon caused her to break away from the heterosexual church world. In her travels, Sylvia became a mother figure to scores of GLBT people.

As the decade of the 1970's began, my life was about to make a dramatic change. My social life diverted from the church world into the hippie counter culture.

1980's

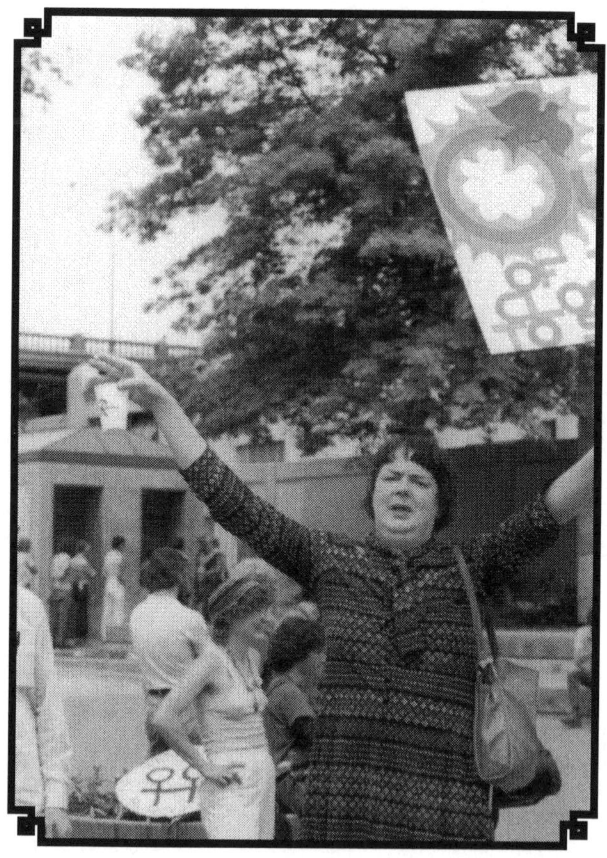

Early days of Portland's Gay Pride 1979

Sins of the 70's

Performing at Darcelle XV
in the 1980s

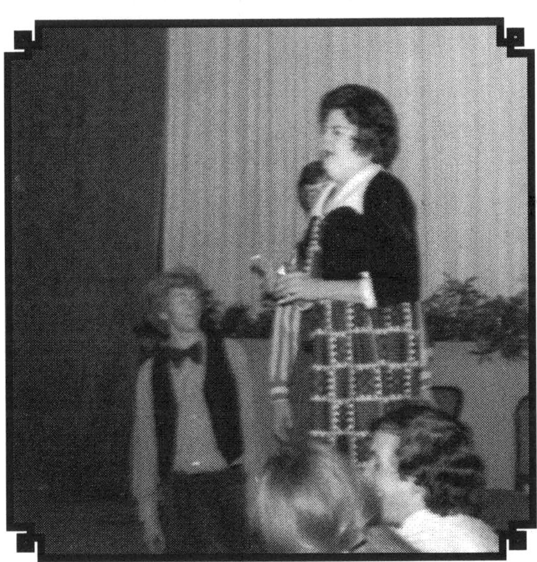

1973 reciting Sophie Tucker at law firm Christmas party

Rockin With Janis
1970-1973

As the decade of the 1970's approached, I was working as secretary to the general sales manager at Crown International Pictures in Beverly Hills. Crown International distributed grade-B films that were marketed to mainly to the drive-in movie circuit.

At Crown International, I experienced sexism. My boss called me in and told me that a new position was being created. The job would include going to private screenings of independently produced films, to determine their marketability for distribution. Some travel would also be involved, visiting district managers in other parts of the country. He asked me to help train the person hired for the position relating to certain aspects of office procedures. I said I would like to be considered for the position. He said that his superior wanted a man for the job.

So, a young man was hired. I showed him the ropes of the business. From him I learned that the job paid $75.00 per week more than what I was making. I took my annual vacation, after being there one year. While on vacation, I sent the company my letter of resignation. I minced no words as to my feelings of being discriminated against because I was a woman. It was while working for Crown International in 1970, that I moved into an apartment on Las Palmas, near Melrose Avenue, in Hollywood. Little did I know that my social life was to take a dramatic turn.

Living directly across the hall from me on Las Palmas Avenue was a long haired hippie, in his mid 20's, named Joe. Joe's best friend and Army buddy, Al, lived in the Echo Park area. Al was married to a girl from Connecticut named Joyce. Even though she lived in the hippie culture, Joyce was provincial. Two teenage sisters, Sue and Janet, had hitchhiked across the country from Massachusetts. Sue and Janet moved in with Joe. Soon, Janet became Joe's 'old lady,' meaning they were sleeping together.

I let my hair grow long and straight, and began wearing flashy psychedelic floor length moo-moo's, with lots of beads. I had found a group of heterosexual people in this culture who liked me. For the next three years, they became my family.

I soon became good friends with Joe, Al & Joyce. They had heard that I was transgender, however I denied it. They probably would have accepted my transsexuality had I told them. However, I wanted to be perceived as a chick. So, in a sense they knew, and yet, because I did not tell them, my sexuality was hearsay.

Janet felt that people who cross dress were putting down their sex. Joe defended me. One day I accidentally overheard Joe and Janet discussing it. Janet said. "Don't expect me to like it, because I don't." In time, however, she adjusted, and was nice to me.

Usually on Friday nights we would party, sometimes at Joe's apartment, and other times at Al & Joyce's little house situated on a hill, overlooking Angelus Temple. Usually they stayed up all night tripping on LSD. Marijuana and psychedelic drugs were in vogue during this time.

If anyone could take the credit for turning me on to pot smoking, it would be Al. One did not take a puff or a drag off of a marijuana joint. Rather, it was called a 'toke.' I did not indulge in LSD and psychedelic drugs. Some in the group occasionally took methamphetamines called "speed," "uppers" or "yellows" . Barbiturates, were called "downers" or "reds." I only smoked pot. At 32 years of age, I knew my own head well enough to know better than to get into hard drugs. People's reaction to drugs varies. Once any substance controls a person, they are on the road to self-destruct.

Living next door to Al and Joyce was another hippie couple, Frank and Kathy. Al and Frank sold pot. In those days an ounce was called a lid. Common phraseology was, "I'm looking to score a lid, man." Both genders called each other "man." The f-word was used in casual every day conversation.

One afternoon, a scroungy hippie purchased pot from Frank and Kathy. Kathy noticed that his shoes were worn out. Kathy said to him, "Instead of buying pot, you need to get yourself a new pair of shoes." The guy replied, "Shoes won't get you high, man."

Joe's brother, John, had hitchhiked across country from Buffalo, New York. Returning to New York briefly, John returned with a pretty, young girl named Anita. Anita and I became good friends, and she called me the big sister that she never had. In time, Joe and Janet moved to the Echo Park area, and I followed suit.

When I was a teenager during the 1950's, I never got into the rock and roll music of that era. During this time of the 1970's, however, I did get into the rock music of that culture. I became an ardent fan of Janis Joplin. She had died from a drug and alcohol overdose in 1970. After her death, her most popular album Pearl was released. I fell in love with the song Me & Bobby Magee. I was toking with friends and rocking with Janis.

Janis Joplin grew up in Port Arthur, Texas, and was a beatnik and a hippie before there was such a thing. Her high school classmates ostracized her as the one who was different. Hence, I related to her in a powerful way. I just knew that had I met Janis when she was still living, there would have had a strong bond between us. The fact that she was not accepted by her high school classmates is documented in the film Janis, The Way She Was. This superb movie includes footage of Janis visiting her 10th high school reunion. Yet, during her short life, she became wealthy by doing what she loved to do.

Janis loved to party, too much. That is why she died before reaching the age of 30. Phrases she often said were: "Why sleep, man? I might miss a party!" and "If you've got it today, you don't need it tomorrow, man. Tomorrow never happens -- it's all the same fuckin' day man!" It was her wish that her remains be cremated and that her ashes be scattered, by air, over Marin

County. Janis loved San Francisco.

Today, on my TV/podcast, I honor her memory every time I do my popular coffee klatch toast. I say, "As Janis Joplin would say, 'Here's to you man.'" And now I say, "God bless you, Janis. I wish we would have met. Someday, I will join you in the hereafter, and we will have a party!"

Between 1971 and 1973 I worked for a photo supply mail order house. After one year there, I returned to the law firm I worked for when first moving to LA in 1964.

Once again, all was well in my life-- until I fell in love. This time the object of my affection was John. In March, 1973, Anita left John and returned to Buffalo, NY. Anita's mother strongly disapproved of John. Anita left him because she could not deal with his excessive drinking. In addition to drugs, John was a hard-core alcoholic. When Anita left him, John was crushed. His drinking increased.

After Anita left, John moved in with me. We were not lovers. John was not in love with me, but he genuinely cared about me. Without Anita in his life. John was lost, miserable, and very unhappy. I was not able to fill the void in his life. This made me miserable and unhappy. I was constantly calling in sick on my job. To put it bluntly, I was a mess.

One day John left my apartment for his telemarketing job in Hollywood, and never returned. I was devastated and my life was in shambles. In grieving over John's leaving, I would sit and listen to his favorite Rolling Stones song Wild Horses, and cry.

On a lonely evening in 1973 after John left, I called Mom, who was remarried to a man named Bill, and expressed a desire to come home. An unrequited love affair had caused me to move from San Francisco to Los Angeles in 1964. And now this pattern was playing itself out again. I desperately needed new surroundings for my broken heart to heal.

I had no money -- only two cats, Kilo & Hookah. And so, with a suitcase, a makeup kit, my two cats in carrying cases, plus $90, I hit the road, and set out to hitchhike from LA to Portland, Oregon. The words of the Rolling Stones song rang in my head, when I thought about John:

Faith has been broken, tears must be cried,
let's do some living, after we've died.

When I began my trek to Portland, I started out hitchhiking up Highway 101. During the flower child era, hitchhiking great distances was common, by both genders. Once I saw a hippie chick at a freeway entrance. She was holding up a cardboard sign that read "I will ball for a ride to Sacramento." (To ball meant to have sex). The first person to pull over and offer me a ride said, "I will take you as far as I am going, but you are going to have to put out." I declined his offer.

On the way to Portland, I ran into a hippie in Salinas. Sitting under a shade tree, we smoked pot together and shared our life journeys. In the song Me & Bobby Magee Janis sings about her time on the road with Bobby. It was in Salinas where they went their separate ways.

One day, near Salinas, Lord, I let him slip away,
he's looking for that home, and I hope he finds it.

In Eureka, an older man picked me up. He said that he would take me to Crescent City. He had a french poodle in the back seat. He said he had been married many years. We went through the Redwood Forest to get to Crescent City. Right in the middle of the Redwoods, he stopped the car and said, "This is as far as I go." I said, "You said you would take me to Crescent City." He replied, "How about a piece of tail?" Angrily, I got out of the car and removed my belongings from the back seat. While I was doing this, he said, "Aw come on. Get back in, and I'll take you to Crescent City." I yelled back, "Go to hell!" He took off.

About five minutes later, a handsome young man who said he was in the Army picked me up. He drove me to the mountain highway pass entrance on the outskirts of Crescent City to enable me to get a ride to Grant Pass, and continue on through Oregon on Interstate 5. He did not make a pass at me. (Darn!).

Upon my arrival in Portland, Mom and Bill picked me up at Quality Pie Shop. When she beheld me with my long straight hair and flashly hippie attire, Mom was shocked. The last time she saw me, when visiting me in LA in 1965, I had dressed conservatively, and my hair was high fashion.

In 1973, Portland was not quite ready for me.

Back In Portland
1973-1975

By 1973, Portland had more than just two gay bars where homosexuals could be open. Besides the bar scene, other community activities for gays and lesbians were forming. While not as conservative as it was in the 1950's, Portland was still on its way to becoming a progressive city.

The old gay hangout, the Harbor Club, was no longer gay. Since its closure in 1965, many other bars catering to gays had come into play. Included was Dahl & Penne, on SW 1st & Alder, at the foot of the Morrison Bridge. In 1973, I visited this establishment a couple of times. I was not yet ready to be involved in the gay community.

When I first got to Portland, I searched desperately for a familial relationship with a hippie group, like I enjoyed in LA. This just didn't happen. The closest I came to it was with my teenage cousin, Sue, her boyfriend Danny, and some of their friends. They were a wonderful group of teenagers who enjoyed pot smoking.

The first weekend I was back in Portland, I hitchhiked downtown. A gay man gave me a ride. When I described the hippie crowd I ran with in LA, he said to me, "You want a bar called the Family Zoo." Upon entering this establishment, I felt right at home. The pot-oriented people were definitely there.

When I called Mom, and asked her if I could stay with her and Bill temporarily upon my return to Portland, she said, "Fine, come on up. You know you are not going to be happy here." When I told my friend Mary that I was moving back to Portland, she also said, "You are not going to like it."

During my first few months in Portland, both Mom and Mary were right. More than just dislike it, I loathed it. I decided that as soon as I had the money, I was going back to Los Angeles where I belonged. When Mom had visited me in LA in 1965, she said, "Here you are not conspicuous. In Portland, you would be." In 1973, I definitely stood out, wearing my hippie attire.

Fortunately, Mom's third husband, Bill, was sympathetic to me. In his wilder days Bill was a biker. Prior to meeting Mom, he partied for days on end on alcohol and speed. By the time he married Mom, he had settled down to a quiet life, working in the office at a large trucking company.

While Bill welcomed me into his home, he did not like my cats. He and Mom had just purchased a new $500 couch. My furniture in LA had been picked up at a dumpster, and so I let the cats claw on the furniture. Kilo was set in his ways; I couldn't get him to stop clawing on Mom and Bill's beautiful couch. Hookah, my other cat, was pregnant. She disappeared for a few days, and when she returned she was no longer pregnant. Apparently she abandoned her kitties, knowing they would not be welcome. When Bill said to me, "You are welcome, but those cats have got to go," I countered by saying, "Those cats are all I have."

Bill told me that if I was going to find a job in Portland, I would have to be more conservative in my appearance. Mom did not like my long hippie-type hair. “On a young girl,” she said, “it looks fine. On you, it looks terrible.” It didn’t take me long to discover that business office employee dress codes in Portland were far more conservative than they were in LA. Mom and Bill gave me money to buy a few conservative clothes. I resumed having my hair done high fashion.

Changing back my appearance, from the hippie look to the traditional office career woman look, made it easier for me to blend in. Casual attire, for both women and men, eventually became acceptable in Portland business establishments. In 1973 however, Portland businesses were just beginning to move in that direction.

Elizabeth, my friend from the Atlas employment agency in LA, had relocated in Portland and was managing a small employment agency. I worked for her in LA as a job placement counselor when she managed an employment agency in LA’s garment district. She hired me to work for her in Portland. Elizabeth offered me a small salary, plus commission, for the placements I made.

Not long before I returned to Portland, the private employment agency business had had some unfavorable publicity due to the unscrupulous business practices of some. In LA, most employment agency fees were paid by employers. Not so in Portland.

Two other women worked under Elizabeth at AA Employment -- Gen and Betty. Unbeknown to me at the time, they became aware of my transsexuality. Years later, Gen told me that Elizabeth had no idea I was trans during the years she knew me in LA. Gen and I became long-time friends. Gen had no problem with my sexuality. Betty, on the other hand, did not like it. During the time I worked with her, Betty did not let on to me that she disapproved of who I was.

Eventually, Elizabeth and I lost touch. Rumor had it that she had relocated in Florida. I heard nothing about her until, years later, in November, 2006, I received an email from her son, Bill. He had been sent a video of one of the Sister Paula podcasts. From Bill's emails, I learned that Elizabeth had passed on.

The following excerpts from some of Bill's email correspondence brought tears to my eyes:

"...reading your first message to me, I looked up at the TV and they were showing a picture of Mt. Hood, as seen from downtown. I looked up at the heavens and told Mom that she was getting through.

Talking to my younger brother, Christopher,....we put together some of Mom's and your history. He remembers Mom kicking Betty out of her life because she was criticizing you.....Mom always accepted you as Paula, her girlfriend. She...always would defend you and your gender. She never questioned your status in all the years she knew you...

[Someone] asked Mom about your history as a transsexual..... She told the woman that she had always loved and accepted you as a woman and that since that's what you accepted yourself as, that it didn't matter at all what you had started life out as. In her mind, you were a woman!

Mom told us about this....in 1977 or 1978...Once Mom knew of your history, you became a hero in our house....

...I always felt that Mom was sad over losing touch with you.... You truly held a special spot in her heart..."

After a few months of working for Elizabeth, I accepted a legal secretarial job at Davies, Biggs, Strayer, Stoel, & Boley. This was a very large law firm in downtown Portland. In fact, it was one of Portland's oldest law firms. Dress codes for women there were very conservative. In fact, I was told that the gals had to petition the firm to be allowed to wear pantsuits. The firm conceded, with the condition that they had to be matching business like suits, and not casual slacks and blouses. In a memorandum "to the girls," Roberta, the Office Manager, wrote: "Attire intended for casual use or at the beach is not proper." Women wearing jeans in the workplace was totally prohibited.

In the Spring of 1975, I decided to move back to Los Angeles. By this time I had purchased a car from Bill, and drove back. During my time in Portland, I had kept in contact with Al, Joyce, and Joe. Sue, Janet's sister, corresponded with me.

In looking back, I can now see that my decision to return to Los Angeles was a mistake. Going back to what once was never works. Furthermore, when I returned to Los Angeles, I was moving out of the center of God's will. I would just as soon delete the next chapter. Yet, I have to tell it all.

In The Belly Of The Whale
1975-1976

The period of June, 1975 through the end of March, 1976 became the unhappiest time of my life. Like Jonah in the Old Testament, I went in a direction contrary to God's Will. By returning to Los Angeles, I was hoping to re-establish my prior life and circle of friends. During the two years since I left Los Angeles, the group of people whom I had considered family had scattered. The Friday all-night parties were no more.

While I was in Portland, Anita wrote me and said that she and John had split up for good. John's excessive drinking had turned his life into a mess. While on a drunken binge, John got into trouble and wound up serving a one year sentence in the LA County Jail. By the time I returned to LA, John had a new old lady named Pat. John and Pat had a daughter, Heidi. While Anita had liked me, Pat did not.

Also, Joe and Janet had split up. Janet and her sister Sue had moved into an apartment in the Highland Park area of Los Angeles. Joe's new old lady was named Susan. Susan did like me and we became very good friends. They had a child named Ivy. Joe had gone to work for a magazine subscription service called Periodical Publishers, closing leads generated by a telephone boiler room operation.

Al and Joyce had a baby boy named Jake. During the time I was in Portland, Joyce had contracted a rare, debilitating circulatory disease. She almost died. Whether or not this was connected to her pregnancy, I do not know. They hired me as a live-in housekeeper and caregiver. This lasted about three months. Being accustomed to an independent lifestyle, I was not able to adjust to the confinement of running a household.

Next, I rented a sleazy pay-by-the-week room at the Las Palmas Hotel in Hollywood. I took some secretarial and typing jobs through temp agencies. They were mostly routine clerical jobs with insurance companies. I became tired of the daily grind of routine office work and wanted to do something different.

At the Las Palmas Hotel, I became friends with Kitty, an aging ex-actress who wore a neck brace. I also became acquainted with a pimp, a prostitute, and a loan shark; all residents of the hotel.

My financial picture was bleak. Often, Kitty and I would panhandle together, working the streets, and supermarket parking lots. Kitty's neck brace helped. Our story was two stranded women. Our standard line was, "Can you spare a dollar? We ran out of gas." Usually on our panhandling expeditions, we got enough money for dinner at a restaurant. Our hotel rooms did not have kitchens.

Although I had a car, I could not afford money for gas to go job hunting, nor did I have money for bus fare; and so, I hitchhiked around town looking for work. One day, on Western Avenue a man picked me up. I told him I was looking for secretarial work. He said, "Maybe we can help each another out. I'll be glad to pay you for some oral sex." This we did, in his car. From there, I got the idea of performing oral sex on men for money.

In the late 1960's I knew a transsexual who worked the streets, turning tricks. It had never entered my mind to do it. Why did I do it as this juncture of my life? I do not know. My career as a street hooker lasted a little less than two weeks. Not being street wise, I became an easy set up for undercover vice squad officers. I hustled in the Sunset/Western area of Hollywood, where female hookers worked in the massage parlors that lined the area.

Each day I would head down to the Sunset/Western area and start hitchhiking. When I got a ride, my story would be that of a secretary, pounding the pavements, looking for a job. Then, I would incorporate into the conversation the fact that I was broke. Sometimes this led up to a pay for play encounter in the john's automobile.

I'll never forget the day I was busted. I was having coffee at a Winchell's donut shop on Western Avenue, near Melrose. Sitting across the room at another table was a young attractive guy, looking like a typical telephone installer. He was carrying a lunch bucket. My customers were usually unattractive, so I naively thought I was going to have my cake and eat it too. The guy smiled and gave me that look. After I got up and left, he followed me out to the sidewalk. He asked me what was happening. I gave him my secretary looking for work routine. I do not remember the details of the conversation which led up to my saying, "Tell you what I'll do. I'll give you some real good head for $15.00." With that, events moved very quickly. Before I knew it, a police car pulled up, and an undercover vice cop got out, and flashed a badge in my face, saying loudly: "You're under arrest for prostitution." And in a flash, I was handcuffed. To this day, I can still visualize in my mind every line of that police badge. On the way to the police station, I learned that the vice officers had been watching me for the past few days as I hitchhiked across Western Avenue.

Like Jonah in the belly of a whale -- there I was, in a men's jail cell. Never before, or since, have I experienced such degradation, accompanied with fear. This was on a Friday afternoon, and unless I could find someone to bail me out, I would be stuck in that cell for the weekend. Although I was allowed a phone call, I was not able to reach Al, who worked in the daytime. I could not call my church friends for help.

There were four men in the cell. One said he was looking forward to later that night, when the lights were turned off. "We've got a 'fish' in here!" he exclaimed. When a new guard came on duty, and saw me there, he said, "What's a woman doing in here?" They all laughed. The cell had one commode, in the open. This was very embarrassing for me, to relieve myself in front of these men. Yet, as the old saying goes: when you've got to go, you've got to go.

Later in the day, the guard let me try again to reach someone by phone. This time Al was home. Since they had booked me as Larry, I had to tell Al about my transsexuality. Al called a bail bondsman and told him that he would put up his house as surety that I would appear in court. Al came down and got me out of jail. After appearing in court, and pleading no contest, which means taking responsibility for the act without admitting guilt. I was fined $100 and placed on two years' summary probation. This meant that I did not have to report to a parole officer. The terms of my probation forbade me to hitchhike.

My friend Steve said to me, "You did a negative thing, and you got a negative result." This was true; yet, it went beyond that. This was more than a mistake, it was a sin. It had to be confessed, followed by repentance. I confessed and repented, and never hustled again. I even stopped panhandling. While being a homemaker just wasn't for me, neither was life on the street. Steve said, "Just go back to working in offices like you did before, and you won't get busted." This I did. Janet said to me, "You should have known better than to pull that," and she was absolutely right.

Even though I had moved out of the Will of God, into flagrant sin, God's hand was still on my life. God only knows what could have happened to me, had I remained in the street life. I shudder to think of what horrible things could have happened to me while I was incarcerated. Even out of this bad experience, God brought about good. My six hours in a jail cell gave me a strong empathy and compassion for people who are confined to a jail cell.

In telling my story, I could have deleted this experience. The Old Testament account of the life of King David includes his sinful affair with Bathsheba, when he plotted the death of her husband. Psalm 51 records David's prayer of confession and repentance. The Biblical account of Jonah tells how he cried out to God from the belly of the whale. God forgave and restored both prophets when they asked forgiveness. And so, I dare not gloss over the sins and mistakes of my own life. Through all of this emerges God's unlimited grace. Grace that exceeds our sin and our guilt. Divine Grace that looks beyond our flaws and faults, and sees our need.

In addition to being forgiven and restored to God's grace, I was about to receive a fresh baptism of the love of God.

Forgiven, Cleansed, Restored

1976

Empty is the stage,
full is the page.
She won't be there anymore,
people won't crowd at the door.
Does the memory of one, bring back the face?
Can you go back there, and recall the place?

Does the message still haunt your head?
Can anyone so great, really be dead?
No, I say they will remember and shed a silent tear.
They will recall her to mind in memory, for many a year.
–Susan Steinwachs

On the evening of February 20, 1976, while visiting with Joe and Susan, I heard the news of the death of Kathryn Kuhlman over the radio. We sat there stunned, not wanting to believe the heartbreaking news that emanated over the airways. The next day, the Los Angeles Times front page headline story said, "Kathryn Kuhlman dies at 66." The news of her death brought heartbreak to thousands of her followers.

My ten month return to Los Angeles had brought me much unhappiness. What helped make it bearable was Kathryn Kuhlman's daily radio programs and her monthly Sunday afternoon miracle services conducted in the Shrine Auditorium. During this period, I joined the thousands of people who waited outside the 7,000 seat Shrine Auditorium every month for the doors to open at 1 pm. When I was down in the dumps, the moment Miss Kuhlman walked out on the stage, my depressed feelings would lift. She literally radiated the glory of God.

During the period June, 1975 through March, 1976, every month someone who was not familiar with Kathryn Kuhlman came with me to her Los Angeles services and experienced the presence of God that permeated through her ministry.

Kitty, my friend from the Las Palmas Hotel, attended a service. When Miss Kulhlman called people up to the platform, exercising the spiritual gift of the "word of knowledge" in calling out healings, one of the workers escorted Kitty to the platform. When Miss Kuhlman touched someone, they usually fell under the power, being caught by a worker to keep them from hitting the floor. Kitty said that when she stood in Miss Kuhlman's presence, she could sense a strong wind that knocked her over. This was the same "rushing mighty wind" described in Acts 2.

One Sunday, Al and Joyce, along with Joe and Susan, attended a service. As they were new to this type of ministry, their lives were greatly impacted. I reserved space for us on one of the many chartered buses that transported folk to the meetings from all over Southern California Once we got there, we discovered that the non-bus folk were seated first on the main floor. Eventually we were seated in a reserved section in an upper balcony.

Susan, who authored the words at the beginning of this chapter, went with me to the Kathryn Kuhlman services several times. In fact, Susan and I were at Miss Kuhlman's last public service at the Shrine Auditorium in November, 1975. In the theater of my mind, I can still see Miss Kuhlman standing there, with upraised hands, looking up and saying, "Nothing in my hand I bring, simply to thy cross I cling." She knew that her life and mission on this earth was soon coming to an end.

Steve, my gay friend from Huntington Park, and his friend Alex, fell in love with Miss Kuhlman, and loved attending her services. In July, 1975, in Steve's home, we enjoyed the national telecast that featured highlights of her famous service in Las Vegas, one of the few times she allowed television cameras into her meetings. Years later, when it was made available, I purchased a VHS tape of this telecast, entitled Dry Land, Living Water. In this service, Miss Kuhlman declared "What America needs is a fresh baptism of the love of God!"

I had first discovered Kathryn Kuhlman in the late 1950's, through her daily radio ministry. For many years, right up to the time of her death, she opened her radio program by saying:

"Hello there, and have you been waiting for me? I'd just knew you'd be there. Thanks. And remember -- no matter what those problems are in that life of yours today, no matter how big your troubles -- as long as God is still on His throne, and hears and answers prayer -- and just so long as your faith in Him is still intact -- everything will come out all right."

During periods throughout my life when I did not attend church anywhere, Kathryn Kuhlman's radio ministry kept the spiritual spark alive in me. After she died, her radio Biblical teaching series continued to be aired. I taped many of her programs on my cassette radio.

Daughter of Destiny by renowned charismatic writer the late Jamie Buckingham, chronicles her amazing life. "Tell it all, Jamie, the bad right along with the good," said Miss Kuhlman when she commissioned him to write her story. At the conclusion of her biography, Jamie Buckingham describes Kathryn Kuhlman as "the John the Baptist of the ministry of the Holy Spirit." She played a strong role in pioneering the mighty charismatic renewal that swept into all churches. Yet Miss Kuhlman did not allow loud and noisy demonstrations in her meetings. The most staid and conservative clergy felt comfortable sitting on the platform alongside Pentecostal preachers.

The west coast memorial for Kathryn Kuhlman was held at the Shrine Auditorium on March 28, 1976. Susan and I attended. A beautiful color photo of Miss Kuhlman was given to everyone. Upon returning to Portland, I purchased a frame for the photo and it is still in my apartment. It is one of my most cherished possessions.

At the conclusion of the memorial service, everyone sang, reverently, softly, and slowly, the song which I sang when a very young child:

Jesus loves me, this I know,
for the Bible tells me so...

As I sat there singing, along with 7,000 people, I received a fresh baptism of the love of God. There was no outward visible demonstration. Yet, tears streamed down my face as I experienced a cleansing wave of restoration that can only be described as pure love. The forgiving power of Jesus became a living reality to me. The next day I left Los Angeles. I knew it was God's Will that I return to Portland.

"Advocate Tom"

1976

Even though my ten month return to Los Angeles in 1975-1976 was an unhappy period in my life, another positive thing that came out of it was the fact that I reconnected with my friend Sylvia Pennington.

I had originally met Sylvia in the late 1960's when we were both job placement counselors for the Nancy Nolan Employment Agency's Hollywood office. Back then, we attended the weekly Monday night charismatic prayer meetings at North Hollywood Assembly of God. Sylvia, a Pentecostal heterosexual woman, had no idea that I was transgender during this period-of-time.

Upon returning to Los Angeles, I had called Sylvia and told her I felt it was meant for her and I to resume our friendship, Sylvia replied, "Yes, I feel that too." The reason for this was not yet clear. She did confirm the fact that God had a ministry for me in Portland.

When I made the decision to return to Portland, I had no money. My car was in dire need of a tune up, oil change, new tires, and other repairs. Also, the battery was running very low. Although Sylvia was not able to give me money, she offered to fill up my tank with gas, using her credit card. I glibly said to Sylvia, "Maybe I'll pick up some hitchhiker on the road who will help me make it to Portland." Since most people hitchhike because they have no money, I was not serious. Sylvia replied, "Well, that's the way it is going to have to be."

And so, not even knowing if my car would last for the trip from LA to Portland, I set out on a faith journey with a tank full of gas and $5.00. Also, accompanying me on the trip were the prayers of Sylvia and some of her friends. Somehow, I just knew that everything would be alright.

Somewhere between LA and San Francisco, when the gas tank was getting very low, I picked up a young couple who were stranded on the highway. They were on their way to a garage to pick up their car that had been left for repairs. The garage was about a mile off of the freeway. They were not able to help me financially. With my gas tank so low, I did not want to drive the extra mile to take them to the garage. Nonetheless, the leading of the Holy Spirit was strong and clear that I drive them to the garage.

While driving to the garage, on the country road off the freeway, I saw a young man walking toward the highway. After dropping the couple off at the garage, on my way back to the freeway, I saw that same young man, still walking on the country road, with his thumb out. I picked him up. His car had also broken down, and he had to leave it at the same garage because some part had to be ordered. He decided to hitchhike on to San Francisco, and pick up his car when returning to LA.

When I told him about my faith journey to Portland, he filled my tank with gas. He also gave me a large sum of cash. By the time I got to Portland, I had gas left in my car, and $13.00 cash. Had I used human reasoning, thinking on a natural plane, with my gas tank being close to empty, I would have dropped the couple off on the freeway. Had I not obeyed the leading of the Holy Spirit to drive the stranded couple to the garage, I never would have met this young man.

When Sylvia visited me in Portland a few months later, I shared this experience with her. She recollected my glib comment about a hitchhiker helping me out. Sylvia said, "When you mentioned getting help from a hitchhiker, something in my spirit clicked. I knew that would be how God would provide for you. Besides," Sylvia continued, "you were backed up with a lot of prayer".

The hitchhiker said that his name was Tom, and that he was a male prostitute. He placed ads in the gay newspaper, The Advocate. At that time, the paper had a special section for model and masseur ads. He serviced a wealthy clientele and usually made anywhere from $200 to $500 in one night. He was happy with this lifestyle. Yet, in conversation, he acknowledged that something was missing in his life. I shared my Christian testimony with him. When I dropped Tom off in San Francisco, I gave him Mom's address so we could stay in touch. I told him I would be happy to return the money he gave me, once I got back on my feet financially.

Three months later, Mom called me and said, "I have a letter for you. The return address says, Advocate Tom, Los Angeles, California. There was no street or PO box address. In his letter, Tom expressed how much he enjoyed my company on the highway. He said that I did not have to pay back the money he gave me. Tom's letter closed with these words, "Paula, you are a beautiful person. Thank you for showing me faith." I never heard from him again.

Years later, in a Portland gay bar, a man told me that his lover, whom he lost to AIDS, often talked about meeting me when he was hitchhiking in California. "He never forgot you," the man said. This could very well have been Advocate Tom.

Well, my car made it to Portland. As soon as I arrived, I pulled into a Denny's restaurant to get something to eat. When I returned to my car, it would not start. The battery had died. I called Mom to come and get me. God kept my car running just long enough to get me home. I said to Mom on the phone, "This is a miracle trip."

The ministry God had for me in Portland, as confirmed by Sylvia Pennington, was soon to begin.

Centenary Wilbur Days
1976-1977

From 1963, when I transitioned my identity to Paula, until 1976 when I returned to Portland, I had lived in my own particular closet. During this time, churches I attended, as well as my employers, had no idea that I was a trans-person. While I maintained my friendship with two gay men, Steve and Alex, I had nothing to do with the gay community. When I returned to Portland in 1976, this was about to change.

In 1968, Rev. Troy Perry had founded Metropolitan Community Church (MCC) the first Christian church to openly accept gay people. MCC's first worship service was held in a small home in Huntington Park, California. It was not long until the growing group moved to the Womens Club facility in Huntington Park. Once the proprietors discovered this church was a homosexual congregation, they were asked to leave. In its early days, the fledgling gay-oriented MCC congregation was thrown out of several other church facilities. Pastor Troy Perry made the famous statement each week to his congregation, "You need to be in church every Sunday so you will know where we will be meeting next week."

Although I did attend a couple of worship services of MCC-LA in the late 1960's, I was not yet ready for open involvement with MCC until my return to Portland in 1976. At that time, I heard that MCC was conducting worship services on Portland's east side at Centenary Wilbur Methodist Church (CWMC). Upon my return to Portland, I was guided by the Holy Spirit to get involved with MCC Portland.

There were two failed attempts to start MCC in Portland in the early 70's. In early 1976, a small group of gay people met for discussion in an upstairs room of CWMC. The group included a formerly Baptist minister, previously married with a daughter.

It wasn't long before the growing circle decided to affiliate with The Universal Fellowship of Metropolitan Community Churches (UFMCC).

Later in the same year, Rev. A. Austin Amerine, a former married Assemblies of God minister, who had also come out as a gay man, moved from San Francisco to Portland. Austin became the founding pastor of MCC Portland. Under his leadership, the group evolved into a structured worship service, and moved from the upstairs room into the main sanctuary of the church facility. Austin's expertise was founding and establishing new churches. His first step would be to find successful business people to serve on the church's first Board of Directors. Austin often said, "You don't build a church from behind a pulpit. You've got to go out into the community, grab 'em by the balls and get them into church." Under Austin's leadership, MCC Portland grew rapidly and it wasn't long before Rev. Troy Perry came to Portland to officiate MCC Portland's recognition as a chartered church.

When Sylvia Pennington predicted that I had a ministry in Portland, neither one of us realized just how profound her premonition was. In the fall of 1976 I started attending MCC regularly. Soon I became church secretary. Prior to moving into its own facility, the church had its "office" on Austin's dining room table. Every week, I would drive out to Austin's apartment, and type the church bulletin on an IBM electric typewriter.

During this time, Anita Bryant led her so-called Save Our Children voters referendum in Dade County, Florida. A gay rights ordinance was consequently overturned. I'll never forget the day, sitting in Austin's dining room, when I saw the news of the outcome flash across the television screen. Austin was very upset. "This is going to set us back," he said.

As I drove across the Ross Island Bridge on my way home that day, suddenly an Old Testament passage in II Kings 6:15-17 flashed into my mind:

"And when the servant of the man of God arose early and went out, there was an army, surrounding the city with horses and chariots. And his servant said to him, "Alas, my master! What shall we do?" So he answered "Do not fear, for those who are with us are more than those who are with them." And Elisha prayed, and said, "Lord, I pray, open his eyes that he may see.'" The the Lord opened the eyes of the young man, and he saw. And behold, the mountain was full of horses and chariots of fire all around Elisha."

And so, even though it appeared that the cause of human rights was defeated by the Dade County voters, the promise came through that "...those who are with us are more than those who are with them."

Actually, Anita Bryant did the gay community an unintended favor. As one politician said, "She made us get off our duffs and do something." The Bryant referendum triggered the gay rights movement into action.

When I first returned to Portland in 1973, I had made contact with Frank, my grade and high school classmate whom I had known since 1951. I saw Frank in 1961 when he visited me in Oakland, California, where he was stationed in the Army. For years, Frank kept his homosexuality hidden, even to the point of denial. He believed that one could not be a Christian and be gay at the same time. Once Frank came out as a gay man, he stopped attending church altogether. By 1976, he had a lover named Mark. Soon Frank and Mark started attending MCC Portland on a regular basis and became actively involved. Soon Frank accepted his homosexuality as a gift from God.

In 1976, Sylvia visited me in Portland. I introduced her to Frank and Mark. Sylvia fell in love with them, and vice versa. At this point in time, Sylvia still had no idea that I was a trans-person. Frank assumed Sylvia knew about my sexuality. Frank said to her, "I knew Paula as Larry." Sylvia's mouth fell open in surprise. I cringed in fear. I felt like hiding. At that moment, I regretted ever making the introduction. There was no more discussion on the issue for the duration of Sylvia's visit to Portland.

Upon returning to Los Angeles, Sylvia wrote me a letter. It wasn't until she was on the airplane, flying back to Los Angeles, that the reality of what Frank had said hit her. She cried on the plane when she thought about the painful transition I must have went through. Sylvia then came to the realization that meeting me was part of God's plan of opening up her understanding of the plight of sexual minorities. She was living with her sister Jeannie. When Sylvia told Jeannie that I was trans, her sister said that things about me that she didn't understand suddenly made sense. Jeannie was very accepting of me. She still liked me, as much as she did before finding out.

Just as Sylvia had predicted that I had a ministry in Portland, in the winter of 1976, I wrote her a letter and told her that God was getting ready to move her into a ministry within the gay community. She responded and said, "Paula, you may think that you wrote that letter. However, God wrote it." My letter had confirmed the Holy Spirit's direction in her life. On New Year's Eve, 1976, Sylvia attended a watch night service at an Assembly of God church in Southern California. During the time of prayer around the altar, while praying in the Spirit, Sylvia thought about the many gay people who had come into her life. Right there and then, she said "yes" to God's leading. Sylvia later said, "Had the pastor of that church had any idea of what was going on at the altar, he would have flipped."

Within the next few years, Sylvia received ministerial credentials in UFMCC. She traveled all over America, staying in the homes of gay people. Not only did she preach at many MCC churches, she also became involved with other gay-oriented ministries that were forming.

Austin often said, "God raised up MCC because there was a

need." I'll never forget a young man sharing his story at an MCC Portland service. His Baptist relatives disowned him when he came out to them as a gay man. He said, "The evening after my church and family threw me out, I looked up into the sky and prayed: 'God help me.' The very next day I found MCC."

At a Sunday service at Centenary Wilbur, a woman named Ann Shepherd addressed the congregation. Her husband Bill was a prominent attorney. Bill and Ann had three lesbian daughters. Ann announced to the congregation the formation of a new group entitled Parents of Gays. She and Bill offered to give counsel to parents of MCC members. Since then, this group has evolved into an international organization called Parents & Friends of Lesbians and Gays (PFLAG). PFLAG continues to play a powerful role in the acceptance of GLBT people.

Another first in Portland's Gay community during MCC Portland's Centenary Wilbur days, was the beginning of Portland's Gay Pride celebration. In 1969, the Stonewall riots in New York City gave birth to annual Gay Pride parades and celebrations in major cities. This coincided with the time in which Troy Perry founded MCC. Now, during the time that MCC was being established in Portland, Gay Pride was beginning to take root in the City of Roses.

Portland's first Gay Pride march took place in 1976. The first two years of Portland's Gay Pride saw about 200 people marching in a downtown parade. MCC Portland participated. Fanatical fundamentalists surrounded us with hateful signs depicting demons and hellfire. One sign said "Turn or Burn." Not only did I verbally yell back at the Bible bigots, I proudly carried a banner that proclaimed: **Out Of The Closet To Stay!**

Today, Portland's Gay Pride celebration draws over 30,000 people. And the event is now called Pride, thereby removing all labels.

One afternoon, in 1978, Austin drove by a historic church building, located on the corner of NE 24th Avenue & Broadway Boulevard. He noticed a For Sale sign on the front lawn. Later, Austin would say, "The moment I drove by that church, I knew that God wanted us to have it." And so, MCC Portland's Centenary Wilbur days were soon coming to a close.

Kissing Frogs

1978-1979

Just as MCC in Los Angeles grew rapidly in 1968, even so did the Portland MCC congregation in 1976. By 1978, MCC Portland moved into its own facility on the corner of NE 24th Avenue & Broadway Boulevard. In 1909, United States President William Howard Taft had conducted the cornerstone laying of this building. Prior to MCC, the building had been occupied by First Universalist Church of Good Tidings, Grace English Lutheran Church, and First Church of Divine Science. By 1977, the Divine Science congregation was down to less than 20 active members, most of them elderly. MCC was able to purchase it at the bargain price of $87,000. It needed a lot of work, but the congregation now had its own space. Other groups in the gay community utilized MCC's facilities, and the church became a major gathering place for Portland's sexual minorities.

My first official title with MCC Portland was when I became the church's first secretary. I was also Austin's personal secretary. Now, instead of typing at Austin's dining room table, I had my own office in the church. This is as close as I've come to being a preacher's wife.

When it came time for the board of directors to approve the purchase of a new typewriter, I requested an IBM Selectric II. When the board considered a less expensive brand, I insisted on the Selectric. One of the board members said to Michael

Hoffman, church clerk, "You and Paula have got to have the best of everything." Mike shot back, "That's because we are the ones who are doing the work." I told the board what Kathryn Kuhlman often said, "The best there is, is none too good for God." I got my typewriter.

In addition to being Secretary, it wasn't long before I had my own column in the back cover page of MCC Portland's monthly newsletter The Chalice. Glen Scott designed a logo for me that said "Paula's Socialight." The column focused on the church's social activities. Eventually, I assumed the position of editor of The Chalice and my column became "Inreach And Outreach."

During its early days, the majority of MCC Portland members were gay men. As the church started to grow, more women were becoming involved. Austin felt that financial priority needed to be given for hiring a woman for the pastoral staff, so I performed my secretarial duties, both for the church and the Pastor, on a volunteer basis. In hindsight, I wonder how I survived financially during those days. Yet, somehow my needs were always met.

Some of the older gay men in the congregation were unhappy with Austin's decision to hire a woman assistant pastor. Dick, a retired policeman, said, "We don't want a diesel dyke as a minister." When Austin hired Rev. Arlene Ackerman to relocate to Portland from Stockton, California, Dick's rapport with Austin deteriorated.

At the time I was disappointed that funds were not available to pay for my services as church secretary. In hindsight, however, I can now see the wisdom in Austin's decision. In a counseling scenario, some people are more comfortable with a particular gender. The very nature of MCC's purpose and ministry mandates that ministers of both genders serve on a pastoral staff.

Arlene started a women's group for social activities for women. Soon, a men's group also started. In my early days of living as Paula -- in church circles where they were not aware of my biological sex -- I was happy being involved with the heterosexual womens' activities, rather than with straight men. In MCC however, where I had come out of my closet, I was happier socializing with gay men rather than with lesbians. When I told Austin that I would prefer being involved in the men's group, he said, "Now Paula, you can't have it both ways. You give half the church a black eye whenever someone innocently refers to you as 'he.' If you want to be perceived as a woman, then you need to be with the womens group." The lesbians welcomed me into their social circles, as a woman, with open arms.

In 1979, Austin resigned the Portland pulpit to accept the position of NW District Coordinator for UFMCC. At his farewell service, he was presented with a large balloon of a frog. Why was Austin given the frog balloon? Here is Austin's classic 1979 article entitled Kissing Frogs, exactly as published in The Chalice:

"In his book Ask Me To Dance Bruce Larson introduces an adaptation of the old story about the ugly frog who was put under the spell of a wicked witch, but later turned into a handsome prince when kissed. (This was shared with him by an Episcopal priest [Wes Seelig] who had used it in a pastoral letter to his congregation.

Do you ever feel like a frog? Frogs feel slow, low, ugly, drooped -- you want to be bright but you feel dumb; you want to share but feel selfish; you want to feel thankful but instead feel resentful; you want to feel great but feel small; you want to care but are indifferent. You want to be challenged by life but you are too froggish to budge. It's like you, too, have been put under the spell of the wicked witch. What is the business of the church? Kissing frogs.

Many of us were once frogs; under the spell of a wicked witch -- turned out of our churches, our families, our society -- rejected as Christians. If the job of the church is indeed to kiss frogs, then we have to look around us and see the frogs. There are old ones, ugly ones, poor ones, dull ones; there are dependent ones; there are unhappy ones. There are frogs that are rejects -- there are frogs that are prisoners -- there are frogs that are rich. Why do we withhold the testimony and witness of the Lord to people around us? If we believe that the task of any church ministering in the name of Christ is to change the lives of people, then we must look at the unlovely, the unloved, and the unlovable, and offer them that 'magic kiss' -- the power which will change their lives.

Stop and think -- where would you and I be if someone had not kissed us? It is not always easy to meet the challenge, or to fulfill this obligation. Those who are most effective in kissing frogs are usually those who have been kissed themselves, and in this kiss received a transforming communicable experience of the living Christ -- in its wake we felt a tremendous passion to pass it on to someone else. In Christ we recognize this as 'compassion' and, really, we are simply following in the steps of Christ when we demonstrate this compassion to those around us.

Another demonstration of this urgency is to share with others that transforming kiss in that we find within us a love for others that is not dependent on being loved, liked, or flattered, in return. This concern for others is the basis for an unbreakable fellowship we feel with others who are also busy kissing frogs.

While it is true that it may not be easy to kiss a frog, still it is made easier when we possess a serenity and a peace not dependent on things we are doing or feeling a need to do. This, in turn, gives one a deep sense of joy.

We are part of the MCC family because somebody took the time to kiss us when we didn't even like ourselves. Therefore, may we never withhold this kiss to others who have suffered, who are estranged or feel they are unlovely.

Yes, the Episcopal priest was right – The business of the church is kissing frogs."

For Such A Time As This

1978-1980

The wonderful thing about UFMCC is that its churches offer a place where people from liberal and conservative, liturgical and evangelical, Christian backgrounds come together and share their various traditions in worship. When we were moving toward the season of Lent in 1979, an MCC member from an Episcopal background called me at the church office. He asked me, "Are we going to get a palm on Palm Sunday?" Being a Pentecostal, I had no idea what he was talking about. I responded, "I don't know. I'll have to ask." To which he replied, "Well, I'll feel cheated if I don't get a palm on Palm Sunday." I fired back, "Well, I'll feel cheated if we don't have a message in tongues on Pentecost Sunday!" We both had a good chuckle over that. I followed through with his request and palms were given out at the door come Palm Sunday.

In his letter of recommendation for my admittance into the exhorter program, Ron Bergeron, a Catholic theologian, said, "I have never seen any concern from Paula about my Roman Catholic trappings, and her evangelical background. That is what I like in Paula." Over the years, I have come to learn and appreciate truths from all traditions and systems of teaching.

The exhorter program was created by UFMCC for those who aspired to become ordained ministers. Later, this was changed to the more clear title of student clergy. Austin asked the exhorter candidates to write an article on some aspect of Christian Social Action. I wrote The Transsexual Plight. UFMCC's international magazine, In Unity, published the article. When Austin put his newly hired assistant pastor, Rev. Arlene Ackerman, in charge of the exhorter program, I wrote a thesis on preaching. My paper was titled Sermons And Their Preparation.

UFMCC's governmental structure also included deacons. "Deacons are an extension of the pastor in various forms of serving in ministry within the local church." (See Acts 6:1-6)

In addition to licensed and ordained clergy in UFMCC, deacons and exhorters also wore clerical collars. The exhorter collar has one stripe on it, the deacon collar has two. When I became an exhorter, I refused to wear a clerical collar. It just wasn't me.

When Troy Perry founded MCC In Los Angeles, he wore a clerical collar. In Troy's Pentecostal background, clerical collars were not utilized by ministers. While UFMCC is a Christian denomination, it is very eclectic. It was Troy's wish that people from liturgical church backgrounds feel at home. In UFMCC's early days, Troy's Pentecostal style of preaching made the evangelical community feel part of the family.

Today, some UFMCC ministers wear priestly-type high-church liturgical robes. Brian Potts, an Episcopalian, sewed and put together (what I call) liturgical costumes for ministers and priests all over Portland. Brian called it ecclesiastical drag.

Whether preaching from a pulpit, or in front of a television camera, I always strive to look my best. Whenever I preach, I insist on a fresh hairdo. I want God to be proud of my appearance. Yet, I wear no clerical garb as such.

While being a minister is a profession, Jesus never intended it to be a status symbol. I have known many who could not wait to have "Rev" in front of their name. In MCC, I knew of a newly ordained minister who demanded, "You will call me Reverend." I am just as uncomfortable being called Reverend as I am with wearing liturgical robes and a clerical collar.

In response to James and John requesting status in God's kingdom, Jesus said:

"You know that those who are considered rulers over the Gentiles lord it over them, and their great ones exercise authority over them. Yet it shall not be so among you; but whoever desires to become great among you shall be your servant. And whoever of you desires to be first shall be the slave of all. For even the Son of Man did not come to be served, but to serve, and to give His life a ransom for many. " Mark 10:42-45.

UFMCC has strict educational requirements for candidates who apply for ordination. Rev. Troy Perry himself, who founded the denomination, would probably be denied ministerial credentials by UFMCC, should he apply today. There are many ministries that could never survive in the framework of a denominational church structure. History reveals many women and men, mightily used of God, who had little, if any, formal education. For example, in the biography of the late Kathryn Kuhlman, Jamie Buckingham wrote, "Theologians had answers, but no miracles. Kathryn Kuhlman had no answers, but her ministry had miracles." Miss Kuhlman often said, "Some people are educated beyond their intelligence."

"God did not call me to be a pastor. My calling is to do the work of an evangelist." (II Timothy 4:5) Paul said:

"For Christ sent me not to baptize, but to preach the gospel: not with wisdom of words, lest the cross of Christ should be made of none effect." I Cor. 1:17

I have studied the scriptures for years, and yet I never did follow through and get a formal degree. Like Paul, "...I come not with excellency of speech or of wisdom, declaring unto you the testimony of God. For I determine not to know any thing among you, save Jesus Christ, and Him crucified." (I Cor. 2:1, 2)

When Austin resigned as pastor of MCC Portland to fill the position of NW District Coordinator, the second Senior Pastor was Rev. Don Borbe. Pastor Don, as he preferred to be called, moved to Portland in 1979 from Philadelphia, Pennsylvania, where he had served as Senior Pastor of MCC Philadelphia.

Austin never once asked me to preach. He often said, "There is only one preacher at Portland MCC, and that's AAA." Pastor Don, on the other hand, had me preach often, many times in the main worship service on Sunday. In fact, Don honored and respected my call to preach; more so than did any other minister I have ever worked with.

One evening in March, l980, while I was working in the church office, the beautiful sounds of a chorus of men rehearsing permeated throughout the sanctuary. This was the first rehearsal of the Portland Gay Men's Chorus (PGMC). 23 men comprised this initial group. In June, 1980, they held their first concert to an audience of about 200 people in the sanctuary at MCC during Gay Pride. At this time there were only three other gay men's choruses in other cities. There are now over 200 choruses worldwide. Today, PGMC has about 150 members, and performs to audiences of over 1,500. 65% of their audiences are heterosexual. In Portland, many city, county, and state politicians support, and attend, PGMC concerts.

One of PGMC's founders was Gary Coleman. Gary was MCC Portland's first choir director, dating back to the Centenary Wilbur days. Today, Gary is still actively involved in the administration of PGMC.

In 1980, MCC Portland held a fund raising auction for its first balloon payment on the church's 15 year mortgage. Deacon Bob Jackson donated an old Ford Falcon automobile. The auction was successful and the church gave the car to me, in appreciation for my volunteer services as Church Secretary. I called it the Godmobile.

During MCC Portland's Centenary Wilbur days, a young man named Jack Hoggatt (aka Jack St. John) played the piano and sang. After moving into the arts and crafts style facility at NE 24th Avenue & Broadway Boulevard, Jack became music director of the local church. Jack is a very talented piano player and composer. Whenever I preached, I utilized Jack's musical talents. He would sing prior to the sermon. And, at a set time toward the conclusion of my message, Jack would play background organ music, a tradition in evangelical circles. And then at the completion of my sermon, Jack would sing an appropriate song. The two of us worked well together. In late 1979, Jack and I put together a cantata entitled Esther The Queen, A Timeless Story. Jack wrote the songs, and I prepared and delivered the narration. Esther was performed at NW District Conference at MCC Portland in November, 1979. We received a long and loud standing ovation.

Over time, I developed strong romantic feelings for Jack. I had the idea of Jack and I traveling as an evangelistic team. The name I created for our evangelistic outreach team was Inclusive Outreach Unlimited. (IOU).

I was becoming well established in UFMCC. This fact is documented in the next chapter.

Love Letters Of 1979

When going through boxes of papers from the past, I came across the following three letters. These missives document some of my accomplishments during my time at MCC Portland, far better than I can. The following letter, addressed to me by MCC Portland's Board of Directors, was read to the congregation by the Pastor in January, 1979:

Dear Paula:

"What a unique individual you are. Your love for the Lord has found expression by your involvement in Metropolitan Community Church of Portland - as an exhorter candidate - as church secretary - and as Editor of The Chalice. In at least one or the other of these capacities, you reach the lives of practically all of the members and communicants of this congregation.

In recognition of your service as church secretary, the Board of Directors has approved a small salary for that position as of January 1, 1979. We hope that you will continue to serve the Lord with the same devotion that you have already shown. As the capacity for love is infinite, we can say, 'We love you Paula' without diminishing the love expressed for anyone else."

Austin Amerine wrote the following letter of recommendation on church letterhead:

To Whom It May Concern,

"Paula Nielsen worked as my Secretary from the fall of of 1976 through June 8, 1979 at which time I resigned as Pastor of this Church to accept the position of Northwest District Coordinator. She worked strictly on a voluntary basis until January of l979 when the Board of Directors voted to offer her some limited financial remuneration. She also served in the capacity of Editor of The Chalice, our local church publication, for a great deal of this time, as well as participating in our exhorter training program (ministerial training).

As a secretary I have found Paula to be dependable, creative and resourceful, particularly with those in which she has great interest. She was usually not afraid of innovative ideas -- only occasionally there were times when she resisted change from the way she was accustomed -- however she eventually showed a good ability to adapt.

As a transsexual she has learned to deal with the innocent but stupid statements people sometimes make. She has learned that these statements are often made simply from a lack of understanding rather than in an attempt to be bigoted or vicious.

It is hard to distinguish and evaluate Paula on all of the things she does because she not only does the things that she is expected to do as a secretary but takes on a multitude of other things as well. If she has any weakness, it is an inability to say 'no', but she usually figures a way to find the time to do everything she is asked to do.

There is little that Paula has been asked to do by me that she has not accomplished. I seldom have to check behind her. Paula is a high producer of high ability and, in my opinion, Portland MCC was lucky to have her working in the Church because along with her talent as a Secretary she showed a great dedication and commitment and feeling of loyalty and love of this Church as a body of believers. She respects authority of those around her. She knows and recognizes the need for confidentiality and has a good sense of propriety in screening information.

If, in the future, the Northwest District of the Universal Fellowship of Metropolitan Community Churches is able to provide any funding for secretarial work, Paula will be the first person to be contacted -- in fact, I would like to take her with me now."

The following letter, dated November 18, 1979, from Rev. Michael England of MCC in San Francisco, was addressed to Jack St. John and myself. It is his response to our performance of Esther The Queen -- A Timeless Story:

Dear Jack and Paula:

"Even though I did not get to say it in person to you, I want to let you know again how very important to me Esther the Queen was. That was for a number of reasons. In the first place, I began to get excited during your introduction, Paula, when I realized that you had actually researched the book of Esther and were sharing some important historical and textual criticism with us and doing it in a clear and uncomplicated way. I thought that the writing of the narration throughout was very beautiful and effective. As, indeed, was your topnotch delivery of it, Paula.

I have really longed to be able to take seriously music in our denomination. We have been borrowing other people's music, and much of it not very good music at that. 'Esther the Queen' was not only very definitely an outgrowth of our special mission and experience, but as music I found it rich and subtle and very, very moving. It's a composition that any musician could take seriously, and it makes me proud to know that you are composing in UMCC and that we can give your work to the Christian Church. So thank you for that.

You are both dynamite people of the sort any congregation would give its arm to have. If I were your pastor, I'd pray to God for the legs to fall off of anyone who tried to proselyte either of you, and I have no doubt that happens frequently. I'd do it myself if I thought I could get away with it, but I can see that you are part of a church which is growing and giving you the kind of support that lets you develop your gifts and share them. I know what a wonderful space that is to be in.

Once again, thanks to both of you for your gift to us at Conference..."

When Rev. Don Borbe was elected by the congregation as MCC Portland's next Senior Pastor, I continued in my position as church secretary.

1980's

COCKTAILS
DARCELLE XV
RED HOT MAMA
PAULA NIELSEN
DARCELLE XV

Shifting Priorities of the 80's

Broken Bread
1980

By the time the year 1980 began, I had arrived as an open, active and viable part of Portland's gay community.

In addition to my work at MCC Portland, I became a writer for the Northwest Fountain, a local gay newspaper that was owned and published by Dave Porter. When he visited the church office, Dave discovered my article The Transsexual Plight that had been printed in pamphlet form. I became Religion Editor for the paper, keeping folk apprised of religious activities in the community. I also wrote community news articles. Over the next several years, I wrote for many other alternative lifestyle publications. Eventually, I had a column of my own, Thoughts From Paula.

Pastor Don Borbe elevated me to full exhortership status. As an exhorter, in addition to preaching, I served in other ministerial capacities, such as consecrating the sacrament of Holy Communion. I also took correspondence courses for college credits through UFMCC's Samaritan Theological Seminary. Among other courses, I especially recall the study on higher and lower Biblical criticism. Even though I never achieved a formal college degree, my lifetime of Bible study gave me a good working knowledge of the scriptures. To this very day, I take Bible study courses on a regular basis.

In addition to our working together in the church services, Jack St. John and I became close friends. One evening, while I was visiting in his apartment, we lay side by side on the bed and hugged. This was not sexual. I left his apartment that night, realizing that I was in love with him. I walked home in a romantic haze. I had dreams of our traveling as a husband and wife evangelistic team. Move over Aimee Semple McPherson, here comes Paula Nielsen St. John. If I were cruising for sexual activity and saw Jack, I would not have been interested. He was not my type. In our culture, if one is in love and/or has romantic feelings for another person, a sexual attraction automatically accompanies it. Over the years, I have discovered that just as one can have sexual feelings for a person without being in love, one can also be in love and not be sexually interested in the object of their affection.

My life has been checkered with unrequited romances. However, the one with Jack was the most powerful. There was a strong, powerful, and mutual bond between us. This, coupled with my lifelong desire to marry and work with a minister threw me into a strong emotional and obsessive space with Jack. Jack had his own issues with chemical dependency.

When one is in love with another person, and the romantic feelings are not returned, they read things into comments made by the object of their affection. One Sunday, I preached a sermon entitled "The Rose." I drove Jack home after church. In complimenting my sermon, he said, "When listening to you preach, I thought to myself she is all mine." And, he often referred to me as "the little woman."

Jack and I discussed our moving to Eugene, Oregon, 100 miles south of Portland. We both liked Rev. David Pelletier, the pastor of MCC of the Willamette Valley (MCCWV) in Eugene. The University of Oregon (U of O) in Eugene was given a mandate to fill some clerical positions immediately. Jack, having worked for the state before, was hired over the telephone. He relocated there while I was still working in the Portland church office. Pastor Don was pushing for a full-time salary for the church secretary position.

Just as the MCC Portland Board of Directors was preparing to increase my salary to a full-time wage, I resigned the position so I could move to Eugene. People close to me advised against my moving to Eugene. Pastor Don said, "I support Jack going down there, but I don't support both of you going." Austin, now the NW District Coordinator, strongly advised against it. He said, "I don't believe God is calling you to work in Eugene." However, my emotional tie to Jack was so strong that wild horses could not have kept me in Portland. I called Jack every day in Eugene. I also called Pastor David Pelletier. David had gone through an unrequited love affair. So I called him for relationship counseling. I was so obsessed with Jack that I even called Sylvia Pennington in Los Angeles to talk about it. In this obsessive space, I was not able to think about anything else.

Part of a Spirit-anointed ministry is "healing the broken hearted." (Luke 4:18). The deep inner pain and heartbreak I have suffered throughout my lifetime has enabled me to be a channel of healing to brokenhearted people. In describing her ministry, Jamie Buckingham wrote in Kathryn Kuhlman's biography:

"No man could have ever loved like that. It took a woman, bereft of the love of a man, her womb barren, to love as she loved. Out of her emptiness, she gave. "

When Jesus fed the 5,000 with two loaves of bread, he not only blessed the bread -- he also broke it. Through the broken heart, and the broken life, God loves and blesses thousands, even as Jesus fed the multitudes. Author Kathryn Keating honors the ministry of Kathryn Kuhlman with these words:

" As in the days of yesteryear, the Master took within His hands the bread and broke it.He for so many years just grasped your life within His hands and thanked God for it. Then most carefully He has broken it, and passed it out to those of us who needed such a life -- and we've been fed.

From we who would have died without this meal, there rises on this day giving thanks to God who broke you, yet who spared your life. And in gratitude to you for though you wept, you bowed your knee to being broken bread, that those of us who hungered could be fed.

This is God's way, has always been God's way. How else could one suffice to feed a multitude?But few of us withstand the breaking in God's hands, so thousands died who might have lived. But if one die, that one bringeth forth much fruit.But if that one lives, that one lives alone. So has God said. So thank we you for being Broken Bread. "

In 1975, I had moved out of God's perfect Will when I returned to Los Angeles. In the summer of 1980, I did so again when I relocated to Eugene. Nonetheless, even when I moved out of God's perfect Will, God forgave, and restored my ministry and used these experiences to bless others. There is no breakage, no loss, no grief, no sin, no mess so dreadful that out of it God cannot bring good. Our God is the Divine Alchemist. God can take junk from the rubbish heap of our lives, and melting this base refuse in the pure fire of His love, hand us back gold. As I relocated to Eugene, my dark night of the soul was just beginning.

Dark Night Of The Soul
1980

Eugene is the second largest city in Oregon, with a population of over 150,000. It is a college town. The city is noted for activist political leanings, alternative lifestyles, and focus on the arts. During the 1970's, UFMCC established a church in Eugene. Services were held in a rented chapel, across the street from the U of O. Rev. David Pelletier and his partner Gary had relocated from St. Louis, Missouri to pastor MCCWV. David's background and seminary training was Lutheran.

Jack and I were both living in Eugene by August, 1980. My stay in Eugene lasted from August until the end of November of that year. During most of this time I stayed with David and Gary. By the time I arrived, Jack had his own apartment. In November, a few weeks prior to moving back to Portland, I rented a pay-by-the-week room in a cheap and seedy motel.

Looking for work in Eugene was more difficult than it had been in larger cities. Whenever I needed work, I could apply at a temp agency, take a typing test, and be sent out on an assignment that same day. Not so in Eugene. The temp agencies had far more applicants than job openings. They did not even take applications from walk-ins. When a temp agency did advertise a job in the newspaper, at least 50 applicants responded. At one law firm, where I answered an ad in the newspaper for a legal secretary, they told me that about 75 people had applied for the position.

I also put in applications at various employment agencies. I told the agencies that I relocated from Portland to work with my church. I listed MCC Portland as my last employer. A gal from one of the employment agencies called me and asked, "Just how is your church different from other churches?" I snapped at her and said, "My religion has nothing to do with my job qualifications. You should not even be asking me that question." and hung up. One of the agencies placed me on a temporary legal transcribing job for the Public Defender's Office. This was a two-week vacation fill-in. It was the only job in Eugene that I enjoyed. Later, I took a telemarketing job, advertised in the newspaper, in the adjoining city of Springfield, selling tickets to a charity event sponsored by the Lane County Sheriff's Union.

During my last month in Eugene, an employment agency placed me with a court reporter who worked out of her home. She dictated deposition proceedings that she had taken down in shorthand into a dictaphone. She was one of the most negative and unpleasant persons I have ever worked for. No one stayed in her employ very long. By the time I left Eugene, she owed me about $200. A few months later she filed for bankruptcy and listed me and two other typists among her debts. I never did collect the money.

If my professional life was unhappy, my personal life was even more so. I put together MCCWV's newsletter and preached in one Sunday service. Jack's musical abilities immensely enhanced the worship services for the small congregation. Often I stayed away from church because Jack was there. It was during this time that Jack and Pastor David jointly composed the stirring inclusive anthem entitled The Church Alive. This magnificent hymn is still used in UFMCC churches worldwide, and is usually sung at major conferences and events.

Jack thought that by moving to Eugene he would be away from his chemical dependency. The ploy did not work. Street drugs were available everywhere. I started hanging out in a small gay bar and got to know a few people. There I could usually find marijuana. As I was so unhappy, my times of getting drunk on booze were increasing. One night a guy gave me some LSD.

Prior to 1980, my only experience with LSD was in 1974 with my cousin Sue and her boyfriend Danny in Portland. Then, I dropped small amounts of windowpane acid twice. I never took a full hit. Trying to blot out my unhappiness in Eugene, twice I dropped acid when I was drunk. Booze and drugs may help some people momentarily forget their troubles; not so with me. The chemicals merely intensified my unhappiness.

One night I wandered into a bar catering to the college crowd near U of O. I got loud, boisterous and bitchy. The bartender called the police. They did not arrest me. They took me to a place designated for drunks. As I sat there loudly weeping, totally brokenhearted and calling out Jack's name, a counselor recognized me from the time in 1979 when I had preached at MCCWV.

Another night, I was hoping Jack and I would do something together. He said that he was going out to a bar to be picked up. Later that night, I got drunk and tripped on LSD. I got in my car and started driving at a high speed all over town. In the car I was driving and shouting loudly. I was angry at God. "Why am I so unhappy?" I screamed out, with tears streaming down my face. "Other people have lovers, but not me. It just isn't fair," I yelled. Suddenly it dawned on me that I had no idea where I was. Never before in my life had I felt so totally and completely alone, enveloped in the dark night of the soul. I did manage to get to a pay phone and called Gary to ask for directions.

Another night when I was drunk, I knocked on Jack's apartment door. I do not recall much, except that he did not invite me in. We yelled and cried back and forth through the door. Jack threatened to call the police but didn't. A girl who lived upstairs came down to see what the loud commotion was about.

On Labor Day, I stayed away from the church festivities and went for a walk by myself in a city park. There were families picnics with people having a wonderful time. At that moment, I wished I had been born a straight person. I felt resentment that I was born between the sexes. This was the only time in my life when I questioned my faith.

A woman bartender at a gay bar told Jack that I had come in one night. She told Jack "I just wanted to reach across the bar and hug Paula, she was so unhappy." That was putting it mildly. My time spent in Eugene was the lowest point in my life. Never before, or since, have I experienced such utter and total misery.

Pastor David was not pleased with my drinking. At his insistence I attended some Live and Let Live gay Alcoholics Anonymous meetings. The support I got at the meetings did not delete my unhappiness. However, my interacting with others who also had a drinking problem did help me. This provided me with a confidential setting where I could share my inner pain, and it kept me from drinking.

Pastor David did understand my pain inasmuch as he had once experienced unrequited love. When it came to my feelings for Jack, David said, "Jack cannot help you with that." I understood this, because a few times in my life when someone was in love with me, I could not help the other person either. Nonetheless, Jack did reach out to me, and tried to help. We met for lunch one day, and he handed me an article he had written. It described my deep inner unhappiness. The article, entitled The Gardener, places me in a garden, badly overrun with weeds, surrounded with broken tools.

"Within moments an inner voice spoke, lovingly, and yet with a hint of irritation, "What has happened here?:

I don't know", Paula replied, distantly. Where has everybody gone? Her eyes were full of tears and she was too tired and unhappy to let them fall. "I just don't know.

I told you I would fix the tools," said the Inner Voice.

Paula lashed out, They break every five minutes. People come to help; they suddenly disappear without a word! Every time I think I've found someone, they fall by the wayside. I'm tired, I'm alone and I'm scared.

Suddenly Paula grabbed a red rose, the only thing growing in that patch of weeds, defiantly closed her eyes tightly, stubbornly set her lips, and waited for the Inner Voice to go away.

A female voice said, It grieves me to see our child so unhappy. What shall we do? In response, the same Voice, but now with a male sound, said, we have given her every tool she needs. She must use them."

But she is so lonely and disillusioned. Maybe the row we've given her IS too hard for her to hoe. We have made her in our image, the Voice replied. And more so than many of our other children, we have given her much of ourselves: Our inclusivity of emotions, our various orientations, our maleness and our femaleness. She is more of total person than the other children."

The other children don't understand her. They ostracize her from their private times. They don't let her get close to them. They withhold their special love from her.

She must depend on Us all the more. Let's fix these tools and see if she will try again.

Suddenly the ground shook and burst forth with fragrant blossoms. Paula, the Voice spoke. Paula, I love you. Flowers blossomed. Weeds disappeared. The tools were again repaired as new.

Again the Voice spoke, People are human. They will fail you. Only I am perfect.

Within seconds, Paula was aware of her surroundings. Introspectively, she took a deep breath and said, I can do it. I'll make it, I know. A peace swept over her. The female Voice said, "She'll make it. The male Voice said, We'll stay near."

As I read this the words of Jesus came to mind:

"I will never leave thee nor forsake thee."

In November the NW District Conference of UFMCC was held in Tacoma. I returned to Eugene from the conference, went to my motel room, packed my bags, and returned to Portland without stopping to say good bye.

While driving back to Portland, lovingly and tenderly the Holy Spirit reminded me of God's promise in I Peter 4:12 & 13:

"Beloved, think it not strange concerning the fiery trial which is to try you, as though some strange thing happened unto you: But rejoice, inasmuch as ye are partakers of Christ's sufferings; that, when His glory shall be revealed, ye may be glad also with exceeding joy."

For the first time since moving to Eugene, I felt inner peace. My dark night of the soul was almost over. I had passed through the storm. My faith in the One who makes no mistakes was stronger than ever before. As I neared the city of Portland, the words of a beloved Fanny J. Crosby hymn came to mind:

Down in the human heart,
crushed by the tempter,
Feelings lie buried that grace can restore.
Touched by a loving heart, awakened by kindness,
Chords that are broken
will vibrate once more.

Returning To Nineveh
1980

When a person moves out of God's Will, unhappiness invariably follows. On the other hand, once an individual returns to where God wants them in the first place and that person experiences Divine restoration, happiness returns. When Jonah was freed from the belly of the whale, he obeyed God and went to Nineveh. A revival ensued. Portland, Oregon was my Nineveh, and still is.

Both in 1975 when I returned to Los Angeles, and in 1980 when I relocated in Eugene, Oregon, I was chasing after relationships that were not to be. I was still searching desperately to find my place in life, as Jean Darnall had discerned back in 1964. Returning to Portland, again I recalled the words of my friend Laura. "Paula, you are like a bowling pin -- you get knocked down and then bounce right back up again." No matter how unhappy situations may be -- and I have had many -- with time, the wounds heal and I move on with my life, happy once again. Depression leaves, and joy returns.

Once I got back to Portland in late 1980, I felt like an oppressive weight lifted. Walking up NE Broadway to the MCC Portland facility, I was singing the line from Hello, Dolly: "It's so nice to be back home where I belong."

Once re-situated in Portland, I called Pastor David Pelletier in Eugene, apologizing for taking off so suddenly without even saying goodbye. Jack was still living in Eugene. "If I had not been in love with Jack," I told David, "I probably could have handled the Eugene experience." David replied, "You would have handled it better."

MCC Portland, of course, had hired another church secretary, and so I set out looking for work. Pastor Don Borbe immediately utilized my secretarial skills, dictating correspondence. The Board of Directors questioned this. One board member said to me, "It isn't fair that you are doing the work that someone else is being paid to do." I responded and said that by doing this work without pay, I was repaying the church for personal phone calls I had made to Eugene earlier in the year.

While still living in Eugene, Jack visited our mutual friend, Thea Nelson. I joined them for dinner. Jack said, "There is only one thing I don't envy you for (in returning to Portland). There is going to be a big hassle surrounding Pastor Don Borbe, and you are going to be right in the middle of it." His prediction proved to be true.

In December, 1980 the MCC Portland Board of Directors asked Pastor Don to resign. To show my appreciation for his support of my ministry over the years, I choose not to elaborate on the details. I stood firm in my support of Don, and still do.

This situation made MCC Portland look bad in the overall gay community. Gay rights activist Jerry Weller said, "What kind of a Christian church would fire their pastor right before Christmas?" Don refused to resign. In January, 1981 a congregational meeting was held in the church sanctuary to a packed out house. The congregation voted him out. While sitting up front with the board of directors, taking notes of the meeting, I was ashamed to be a part of it.

Rev. Claudia Vierra, then working with MCC in Boise, Idaho, came to Portland for three days a week to serve as interim pastor. Although she felt that Don should have resigned when the board asked him to, Claudia made an effort toward reconciliation between Don and the church. She preached a sermon on forgiveness and told the congregation, "This church is at least 50% responsible for what happened." She invited Don to speak, and he accepted. While this helped somewhat, the damage was done. The sad ending to this debacle was that Don resigned as a minister in the UFMCC.

Another tragic public experience occurred at the meeting where Pastor Don was ousted.

Deborah was Jewish. Her partner was Christian. Deborah became very active in MCC Portland. She wrote a wonderful article for The Chalice entitled A Jew In A Christian Church. While perhaps not Christian theologically, Deborah practiced Christ's love. Her contributions to the life and ministry of MCC Portland were numerous.

UFMCC was established as a Christian denomination. Due to its very nature of being inclusive, it should have been interfaith. To be an MCC church member a person is required to subscribe to the Christian faith. People of other religions are classified as friends. Friends can be active in the local church, and even serve on committees. But they cannot serve on the Board of Directors or vote in congregational meetings.

At a UFMCC General Conference in 1976, the Portland church had put in a bylaw proposal that would have changed this. The proposal failed to garner enough votes to pass. Had this passed, friends would have had full participation, with the one exception that they could not vote on issues related to changes in faith, doctrine or theology.

Unbeknown to anyone, Austin had allowed Deborah to vote in congregational meetings. At the meeting surrounding the removal of Don Borbe as pastor, when the clerk compared the number of members present who were voting, there was one name too many. When this was brought out, a board member said: "I hate to say this, but Deborah cannot vote." Many members, including myself, were very unhappy about this. Member Ron Powell pointed out, "Deborah served on the committee that brought Don to Portland." Deborah was denied taking a part in this decision of the church. The Board's rationale was, "If we go against UFMCC bylaws and allow Deborah to vote, the outcome of this election could be declared invalid."

Later, a MCC Portland board member wrote to the Board of Elders of UFMCC, relating what had happened, to no avail. A MCC minister said, "We are inclusive if you are a Christian." I disagree. Once you say "...we are inclusive IF..." you are no longer inclusive. Along with some others, I felt that this was blatant discrimination. Church bylaws should be guidelines and not cold unbending arbitrary rules. The scripture says:

"The letter killeth but the Spirit giveth life." (II Cor. 3:8)

After the removal of Don Borbe as pastor of MCC, and the church's treatment of Deborah, I stopped attending church altogether. I still listened to Kathryn Kuhlman daily on the radio. My faith in God was intact. My confidence in organized religion was not. My priorites took on a major shift.

Lavender Shingle
1980-1982

In January, 1981 the Northwest Fountain published an article entitled Lavender Shingle Goes Up. Featured was a photograph of myself, alongside lesbian lawyers Katharine English and Janet Metcalf. This was Portland's first law firm to openly advertise Serving The Gay Community.

In 1992, Oregon's leading newspaper, The Oregonian, published a cover story about me on the front page of the Living section. The article was entitled Maverick Ministry. It was informative and very supportive. In the article, Katharine English was quoted as saying, "I learned tolerance from Paula." Katharine was referring back to 1980 when she hired me as the first secretary for her newly established law firm, English & Metcalf (E&M).

When Katharine and Janet opened their office, the phone started ringing off the hook. Katharine said, "We've got to get a secretary in here." Katharine called MCC. They told her about me. I had just returned from Eugene. "There's only one thing," said Pastor Don, "Paula is TS." Thinking that TS was some kind of physical disability, such as multiple sclerosis (MS) Katharine said, "Great. Send her over!" She thought, "We will not discriminate on the basis of disability."

When Janet told Katharine that TS meant transsexual, she hit the ceiling. "You mean, Paula is a man. This is a lesbian law firm, and I won't have a man working here," Katharine exploded. Janet replied, "No, Paula is not a man, she is a transsexual. We do not discriminate. If you won't work with Paula, then I won't work with you." And so, reluctantly, Katharine said, "All right, we'll try it." It was years later when I learned about this pre-hiring conference between the two lawyers. After I worked for the firm for one month, so delighted was Katharine with my secretarial abilities that she wrote a glowing letter to The Downtowner, a local tabloid, that won me the paper's Secretary of the Year award. My photograph appeared with the article that included Katharine's comments.

The firm grew rapidly. By this time, Jack St. John was preparing to move from Eugene back to Portland. I suggested to Katharine that she consider hiring him. Her reaction was negative. By now she had accepted me as a woman. Still she did not like the idea of a man working for the firm. She wanted to hire a lesbian.

I knew that Katharine would like Jack. While Katharine and Janet were out of town for a conference, I had Jack come in to organize Katharine's files. My hunch that Katharine and Jack would like each other proved accurate. Katharine loved Jack. She said that he was everything she ever wanted in a secretary. Jack wound up becoming a paralegal for the firm. While Jack and I worked well together in MCC worship services, now that we were working together five days a week, we squabbled constantly. Had I gotten my wish in Eugene for Jack and I to be lovers, it would have been a total disaster. Someone once said, "Be careful what you wish for, you just might get it."

Truly, the Lavender Shingle proudly sporting the name English and Metcalf paved the way for other attorneys to come out in open support of gays. Lavender Law was moving full steam ahead. The combination of two lesbians, a transsexual, and a gay man was definitely making its mark on the Portland law community.

Not only were Katharine and Janet partners in their law firm, they were also lovers in their personal life. In 1980, they had been together for a year. They established a household in which they raised Katharine's two sons, Greg and Nathan who were then, and are now, heterosexual.

Katharine's law practice focused on domestic issues, such as divorce and child custody cases. As a trial lawyer, she was instrumental in securing child custody rights for many lesbian and gay parents. She was also instrumental in convincing many Circuit Court judges that homosexuality itself, is not a valid reason to deny someone custody of their children. She became a specialist in helping the LGBT community with its unique challenges in the legal system. She also did probate work for lesbians and gays, and wrote their wills and other legal documents such as powers of attorney, etc.

Janet's specialty was appellate court briefs, legal documents filed with the Court of Appeals and/or Supreme Court. She also represented defendants in criminal cases. Both lawyers were very successful, well-accomplished, and highly regarded in their respective fields of law and in the courts, as well as in both the gay and straight communities.

In March of 1981 I started performing at Darcelle XV (DXV), a Portland cabaret featuring female impersonators. While working for E&M in the daytime, I was performing at night in the Tuesday night "Catch A Rising Star" show at DXV.

In 1984, the lesbian law firm closed. Katharine's application to serve as a referee for the Multnomah County Juvenile Court came through. Janet decided to further her legal education. Jack decided to relocate to the San Francisco Bay Area to further his seminary education. By this time, I was working for DXV full time. I jokingly said, "Now that I am in Portland and Jack is in San Francisco, we get along better than we ever did".

Although Katharine and Janet went to separate jobs, they remained lovers. After being together for 23 years, Katharine and Janet split up. Katharine moved to Salt Lake City and married her high school boyfriend. She considers herself to be bisexual. Today, Janet is an appellate lawyer for the Attorney General's office; writing and filing appeals briefs on their behalf.

I had moved to California in the early 1960's. My dream then was to be a professional entertainer at Finocchio's. This dream did not find its fulfillment there. My desire to be a professional entertainer was to come true about twenty years later in Portland at Darcelle XV.

Trendsetters - Darcelle & Roxy
1981

"Not In Portland Boys" was the headline of an early 1950's news story in one of Portland's local newspapers. Included with the article was a photo of a group of female impersonators who performed at a night club called The Music Hall. As part of "cleaning up the city", Portland's "hatchet Mayor," Dorothy McCullough Lee, shut down the popular night spot, claiming that it corrupted morals. She literally drove the drag entertainers out of town. Many of the booted-out performers migrated to San Francisco.

In the late 1960's, Walter Cole and Roxy Neuhardt, started an innovative female impersonation cabaret show bar that gained acceptance in Portland's heterosexual community. A city that had traditionally been conservative was becoming liberal and progressive. This came about because of two progressive pioneers whose combined talents and efforts helped make it all happen.

Walter Cole was born in Portland on November 16, 1930. When he was eight years old, his mother took him to a downtown movie palace, the United Artists Theater, to see the 1939 MGM civil war classic Gone With The Wind. In the final scene of the first half of the long movie, Scarlett O'Hara returns from Atlanta to find her beloved plantation, Tara, ravished and in ruins. Hungrily eating a radish, she looked up with fiery determination and clenched fists, declaring, "As God is my witness, I'll never go hungry again!" This fueled a strong impression in young Walter that would remain with him for the rest of his life. Like Scarlett in the film, Walter possesses the strong drive of a workaholic.

Upon graduation from Lincoln High School in 1949, Walter married a woman named Jeannette. The couple had two children. He was not happy working on regular day-to-day routine jobs. By the mid 1950's, he established a popular hangout coffee house for college students and beatnik poets near Portland State University. In addition to selling coffee, customers purchased souvenir cups. The business was very successful.

Roxy Neuhardt was born in Montana in 1935. Prior to settling down in Portland to work as a dancer at the Hoyt Hotel, Roxy ran a dance studio in Salt Lake City, worked as a backup chorus boy in Las Vegas, and performed at Bimbo's 365 nightclub in San Francisco.

Walter met Roxy at a Portland gay bar. It wasn't long before Walter decided that Roxy was the man he wanted to spend the rest of his life with. Coming out as a gay man to his family, Walter separated from Jeannette. Nevertheless, Walter and Jeannette have remained friends to this day. Later in life, Walter would say, "I am deeply sorry for any pain this brought upon my family. I am NOT sorry I told the truth."

After running the coffee house, Walter decided to go into the tavern business. In 1967, he purchased Demas Tavern in a seedy area of Old Town. His first patrons were primarily lesbians, and business was slow. It was Roxy who initially had the idea of turning the establishment into a cabaret show bar featuring female impersonators. Having patronized the world famous Finocchio's in San Francisco, Roxy said, "If it worked in San Francisco, it should work in Portland as well."

Soon Walter met Jerry Ferris, aka Tina Sandell, who performed at a nearby bar called The Magic Gardens. Walter, then going by the stage name Madam D, teamed up with Tina to do shows at Demas Tavern. A table top was set up as a stage; the spotlight was from a slide projector. Patrons paid a 50-cent cover charge which included two glasses of beer. Tina worked with Walter for the rest of her life.

Walter had an innate ability to entertain. Friends came to his home for "waffles with Walt." He also had a flair for acting, and appeared in plays at the Portland Civic Theater. Roxy perceived

Walter as a drag queen hostess, wearing ultra-high fashioned wigs, dressed in glamorous costumes with exaggerated jewelry, a ring on every finger, and long red fake fingernails. While in Las Vegas, Roxy had worked with a film actress named Denice Darcel. With a slight change in spelling, Roxy suggested the name "Darcelle" for Walter's stage persona. The name stuck, and soon became a household word thoughout Portland.

Darcelle and Roxy's combined talents and energy transformed Demas Tavern into Portland's most glamorous and popular cabaret show bar. Doing the remodeling themselves, they took down a middle partition wall, which had divided the bar from a pool table. A stage was constructed. All of the stage lighting and wiring was done by Darcelle. Production costumes were all made by Darcelle. Roxy staged and choreographed the production numbers, many of which remained in the lavish revue for years.

Roxy joined Darcelle and Tina in the show. Roxy's act was tap dancing in a tuxedo. The number got mild and polite applause, at best. One night the audience did not respond at all. The next night Roxy got into full stage glamor drag and performed the same tap dancing routine. The audience went wild with thunderous applause. Roxy's stage persona was transformed from Fred Astaire to Ginger Rogers. Soon Roxy developed a slapstick act where he tap danced on roller skates, which also brought down the house.

And so, a lavish revue, later named Darcelle XV & Company, began. Darcelle's bass voice boomed out of the sound system, announcing: "Good evening, ladies and gentlemen! Walter presents -- That's No Lady, That's Darcelle XV & Company."

A local newspaper, Willamette Week, did the first feature story about the newly established show bar. Heterosexual patrons started filling the club. Darcelle XV soon became Portland's most popular place to celebrate special occasions, or just to have a fun evening on the town.

By early 1970, 20 years after the Dorothy McCullough Lee

era had ended, female impersonation became an accepted form of entertainment. In 1980, Darcelle XV Productions created a national drag beauty contest called LaFemme Magnifique. Local celebrities served as judges for the event, including Portland Mayor Vera Katz.

Darcelle purchased a historic home in NE Portland. During the era of prohibition in the 1920's, the basement of the house, with a separate entrance, had been used as a speakeasy. By the 1950's, it had become a house of prostitution, and it was shut down by Dorothy McCullough Lee. Darcelle and Roxy's creativity turned the two story house into a showplace of elegance.

When Bud Clark became Mayor of Portland in 1984, Darcelle was asked to M.C. the Mayor's Inaugural Ball, which drew thousands to Portland's Memorial Coliseum. Walter Cole and Bud Clark had been high school classmates at Lincoln High school.

Because of the numerous contributions of two trendsetters, Darcelle and Roxy, gay people are now accepted in social circles that had traditionally rejected them. History will say of these two creative personalities, "Portland is a better place, because Darcelle and Roxy lived and worked there."

Drag City
1981

Throughout the decades of the 1980's and 1990's, I was active in Portland's drag community. My story would be incomplete without including some of the colorful and wonderful personalities with whom I had become involved during this 20 year time span.

The November, 1981 issue of the Northwest Fountain featured a cover story called It's Drag City, Man! One of my earliest show business photos filled the cover.

The term "drag" basically means any attire that you do not wear in everyday life. Using this definition, it is impossible for one to "live in drag." When I am in everyday female attire, under the identity of Paula, I am not in drag. On the other hand, when performing on a cabaret stage, wearing a show business costume, then I am in drag.

In 1958 some frequent patrons of the original Half Moon Tavern, situated on Portland's waterfront, came up with an idea to spoof Portland's annual Rose Festival celebration. The resulting show was a big success, and eventually evolved into a social phenomenon called The Imperial Sovereign Rose Court (ISRC). Over time, a fantasy imperial kingdom was devised. The "court system" is still alive today in several states and cities.

Many honorary titles were devised over the years, the main monarch of the Court being the Empress. Later, the position of Emperor was created. Usually the Empress is a drag queen, and the Emperor is a man in male attire. There have been a few exceptions where the Empress has been a biological female, a "drag queen housed in the wrong body." One of the outstanding emperors was a biological female, i.e., a "butch" lesbian. Each monarch is expected to do community service, fundraising, and to establish long range beneficial programs for the city, and to represent Portland in other cities' Court functions.

Each year a popular vote election is held among those approved by the Court's Board of Directors as candidates for the positions of Emperor and Empress. On election day, parties are held in gay bars all over Portland. People go to the polls to vote. A CPA firm tallies the votes. Like the Academy Awards, the sealed envelopes, announcing the winners, are opened and read at the annual Inauguration Ball. Often I would be asked by the reigning Empress to do the invocation for the annual event.

Included in this informal hall of fame is Vanessa XIII Van Richards, whose stage name became The Vanessa. Vanessa hosted open drag shows in the back room of Dahl & Penne's bar for many years. Vanessa was instrumental in starting the ISRC in Portland. Esther Hoffman Howard XXIV was the first monarch known to die from AIDS in 1982. The famous Portland food bank Esther's Pantry still offers groceries to people living with HIV and AIDS. The ongoing acts of kindness to the needy memorialize Esther.

Some monarchs became institutions of service to the community, serving the Court far beyond the years of their actual reigns. The best examples of this is are Darcelle and Vanessa, although there are many others. Each Empress serves officially in the capacity for one year. However, they retain their official title for life. Most famous of all of these Oregon monarchs is Darcelle XV.

In 1972 Darcelle ran for the coveted title and lost. Never one to give up, Darcelle ran again in 1973 -- and became fondly known as Darcelle XV." The XV means that Darcelle is the fifteenth Empress. In 1974, the name of Demas Tavern was changed to Darcelle XV. At the conclusion of the shows performed by Darcelle XV & Company, Darcelle gives the audience a chance to ask questions. Following are the three questions most frequently asked:

Q - How do you get into that dress?

DXV - How do you get into this dress? You might start by buying me a drink.

Q - Where's the beef? Where do you put it?

DXV - You notice we smile a lot on stage and never sit down? Now you know where it's at.

Q - What does the XV stand for?

DXV - In 1973, I was elected the 15th Empress of Portland -- an honorary title.

The Darcelle XV & Company show runs Wednesday through

Saturday nights. On other nights, the ISRC and other gay community functions are held at Darcelle XV. Most of the events are fundraisers.

Each year, the newly elected ISRC monarchs bestow honorary titles to people in the community. The event is called Investitures. In 1987, Rose Empress The Pearl XXX elevated me to the position of Best of the Red Hot Mamas -- Never Last. In 1993, Empress Maria XXXVI honored me with the title of Keeper Of The Spiritual Vision. In 1995, Empress Misha XXXVIII bestowed upon me the title of Royal Minister to the Beauty of the Rose. These wonderful titles acknowledge my work as an entertainer, and my calling as a preacher of the Gospel.

I never ran for an elected title and position in the ISRC. Nonetheless, I played a prominent role in "drag city." At Darcelle XV, I was Portland's Own Red Hot Mama.

Portland's Own Red Hot Mama

1981

Soon after graduating from high school in 1956, I discovered Sophie Tucker's comedy record albums. Her show business career had started in 1904. By the 1920's, she became a national vaudeville headliner. Theatre marquees gave her star billing as "The Last Of The Red Hot Mamas." With the demise of vaudeville, Sophie performed her material in night clubs. Her songs were written for adult audiences. In her autobiography, Sophie insisted that the risqué talking songs, accompanied by music, were not dirty. I agree. The songs were risqué in a fun way, dishing out saucy advice. Right up until her death in 1966, she was still The Last of the Red Hot Mamas. She loved poking fun at herself:

"Not being young and beautiful, doesn't bother me even slightly.

And you wouldn't believe me if I told you, what this babe still does almost nightly."

She also loved to josh about her weight:

"If your figure is plump and dumpy, don't you try to flatten it. Remember that the choicest beef, always has a little fat in it."

I loved Sophie's songs and as an ardent fan, I listened to her albums enough so that I knew them by heart. Throughout my lifetime, I often recited her songs at parties. As I grew older, I maintained this fun attitude, and I still do. It has helped me maintain my sense of humor.

My dream of being a professional entertainer was put on the back burner in the early 1960's when I lived in the Bay Area. Nevertheless that dream never left me. My life is proof that if you cling to your honorable goals and dreams long enough, sooner or later they will come true.

When Portland Town Council (PTC), a political gay rights activist organization, used MCC's facilities for a fund raising dinner one night in 1979, Darcelle XV was the invited speaker. I was helping serve food at this event. Rev. Denis Moore was an MCC minister. His partner Dan Reed was billed as "Dana" in the Darcelle XV revue. From Dana I learned that Darcelle was very impressed with the things that I was doing at the church. "Every time I go out there Paula is always working. She has a heart of gold," said Darcelle.

During this same year, Christine Jorgenson was billed for a three night engagement at Darcelle XV. Rev. Arlene Ackerman got a group of us together after church one Sunday night to see Christine's show. This was the first time I darkened the doors of the popular night club.

In March, 1980, the Counseling Center for Sexual Minorities (CCSM), a gay hot line, was doing a community fund raising show on a Sunday night at Darcelle XV. The show, hosted by a local drag performer known as "Fairy Tyler Moore", consisted of talent from a variety of gay organizations, including MCC Portland. Having done my Sophie Tucker recitations at church functions, I was asked to be in this show. The music was provided by piano player Joe Anderson, along with a drummer. For my act, Joe learned the music from the Sophie Tucker records.

And so, on that memorable night in 1980, I made my first appearance on the Darcelle XV stage. They brought me on as a "Sophie Tucker act". When I hit the stage, I was greeted by loud thunderous applause. I boomed out the intro to the song Never Let The Same Dog Bite You Twice, declaring:

Brothers & Sisters -- Hallelujah!
Here's Sister Paula -- gonna do some preachin' to ya.
My lesson for today, ain't from the Bible
Its for the gals whose man ain't been reliable...

The other Sophie Tucker number I did that night was the popular Mr. Segal, Make It Legal For Me, about a gal knocked up out of wedlock. This fit in well for a hotline fundraiser. Darcelle and Roxy were impressed by my stage persona. Roxy approached me with the idea of making an occasional guest appearance in their show.

Before this happened, I had moved to Eugene for four months. After my return to Portland, while working at E&M as a legal secretary, I made appearances in local gay bars, reciting Sophie Tucker material. Darcelle and Roxy saw me perform at Wilde Oscars, a watering hole and eatery very popular with the gay community at the time. Later, Darcelle would say, "When we saw Paula doing her fun Sophie Tucker routine, we fell in love." Roxy said, "Listening to Paula do Sophie was very entertaining. I saw Paula as a potential fill in for Darcelle when we would occasionally go out of town."

In March of 1981, Fairy Tyler Moore hosted another CCSM benefit at Darcelle XV. Again, I was asked to be in the show. I noticed a flier on the table, advertising a Tuesday night show at Darcelle XV called Catch A Rising Star, describing it as a "showcase for new talent." I asked Roxy about the possibility of my being in this show. He was very interested and supportive. Both Darcelle and Roxy were glad to have me join the Tuesday night cast. In 1984, the Monday Night Burlesque show relocated in Reno, Nevada. This gave Catch A Rising Star both the Monday and Tuesday slots.

The first time I walked out on stage in the Tuesday Catch A Rising Star show, I was introduced as "the male Sophie Tucker." I objected to that billing, and so it was changed and I became "Portland's Own Sophie Tucker." Many younger members in the audience had no idea who Sophie Tucker was. Eventually I changed my billing to "Paula Nielsen -- Portland's Own Red Hot Mama."

The Tuesday night show was hosted by a drag performer named Champagne. My spot was in the middle of the show, breaking the pace from lip syncing party routines. I opened with a Sophie Tucker song, did some standup comedy monologue and then closed with another Sophie number. About a year later when Champagne left the show, I was given the hostess spot. Soon I became a fill-in for Darcelle's star/hostess spot in the Wednesday through Saturday Darcelle XV & Company show. Faithfully working the small weeknight audiences, I polished my act. By the time I was able to perform on weekends, I was wowing the audience, performing for the packed out house.

Piano players Joe Anderson, Ron Snyder, and Jack St. John recorded the piano music of Sophie Tucker's comedy songs for me. I performed the routines live with the taped music.

It was not necessary for me to develop a night club act, once I hit the Darcelle XV stage. My show business preparation took place over a 25 year time span. Reciting the routines I had memorized from Sophie Tucker record albums just came natural to me. My act consisted of standup comedy banter, along with old-time standard songs such as Hello My Baby, and Dark Town Strutters Ball. This, coupled with Sophie Tucker's classic risque comedy songs, resulted in top drawer entertainment.

Dora Jar, a local drag personality, suggested that I do a Shirley Temple routine. I lip synched a medley of Shirley Temple songs, dressed as a little girl. The act was well received. Jumping and tap dancing across the stage knocked the wind right out of me. I also developed a Madeline Kahn routine, lip syncing the bawdy song I'm Tired from the Mel Brook's film Blazing Saddles. Another lip syncing number that audiences loved was a medley from a Mae West album when she performed in Las Vegas, They Call Me Sister Honky Tonk - Frankie & Johnny.

My lifelong dream was to see my name on a marque. While Darcelle was out of town, the cabaret marquee would read:

PAULA NIELSEN -- RED HOT MAMA.

Instead of preaching from behind a church pulpit, I was helping people forget their troubles on a night club stage. As Sophie said:

Let's fill the world with our laughter,
that's the language everyone knows.

Bigger & Better Than Ever!
1982

Throughout the decade of the 1980's, my priorities had shifted from church involvement to show business activities. Some of the folks at MCC Portland felt that I was way out in left field.

Entertainment is one of the methods that God uses to help and bless people. Some of history's most successful evangelists were also gifted entertainers. One classic example is Foursquare evangelist Aimee Semple McPherson, who presented full stage sacred operas in Los Angeles at her 5,000 seat mega church, Angelus Temple, in the 1930's and 40's. Christian television networks today feature scores of charismatic preachers who preach, perform, and entertain. Their stage presence and delivery of God's message hold the attention of all people. There are many gifted actors, actresses and entertainers who also have their religious work.

In early 1982 Jack St. John decided to present another performance of Esther The Queen, A Timeless Story at MCC Portland. He asked me to do the narration. One of the Board members objected because I was no longer attending church. I talked to the pastor about it. After discussion and prayer, he decided to let me do it.

Sunday evening, March 7, 1982 is one of the most memorable evenings of my life. In the same night, I utilized my gifts and talents, both as a preacher and as an entertainer. At 6 pm, MCC Portland presented Esther. The cantata featured the MCC Portland Choir, directed by Jack St. John. I delivered the narration. Darcelle and Roxy were in the audience. Later on that same night, at 8:30 pm, I presented my first one person show at Darcelle XV. Jack St. John was the piano player. Jack also did a guest spot in the show with his wonderful singing. The show was named after a Sophie Tucker record album and song, "Bigger 'n Better Than Ever!"

For years, the Darcelle XV & Company show staged three performances on Friday and Saturday nights, 8:30 pm, 10:30 pm, and 12:30 am. The 12:30 am show usually brought in people who had already been partying elsewhere earlier in the evening. When the law started cracking down on weekend late night drunk drivers, the crowd for the 12:30 am show dwindled. Darcelle then introduced a midnight weekend show with male strippers called The Men of Paradise. The Darcelle XV & Company 10:30 pm show already drew large bachelorette parties. The combination of the female impersonation revue at 10:30 pm, followed at midnight with the male strippers, was very successful. I emceed the midnight male stripper show for its first three years. When not performing in the earlier weekend shows, I was the camera girl and took souvenir polaroid photos of Darcelle with the customers. In the daytime, I assisted Roxy in the office with the payroll and banking on Mondays as well as bookkeeping and answering phones throughout the week.

Soon my act became popular for outside special occasion events, especially 40th, 50th & 60th birthday parties. Some of these parties were held in private homes; others in bars or taverns. When the guest of honor was male, I would often be introduced by the host as his "ex-girlfriend." Usually the guest of honor was a good sport about it. A couple of times, the person for whom the party was being given did not see the humor in a female impersonator roasting them. At a birthday party held at a Greek restaurant, the man said, "Don't come near me faggot." I still did my act, and got paid.

From time to time, I worked private bachelor parties with female strippers, and bachelorette parties with male strippers. I usually did a Sophie Tucker routine, did standup comedy monologue, and then brought on the dancer(s). Blitz Weinhard beer hired me to put together a special package show for a company birthday party. Accompanying me was The Regine, a female impersonator, and Elizabeth Wildfire, a female stripper. I did not tell the audience which performer was the drag queen, and which one was the real woman. Of course, after Elizabeth Wildfire took off most of her clothes, they knew that she was, in fact, the real woman. If the tips were generous, she even took off her G-string. Elizabeth worked as a receptionist in the daytime, and was married. Her husband knew she worked at night stripping. At the conclusion of the show, a man said to me, "Darn, I'm disappointed."

Then, pointing to The Regine, he said, "I was hoping that he was the real woman!"

On Sunday nights, cast members of the Darcelle XV & Company show would occasionally put together a one man show. In 1983, my 45th birthday Sophie Tucker show at Darcelle XV was especially meaningful to me. Christine Jorgenson was in town for a political fund raising event. She stayed at Darcelle's home in the guest room. Christine came to my show. She loved it. I shared with the audience the fact that, as a teenager, Christine's story played a strong part in my discovering my transsexuality.

Throughout the 1980's, my career as an entertainer was moving full steam ahead. I teamed up with a local piano player, Ron Snyder, and performed a show to a packed house at the Coaster Theater in Cannon Beach, a small artsy town on the Oregon Coast. During the same decade of the 80's, I went on the road, via Greyhound Bus, on weekend bookings in California. Friday, Stockton; Saturday, Modesto, and Sunday, Sacramento. My show was well received in all three cities. Another out of town gig was at a complex in Colorado Springs. This was a much younger crowd and was definitely not a Sophie Tucker audience. Early on at Darcelle XV, I learned that there would be an occasional audience who would not like the kind of material I presented. Terry Kaye, the Show Director, said, "Now and then you will get an audience which just isn't buying what you are selling. But you don't think about them, you think about the other 90% who do like you."

The NW Fountain expanded its operation to Tacoma, Seattle, and Vancouver, BC. Dave Porter, editor and owner of the paper, got me a one week booking at a small show bar in Vancouver, BC, called Faces. There I met many new friends.

Soon I developed a three man roadshow called Paula Nielsen & Friends. "For five years in a row, we performed in small towns on the Oregon Coast to very responsive audiences. Two other performers from Catch A Rising Star who were young and pretty, worked with me. Their names were The Regine, a Hawaiian; and Meesha, from Peru. They worked with me on most of the engagements. Two other performers who sometimes worked in this show were Myra Simms and Lana Lazanne, At bars in Cloverdale, Yachats, and the Lincoln City Elks Lodge, the show was a smashing success. The combination of me, the big Red Hot Mama, along with the young, petite, and pretty performers, brought down the house.

My years of church involvement and Bible study, coupled with years of show business training from Darcelle and Roxy, all came together in 1987. My friend Swifty, Darcelle's live-in housekeeper and janitor, often did numerology readings for people, whether they asked for them or not. He said that my numerology chart stated that I can be a preacher or an entertainer, but that I could not do both. I responded by saying, "Oh yeah? Just watch me!" I was destined to become an openly trans evangelist, preaching the gospel on public access television.

My 30th High School Class Reunion

1986

In the summer of 1986, I was drawn to the listings of high school class reunions in the newspaper, something I rarely read. The 30th reunion of the Gresham Union High School (GUHS) Class of 1956 jumped right off the page. Before calling the contact listed in the announcement, I told Darcelle, "I am going to perform at my 30th high school class reunion." Upon contacting Bill Hougen, chairperson of the planning committee, I was booked as a "comedy presentation" for the main dinner at the Red Lion in Jantzen Beach. Many of my high school classmates who had rejected me were about to behold me decked out in a flashy red sequin costume, a high fashion blonde wig, high heel shoes, large false eyelashes, and glittering with large rhinestone jewelry.

Upon arrival at the reunion, we were given a photograph from the class high school yearbook to pin on our lapels. One could then make the comparison as to what he or she looked like in 1956, as compared to 1986. Obviously, my looks had changed since 1956. Enter the effeminate young man who was teased and ostracized, decked out in high-glamor stage drag. We were allowed to bring a spouse or friend with us. I did not make my entrance alone. I was escorted by my friend Keith, a waiter at Darcelle XV who was young and handsome. I wore a beautiful corsage given to me by the owner of Irv Lind Florists.

A woman who was obviously three sheets to the wind from the effects of alcoholic beverages staggered up to me. She stared at my high school yearbook picture pinned on my shoulder, and then looked back up at me. Slurring her words, she asked, "Oh my God! Are you HIM?" I responded by laughing, and said, "Yes, I am happy to say that I am," and walked away. This incident reminded me of a question once put to me at Darcelle XV by a woman tourist from Australia. She asked, "Are you a 'shim?'"

While in high school, I did not socialize with my classmates. Yet, I did have a few secret crushes on some of the guys. I had even fantasized about what it would be like to have be sexual with some of them. And now, 30 years later, those fantasies evaporated. By 1986, the same guys who were so good looking and well built 30 years before had become fat and bald.

While we were standing around socializing prior to the evening's program, a male classmate from my grade and high school years was standing there obviously drunk, with a cocktail in his hand. He came up from behind me and raised up the back of my dress, to see what was underneath. I just smiled and walked away. After 30 years, he was still a jerk.

For my act, I opened with the Sophie Tucker song Red Hot Mama. Following the song, I commenced to do standup comedy night club monologue. It did not take long for me to realize that this was NOT the venue for telling risqué jokes. Some of the people, sitting around large round tables, kept their back to me. Others had frowns on their face. A few looked shocked. Their disapproval of me 30 years ago had not changed.

Nevertheless, there were others who obviously enjoyed my act. Some were too inhibited in this setting to let the others know they were having a good time. There were some who did laugh loudly in such a way as to defiantly let the others know that they liked me. Oh yes -- it was definitely a mixed bag group. My show business training from Darcelle and Roxy taught me never to be intimidated by an audience. Darcelle often told me, "If you don't get the reaction you want, just keep right on going just like they are responding." In talking about stand-up comedy, Joan Rivers once said, "With a good audience you can't say anything wrong. With a bad audience you can't say anything right."

Consequently, I digressed from the frivolous and risqué, and started reminiscing about my high school days. I mentioned some of the high school teachers who had played a profound role in the formative years of my life. Little by little, I moved into a serious vein. Before I even realized what was happening, it suddenly dawned on me that I was preaching. I shared with them my lifelong friendship with Jesus, who understood and accepted me when it seemed like no one else did. I proclaimed, "I've always believed it, I believe it now, and always will believe it." This led in perfectly to my serious closing song The Rose. I walked off the floor, with my head high, and with dignity. The entire performance was videotaped.

After my performance, a female classmate, whom I had known in grade school, walked up to me and said "You've got guts." In talking about those years, she said to me, "We were cruel to you." A cocktail waitress made it a point to let me know how much she admired my courage and fortitude in opening up to my high school classmates.

Over the next year, I was invited to entertain at three private birthday parties for classmates who had seen me perform at the reunion. They loved my Sophie Tucker material. And I received a very supportive letter from Bill, the classmate who chaired the planning committee for the reunion. Following is an excerpt from his letter:

"We have the same God....but live in different cultures. You.... grew up somewhat confused about your assumed traditional role in society versus your overwhelming need to be someone else....I believe that his is an innate compulsion that no amount of.... counseling could have overcome. It was simply you. You needed to find out how to become yourself in spite of the rules of society....You....clearly know who you are and have the confidence and self-respect of one who has come to terms with the world." That night in 1986 , as I stood there in full show biz drag attire, preaching the Gospel, the seed was planted for the concept of a drag evangelist. This evening was the start of a powerful turning point in my life.

An Unexpected Visit

1986-1987

Direction from God often comes at unexpected times and unusual places.

In the spring of 1986, a veteran lesbian Pentecostal evangelist paid an unexpected off hours visit to Darcelle XV. She was Rev. Naomi Harvey who had just started a charismatic church in Portland. Services at her Living Communion Fellowship were being held in a private home at the time, and it wasn't long before the congregation had signed a contract to purchase a church facility in SE Portland.

Naomi's own words about this visit are paraphrased here from her biography A Miracle Woman -- The Naomi Harvey Story written by Darlene Bogle. Pastor Naomi says:

"I was organizing the programming for my new televised ministry on public access television - Fellowship in Song - when I heard God clearly say to me, 'Go down to Darcelle's!' We had been advertising and making our congregation's presence known for several months. I had been working to have our services televised so we could reach beyond the walls of our church.

This was on a Tuesday, when the Club is dark, and when I arrived about 2 pm, the female impersonators were inside, rehearsing, refining their routines, and mending their costumes. The doors were locked, however I heard voices coming from inside, and knocked loudly on the wooden door. I was allowed in, with some obvious reluctance.

I know this is going to sound strange to you, the Spirit of God has sent me here with a message for you," I said. One of the performers scoffed, "God's got a message for us? What is it - Stay out of My church?"

"Just the opposite." I responded.

Naomi watched the performers closely for their reaction, sensing that some might be bitter and hurt about previous religious negativism. She introduced herself and told them about the accepting nature of her church. Naomi gave them fliers about the time of services and location of the church. Assuring them that God loved them very much, they were welcome at the church anytime. As Naomi started to exit the Club, she took notice of me among the group.

"I started to leave when I noticed Paula. I had met her on a previous visit to Darcelle's. The Lord gave me a word of knowledge concerning her, and I told her 'Paula, the Lord has called you into the ministry. He has gifted you as a speaker and has never removed His calling, even though your life has gone in a direction you never imagined.' "

I fought back tears. I told Naomi that I was twelve years old when I knew my calling was to the ministry. Rev. Harvey invited me to come to her house, and to be on the church program anytime. She said I had a message for God's people, many of whom were my co-workers at the Club! I asked if she was really serious about my ability to step out in ministry. She assured me that she was, and would help me in every possible way. She left by saying that she expected to see me the next Sunday at church.

This was a few months prior to my high school reunion. It was the Holy Spirit that led me to perform and simultaneously preach the Gospel to my former classmates, and to come out as a born again Christian and a transsexual. My public ministry began at that event. God confirmed my call to preach through Pastor Naomi.

Naomi also invited me to minister on her public access program. Two segments of Fellowship in Song were taped, featuring me. On one of the programs was a clip of me preaching at my high school reunion. These programs were aired in December of 1986. With Naomi's encouragement and technical help from her church, I launched my own television cable outreach exactly one year later in December of 1987. Naomi was my guest on the initial program.

What started out as a local cable access TV program was destined to become a worldwide ministry.

Changing The Image
1987-1988

In early 1988, the Portland GLBT newspaper, Just Out, ran an article entited: "Sister Paula, Drag Evangelist." The article opened with these words:

"Television evangelism. Usually these words evoke images of people such as Oral Roberts and Jim and Tammy Faye Bakker preaching the Word of God to hundreds of lost souls in a big studio church. These words mean condemnation of.... gay lifestyles...

But a new approach of evangelism is being taken on Portland community-access cable television. A transsexual is helping to spread the Word with a not-so-typical video approach. Sister Paula....also works as an entertainer at Darcelle XV and writes a column for the gay newspaper City Week."

In December of 1986, my friend Pastor Naomi Harvey had invited me to appear as a guest on two of her "Fellowship In Song" cable access television shows. The television studio was located less than two miles away from my alma mater, Gresham Union High School. My grade-and high-school classmate Frank, who was now attending Naomi's church, interviewed me on one of the programs. On the second program, taped on the same day, Naomi interviewed me.

Pastor Naomi and Frank picked me up at Darcelle XV and drove me to the studio. Up to this time, I had never heard of public access television. I had previously been involved with UFMCC's ministerial training program. At MCC Portland I felt like I was preaching to the choir. Furthermore, my ministry gift (Ephesians 4:11) and calling is to "do the work of an evangelist" (II Timothy 4:5). I wanted heterosexual Christians, particularly those in evangelical and charismatic churches, to hear the message of liberation that God had called me to preach. Television was a perfect venue for that. People will watch, and listen to, things on television that they would never go to see in person.

On one of the programs, Pastor Naomi sang a song and dedicated it to me. She said, "Paula, the first time I heard this song, right away you came to my mind." Listening to this powerful song, I just felt that God had inspired the writer of the piece to write it just for me. The song was Changing The Image, written by a well-known evangelist, Nancy Harmon.

Darkness filled my lonely life, until You came.
A ruined life, broken dreams, brought me shame.
Memories bound me to the past, kept haunting me,
Then Jesus came, took my hand, and lifted me.
So lovingly, and tenderly, He's changing me,
to an image where He sees Himself in me.

I was so moved by this song that one year later, in December, 1987, I titled my program Changing The Image.

My years of Biblical training and study, coupled with years of professional show business training, were all coming together to produce the image of a transsexual evangelist. This title was ideal. I was not knowledgeable on copyright laws. Without asking Nancy Harmon's permission, we played her song on the credit roll at the conclusion of each program. An unexpected development was to alter that.

A letter, dated February 5, 1988, from Nancy Harmon, was addressed to Multnomah Cable Access. It was written on letterhead, featuring a large heart, stating the title of her television program Love Special. The stationery called her evangelistic outreach "A Ministry Reaching People." In part, her letter said:

"...we request that you delete from your television programming and format the song, 'Changing the Image,"both in name and song, and whether in video or audio."

In a letter dated February 12, 1988 to Nancy Harmon, I replied:

"The same Holy Spirit that inspired you to write this song is the same Holy Spirit that made the song so real and personal to my own heart, and helped soothe the pain of my own personal struggles in life...

And what the Holy Spirit has done for me through your wonderful song is something that neither you, or your lawyers, or religious co-workers, can take away from me. GOD gave it to me -- and you cannot take it away from me, when addressed on a spiritual level.

You and I preach the same gospel of Jesus Christ -- centered in John 3:16. THAT you do not have a 'copyright' on."

In another letter to me, dated February 17, 1988, Miss Harmon said:

"We cannot allow songs that God has given (which you yourself said) to be indoctrinated into a message such as you preach."

I responded that the message "I preach is John 3:16 -- the same message that she proclaims."

Another letter, this time from Nancy Harmon's attorney, dated February 25, 1988, said:

"My clients, as Christians, find the connection of Miss Harmon and her song with a television show dealing with abnormal sexuality morally repugnant and personally embarrassing. Miss Harmon is well known in the religious musical field. The connection of her song, with the song title or her voice with such a program has been viewed by some as her endorsement of activities they consider repugnant and sinful. This use has caused harm to Nancy Harmon much beyond mere commercial usurpation of her property. Some members of her ministry congregation believe she endorses abnormal sexual practices. She is, in short, being cast in a false light.

We would further maintain that the title 'Changing The Image' belongs exclusively to Miss Harmon. She is very well known both nationally and internationally in religious broadcasting and musical fields. The title 'Changing The Image' has acquired a secondary meaning in those circles which relate the words of Nancy Harmon."

My response to this letter, dated March 1, 1988, said:

"My television show does not deal with 'abnormal sexuality,' nor does it describe any sexual practices, 'abnormal' or otherwise...The fact that I am a transsexual does not, in and of itself, mean that I am abnormal. It is the firm opinion of many medical and scientific experts that transsexuals are born that way. My television ministry is an evangelical and charismatic outreach to people who have been rejected by society, and their churches, because of their sexuality..."

My lawyer advised me that while Miss Harmon could prevent me from use of her song, I could still legally maintain Changing The Image as the title of my program. Alex Quinn, Manager at Multnomah Cable Access, said to me, "Paula, people are watching your program because of you. It doesn't really matter what you call it."

While I was living in Eugene in 1980, one of the women at MCCWV started calling me "Sister Paula." More often than not, she called me Sister, even as Aimee Semple McPherson's followers called her that years ago. The name stuck. I decided to rename my program "Sister Paula."

On March 2, 1988, the Oregon Gay News ran an article headed Nielsen TV Show To Continue; Pressure Prompts New Name. In part, the article said:

"Portland transsexual, writer, entertainer and evangelist Paula Nielsen will present another series of cable television evangelical programs, but the name of the presentation has been changed after an evangelical song writer objected to the use of a hymn she authored.

Originally called 'Changing The Image' Nielsen's show will be called "Sister Paula" in its next presentations. The taping of the next ten programs begins March 6.

The response to the first series of ten shows has gone far beyond my expectation," Nielsen said.....

According to Nielsen, the show will no longer use the title "Changing the Image" after objections from Nancy L. Harmon who authored a copyrighted song of the same name that was used in the show.

Nielsen said that she had originally chosen the name because the image that people see and the image God sees are totally different.

Nielsen said, "While Harmon does have the legal right to make me take her song off the show, the law does not require me to change the show's title."

However, she said, "out of respect for Harmon's ministry, I have decided to 'go the extra mile and change the title in the new series...."

When she heard about this conflict, Margie Boule, a popular columnist for The Oregonian, Oregon's leading newspaper, interviewed me and Nancy Harmon's lawyer. The following Sunday her column was headed *Drag Preacher Can't Change Image.* Margie Boule objectively stated the facts from both points of view. However, her column was sympathetic to me. When interviewing me, she said: "Paula, you are the only evangelical I like."

This conflict resulted in my first major local publicity. This would soon expand far beyond the Portland area.

1981

1996

The Gay 90's

AIDS Ministry at The House of Light

With movie star Fred Willard

Sister Paula in West Hollywood

Lifestyles Of The Poor & Famous
1990-1994

As the clock struck midnight ushering in a new decade at the New Year's Eve celebration at Darcelle XV, a voice on the loud speaker boomed out and exclaimed, "We are now entering the Gay 90's." Little did I know that this decade would throw me into international fame and recognition. Did it make me rich? Hardly. During this same decade I was also involved in ministry to people with AIDS.

After my first two local public access programs were aired in late 1987 and early 1988, someone called in on a radio call-in show and said, "There is a female impersonator on television, preaching the Gospel. This must be coming from New York or Chicago, it couldn't be from Portland." I was amazed at how quickly my local public access program became known internationally, even before ten shows were made.

It didn't take long for me to discover that my audience consisted of every type of person you can imagine. From the beginning, folk from all walks of life, all religions, both liberal and conservative Christians, and even those who consider themselves atheists or agnostics told me how much they enjoyed my program. Over the years, right until this very day, people have said to me, "Sister Paula, you are the only religious program we watch."

The television tabloid PM Magazine did a local segment on my ministry and the segment was chosen to air on the national version of the program. They interviewed me in my apartment and filmed me performing at Darcelle XV, including my Shirley Temple routine.

In 1990, while I was in the hospital with viral pneumonia, I received a telephone call from Rose at Multnomah Cable Access. She informed me that a national program called Access America, hosted by movie star Fred Willard, was receiving tapes of public access programs from all over the country. One program would be selected in the Pacific Northwest, for Fred Willard to travel to the local town and appear as a guest on the show. Those selected from different parts of the United States would then be flown to Minneapolis to appear on the national Access America program. About 400 tapes were submitted from various public access facilities throughout the Pacific Northwest. Out of all of those programs, the Sister Paula show was selected.

Fred Willard flew to Portland and appeared on two programs with me. This got media coverage in The Oregonian. In an interview with TV Host magazine, Willard said, "When I first heard of Sister Paula, I thought 'who's she kidding?'" After meeting me, and appearing on my program, Willard said, "Sister Paula reminds me of my Christian aunt."

When promoting the Access America show, aired on the Comedy Central Network, Willard appeared on several national talk shows. In any interviews Willard did about public access television, both on television and the printed page, he always mentioned me specifically. He became a fan of my ministry.

In 1992, People Magazine did a cover story on public access television. From hundreds of programs aired throughout America, four shows were selected to be featured in the article. Sister Paula was of them. This set off a chain of events throughout the decade of the 1990's, in which articles in many major publications were written about me. I was invited to appear on many national television programs, including the international British Broadcasting Corporation (BBC).

The BBC in London requested clips of some of my programs for a show called "Saturday Night Clive." (Clive was the name of show's host.) They also interviewed me via satellite from a major Portland television station. I was transported to and from the studio via limousine. On the satellite interview, wearing a glamorous show business costume and a high fashion wig, I shared with the audience that my first experience as an entertainer was when I was nine years old on my Grandma's farm in Sherwood where I entertained the cows on a tree stump using a coffee can as a microphone.

In his opening comments, Clive said, "Transsexual evangelists are a vocal minority in America." At the conclusion of the clips and satellite interview, Clive said, "Well, it seems like Sister Paula and God understand one other. Which just leaves us." When the segment was completed, with the plug still in my ears, Clive did not know that I could still hear his comments to the crew. He said, "She was fabulous -- THANK GOD."

The producer of the Jenny Jones show, originating in Chicago, invited me to appear on her show. I was not paid to appear on the program. Traveling expenses, hotel, and food per deim were provided. I was picked up at the airport by limousine, transported to the elegant hotel where I spent one night, then transported to the studio; and from there, back to the airport.

Next, came an invitation to appear on Joan Rivers. The same arrangements were provided as with Jenny Jones. I stayed at the Paramount Hotel, two blocks off of Times Square. Upon arrival, and after checking in at the hotel, I set out for Times Square in search of something to eat. Lo and behold, there were those Golden Arches of McDonalds, and that is where I ate.

Upon returning to Portland from New York City, I received a call from a woman representing Geraldo Rivera's show. On my telephone voice mail recording, I sang the gospel chorus Oh What A Mighty God We Serve. The gal from Geraldo said she represented the mighty Geraldo. "We could do an entire show just around you," she said. By this time I had learned to scrutinize every word spoken by media representatives. For example, she said "we COULD do a show around you..." She did not say that they WOULD do it. At any rate, I thanked her for calling and declined the invitation. Why I turned it down, I don't know.

The next invitation came from a national Canadian show called The Shirley Show. This was an hour-long segment called Outrageous Drag Queens. There were five of us on the program, and each one of us entirely different. I got the a better exposure telling my story on this show than with Jenny Jones and Joan Rivers combined. They even had me lead the audience in singing, He's Got The Whole World In His Hands. I added a verse: "He's got all the pretty drag queens in His hands."

A few months later, the producer who had set me up to travel to Toronto, Ontario, Canada, to appear on The Shirley Show, called me again. He said that he was now working with Jerry Springer. They were getting ready to do a show with both white and black supremacist groups. They wanted me to come on the program, with each group on either side of me, as a transsexual preacher, to preach to them. I angrily declined. "My safety was not taken into consideration. God protects me, but I am not going to overwork my guardian angel. I would like to return home to Portland minus violent acts being perpetrated on me."

During this time, a gay man named John Applegate was producing and preaching on a public access show in Seattle called Gays For Jesus. He turned tapes of my programs in for airing on Seattle Public Access, and I did the same for him by turning in his programs for airing in Portland. By 1994 my public access program was soon to expand from the Pacific Northwest to three different public access facilities in Southern California. Before this happened, God led me through a storm experience deep in the heart of Texas.

Deep In The Heart of Texas

1994

You're going! Although I did not hear a voice, still the direction from God was clear as I stood in the Portland post office in July, 1994. I was reviewing materials I had just received about the 1994 Advance in Houston Texas, slated for October 17-23. Advance is another term for camp meeting. Advance Christian Ministries was a charismatic ministry, consisting of GLBT Christians from independent Pentecostal congregations nationwide. In 1990 I had been a guest speaker for this annual event when it was held in Fort Worth, Texas. The gift of faith (I Cor. 12:9) went into operation and the financial means for the 1994 trip soon fell into place.

I thought I knew why God was directing me to travel to Texas. I prepared several VHS tapes of 60-minute Sister Paula television specials, and literature explaining my ministry. I visualized new direction for my ministry in evangelism, thinking that my exposure at Advance would result in bookings to preach in various churches from coast to coast.

The direction and spiritual renewal DID happen, but not for the reason outlined above. Once again I was reminded of the fact that my ways are not God's ways (Isaiah 55:8) and that often life's most powerful and profound lessons come through times of trials and tribulations.

Little did I know what was in store for me when I embarked upon the airplane on Monday October 17, 1994. I was about to become keenly aware of the fact that "...the Lord hath His way in the whirlwind and the storm..." (Nahum 1:3) The foundations of my faith were to be tested and my faith strengthened.

"Welcome to Texas, Paula!" exclaimed Tom Hirsch, Director of the Advance, upon my arrival at the Circle C Ranch. My response was, "Is there anyone here named Noah?" It was already pouring rain and a lake had already begun to form right in the middle of the campground. The beautiful new van that had been rented to transport those attending Advance had already gotten stuck in the mud.

Initially we all felt that the rain would soon subside and we would get on with our preparations for the week ahead. Nothing of the kind. Thunder and lightning increased and the pounding rain came down harder and the waters all round us, created by the rain, kept getting closer to the house we were in. By the time we were forced to evacuate the grounds, the rented van was buried in water with its rooftop barely showing. A brother and sister looked up and shouted, "We are now going to take authority over this storm in the name of Jesus!". The more they commanded the storm to stop, the worse it became.

While about 180 people had registered for the conference, 46 of us had arrived on that first day. The others were called by telephone and told not to come. Half of us were on the road side of the rain induced lake on the grounds. The rest of our group were stranded on the other side of the lake. The water came up to the average person's shoulders. Our group left in a caravan of cars. The others were not rescued until two days later. Fortunately, there was a cabin on higher ground untouched by the floodwaters that contained food that had been brought in for Advance.

We were given directions to the nearby New Caney Middle School. To get there, we had to cross a bridge. The flood waters were covering the bridge. Those in a van and truck ahead of us barely made it across; the rest of us didn't even try as the waters were rising rapidly. And so, our little procession of three cars with six people each -- one car included a mother and her baby -- turned around and headed back, looking for a safe place to park for the night. Three times we had to move on as the flood waters kept rising. We finally found a place where it was safe to park. Cramped in cars with no room to stretch out, there we spent the night. The words of the hymn Lord Plant My Feet on Higher Ground took on a special meaning for us.

In an attempt to be humorous, I pointed out to the group that we were in Texas Chainsaw Massacre and KKK territory. "Thanks for sharing that," said one of the gals in our car. While we were parked on the road, the rain had subsided. I drifted off into a fitful sleep, asking God to not let it rain anymore. 30 minutes later, I awoke to the rain pouring even harder and the light beams from the lightening so strong that you could actually see everything in detail when it flashed.

I was angry at God. Then, the inner voice of the Holy Spirit lovingly said to me, "Paula, you are safe and warm. No harm will come to any of you who are here for Advance." Then my attitude shifted and I started singing the song Keep Me Safe 'til the Storm Passes By and I felt secure in the hollow of God's hand.

In the morning folks from the neighborhood brought us coffee and a lady who lived nearby invited us into her home. While her yard had standing water, her home was untouched by the flood. Not only did the friendly lady fix us coffee and some food, she also let us use her bathroom and shower. While putting on makeup, I was gently reminded by the Lord of the fact that He had even provided a place for me to put on my makeup. My makeup kit always remains in my purse when traveling.

Soon we were rescued by rowboats and were transported across three miles of flood waters. While we were riding in the rowboat, the Lord reminded me of that blessed song from my youth:

Launch out into the deep, oh let the shorelines go.
Launch out, launch out, in the ocean Divine,
Out where the full tides flow.

While the memory of that song caused my heart to rejoice, the sights of rooftops of homes barely showing above the massive expanse of flood waters created a sadness within.

We were finally taken by school bus to the New Caney Middle School. That night at New Caney scores of people, all ages and family sizes, many with their pets, were being brought in where it was warm. Restaurants from the area donated food and emergency supplies from the Red Cross, and others, came flowing in.

And there we were, a group of lesbian and gay Christians, ministering to the elderly by getting them food and helping them with other needs. One lady was sitting there weeping. I gave her a hug. Many people told me that all of their material possessions were swept away. The Red Cross had set up disaster relief for the flood victims. An opportunity for ministry presented itself to us. A woman from the Red Cross asked Tom Hirsch, "Is this a gay group?" Fear shot through Tom like a bullet. Tom hesitated, and then meekly replied "Yes." The woman responded, "Not to worry. I am a lesbian." Tom breathed a visible sigh of relief.

Our group had a hallway blocked off for us and there we slept that night on the floor. While sitting on blankets and sleeping bags, we had an informal worship service in the school hallway. Pastor Tom delivered a stirring message centered around the theme of the Advance: Go Ye Into All The World. He focused on the fact that our world is wherever God puts us.

So many people feel that to go into all the world, traveling is necessary. While we dare not minimize the importance of national and overseas missionary evangelism, the application of Acts 1:8 stresses the fact that before we witness "unto the uttermost part of the earth," we begin in "Jerusalem." Our Jerusalem could very well be our home church. Does our ministry touch lives there? Those aspiring to be evangelists feel that it will be necessary for them to travel. The inexperienced see the travels of an evangelist as glamorous and exciting. What they learn later is that this form of evangelism is very lonely. When someone sings, "I'll go where you want me to go, dear Lord..." they often fail to realize that where God leads is not always where they may want to be.

However, through Pastor Tom that day in an evacuation facility in Houston, Texas, God revealed to me that I was already taking the Gospel into the world through the Sister Paula television ministry and through the places in Portland where God had already placed me for ministry. I realized that I had my mission field already laid before me, I just hadn't recognized it.

Looking back to that day in July, 1994, when the Holy Spirit had directed me to register for Advance in October, like those whom Jesus commissioned prior to His ascension, God was sending me into my 'all the world.' Through Pastor Tom the Holy Spirit was directing me to throw all of my energies into ministry wherever I am at any given moment.

As we shared and took turns praying, the Holy Spirit directed me to quietly say "peace be still," not only to the storm but to the hearts of its victims. The rest of the evening and throughout the next day when I flew back to Portland, it did not rain. As the initial flood crisis was subsiding, and people's prejudices came back to the forefront, Tom became fearful for my safety. Arrangements were made and I was the first one to be transported to the airport.

While I winged my way back home, my thoughts went back to that first night in Texas when some of my colleagues in ministry were vigorously commanding the storm to stop. I was reminded of the fact that we do not command God to do anything. We submit ourselves to the One who spoke the worlds into existence and who controls the elements. When Jesus stilled a storm He made no demands. He gently and quietly spoke the Word of authority and the elements had no choice but to obey.

When the plane descended into the Portland Airport, and I anticipated going to my small room with its comfortable easy chair, warm bed and my little kitty cat waiting for me, I thanked God that I had a home to go to, and also prayed for those in Houston who lost their homes. I thanked God for sending me to Houston, thereby providing me with an opportunity to minister to the broken hearted there. God renewed within me a deep dimension of spirituality for ministry and gave me fresh Biblical direction for the days that lay ahead.

No invitations for preaching engagements developed at this conference. Rather, about one week after returning to Portland, I received a phone call from Tom and Richard, two gay men, who produced a Christian GLBT public access television program in Hollywood. They had heard about my television ministry through someone who had met me at the Advance in Texas. Tom and Richard invited me to come to Hollywood, and appear on their public access program. This opened up new avenues and doors that never would have happened had I not obeyed God's leading to fly to Texas.

Spotted In Boys Town
1995-1998

As the airplane made its landing at LA's Hollywood-Burbank airport, the theater of my mind harkened back 19 years to the spring of 1976, when I had left Los Angeles for good and returned to Portland.

As I exited the jet in Burbank, Tom and Richard greeted me with open arms. They had made a reservation for me at The Hollywood Celebrity Hotel on Orchid Avenue, one half block North of Hollywood Boulevard, near the historic Grauman's Chinese Theater. When I lived on North Highland Avenue back in the 1960's, this hotel was a small two-story pay by the day, week or month apartment building, housing folk who were seeking a career in the movies. Since then, it had been remodeled, and turned into a tourist hotel, with all of the amenities and yet inexpensive. The Hollywood Celebrity Hotel was to become my home away from home for the next five years, as I made trips back and forth between Portland and Los Angeles to film my program at the public access facilities in Santa Monica, West Hollywood, and Hollywood and to appear on national and international shows for the British Broadcasting Corporation (BBC). This all occurred because I had obeyed God's bidding to attend the Christian Advance retreat in Houston.

After checking me in at the hotel, Tom and Richard took me to the public access TV studio in Hollywood. In addition to producing their own weekly gay Christian television program, they also aired GLBT religious programs that had been produced in other cities. They called this collage of programs The Grace Network.
I was soon to learn that the cable access facilities in various cities did things differently. In Portland, a producer had to recruit his or her own crew; whereas in Los Angeles, the studio itself recruited and trained folk to learn television production. This presented an opportunity for folk who desired to break into television production to get experience and training. They would sign up, indicating what days they were available to volunteer, and then take luck of the draw, working on the crew of whatever program happened to be scheduled on that particular day.

Let's Meet Paula was the title of the first segment in which Tom interviewed me. When the filming was complete, Tom and Richard transported me to Century Cable in Santa Monica. It was there that I met Mike Haboush, fondly called "Mike-o" who was to become a lifetime friend.

Mike-o was an attractive young man, who had moved to Southern California from Pittsburgh. He had worked as a go-go boy in gay bars. And he got bit parts in independently produced movies. When I met Mike-o he was Program Director for Century Cable Public Access. He also was the sound DJ at The Revolver, a popular gay bar in West Hollywood.

Prior to going to LA, I had sent Tom a tape of one of my programs. He had given the tape to Mike-o. Mike-o expressed an interest in having me appear as a guest on his public access program Upbeat. Not only did we film two shows that first day, but Mike-o filmed me doing a commercial plug for The Revolver, which was played on the video screen in the bar nightly.

After the filming, we all went to a fun and inexpensive funky hang out restaurant on Santa Monica Boulevard in West Hollywood, the Yukon Mining Company. I had a wonderful time, holding court with a fun group of people. I was well on my way to becoming a celebrity in West Hollywood, also known as Boys Town. After a few trips to LA, I became well known there, and like the movie stars, folk would say that they had “spotted” me on Santa Monica Boulevard.

The Rev. Elder Nancy Wilson was pastor of MCC-LA, which was housed in the West Hollywood headquarters for UFMCC. She booked me to preach at MCC-LA. Rev. Elder Troy Perry, moderator of the denomination which he founded in 1968, had his office there.

On one of my trips to LA, I casually dropped in at the UFMCC headquarters office. Troy Perry greeted and welcomed me with open arms. I autographed a lithograph publicity photo for him and he placed it on his office wall. Troy took me to lunch on Santa Monica Boulevard. I was recognized by many people both on the street and in the restaurant. People came up to our table and I gave them autographed publicity photos. A man came over to our table and said, “The other day a friend said that he spotted you on Santa Monica Boulevard.” Yep, I was a star, and I loved the celebrity recognition.

The following year, in his opening sermon at an UFMCC General Conference in Australia, Troy told the audience about our experience that day in West Hollywood. He jokingly said that usually the public’s attention was focused on him. On that day, Troy said, “All eyes were on Sister Paula.”

Bea Arthur, star of the TV series Maude and Golden Girls saw my program on Century Cable, and became a fan. She was a very close friend of the famous "male actress," Charles Pierce, known for his live impressions of stars such as Joan Crawford and Bette Davis. Charles Pierce and I became friends. Bea Arthur was very supportive of the gay community and did pro bono appearances at fund raisers for GLBT causes. I wrote her a letter asking her to appear as a guest on my program. She left a message on my voice-mail stating that she was not comfortable doing talk shows. Many of my coworkers at Darcelle XV listened to the voice-mail. Lani, a cocktail waitress said, "I listened to Maude on Paula's voice-mail."

During this five year period, I appeared on two major television programs. The international reality show Strange Universe filmed a wonderful segment about me, hosted by producer Trev Brody. Trev was an attractive gay man. As we walked down Hollywood Boulevard in front of the television camera, Trev asked me, "Do you think of Hollywood as the 'sin city?'" I responded, "No, I think of it as the 'FUN city.'"

"Sister Paula is The Trans Evangelist," exclaimed the teaser promo clip for the Strange Universe segment. Immediately, I changed all of my publicity materials from America's Drag Evangelist to The Trans Evangelist. Back in December, 1987, when I first started producing my program, I used the term "drag evangelist" to distinguish myself, even though I do not consider myself to be a drag queen. "Trans Evangelist" described me to a 'T.' Thank you, Strange Universe for bestowing that title on me. I was shocked that I had not thought of it myself.

When this segment was aired, I got a phone call from Joe, my hippie friend from the early 1970's, who had lived across the hall from me in the apartment building on Las Palmas in Hollywood. Joe had moved to Texas. He said, "The minute I heard the TV announcer saying 'The Trans Evangelist,' I knew that was you." From Joe I learned that four years previous my friend Al had passed away from a liver ailment. I cried, remembering how Al had put up his house back in 1976 in order to bail me out of jail. About a year after the Strange Universe segment was aired, Trev Brody was tragically gay bashed, resulting in brain damage. After this tragedy, I never heard from Trev again.

A BBC program called TV Pizza flew me to Hollywood to film a segment with them. The program featured various unusual television programs and personalities in America. It was filmed in a producer's home in Hollywood Hills. On the show I was asked what I thought about Tammy Faye Bakker. Aware of her support of the gay community, I complimented her. As I was preparing to leave the taping, Tammy Faye herself walked in. We had a pleasant momentary conversation, in passing. Tammy Faye and I were featured on the same segment, albeit not together. She looked the same as on TV only, like Joan Rivers, she was very short. I towered over her.

Tammy Faye was very loving and supportive. This was at the time she had been diagnosed with colon cancer. She had passed through the storm of her husband's infamous trial. At this time, Jim Bakker was in prison, and Tammy Faye had remarried. In Tammy Faye I sensed a person who had experienced much inner emotional pain, and yet one whose spirit had triumphed. When Jim and Tammy lost their PTL empire, the gay community supported them.

After this, when people asked me what I thought about Tammy Faye, I said, "That woman does not have a prejudiced bone in her body. She is a true and loving Christian, who came forth from her fiery trials with her faith still strong and intact." I sent Tammy Faye a copy of my printed testimonial sermon entitled The Wall of Fire. She answered back, saying that she would love to hear me preach. Today, her son Jay Bakker is very open and vocal in his support of the GLBT community.

During the decade of the "gay 90's" my transsexuality had become nationally and internationally known.

Mass In The Time Of Aids
1990-2000

Throughout the decade of the 1990's, in addition to appearances on national and international television shows, I experienced some of my most powerful and profound spiritual experiences in AIDS ministry.

Commencing in the early 1980's, the number of people who succumbed to this fatal disease were legion. Included in my first public actress television crew, in December, 1987 were two gay men who had relocated to Portland from San Francisco. The reason they relocated was the fact that, in San Francisco, they were attending at least two memorial services weekly for friends they had lost to AIDS. This was more grief than they could handle.

At the onset of the pandemic, my friend and employer, Darcelle, was fearful that the spread of the disease would scare the nightclub's heterosexual customers away. Myra Sims was the first performer at Darcelle XV to die from AIDS. Darcelle didn't want this fact known publicly. Darcelle has since promoted and supported numerous fundraisers for AIDS causes, and continues to do so today.

It was in 1991 that I became personally involved in AIDS ministry, starting out by working as a volunteer receptionist at a facility, called the HIV Day Center. A project of Ecumenical Ministries of Oregon (EMO), the Day Center provided free lunches, along with many other daytime activities for its clients. Most of the churches connected with EMO were liberal congregations. Many of the people with AIDS (PWAs) were rejected by friends and relatives, and some were even excommunicated from their churches. The Center gave them a safe haven where they could find acceptance and love. The Center's Director, Tina Tomasso Jennings, was a loving and caring mother figure for the clients. Father Gary McInnis, a Catholic priest, prepared the daily meals. On April 1,

1993 I was presented with the HIV Day Center Volunteer of the Year award.

In connection with his ministry to PWAs, Father Gary founded a local church called Journey Catholic Community. The weekly Mass was held every Sunday night at St. Stephens' Episcopal Church. Both GLBT and heterosexual people are involved with Journey.

At a time when many evangelical preachers were delivering a searing message of hate, proclaiming that AIDS was God's punishment of GLBT people, Father Gary conducted Mass in the Time of AIDS weekly at the HIV Day Center. Candles were lit and prayers were spoken. An icon displayed said:

"Console, comfort and deliver, O Lord, all afflicted with AIDS."

In addition to being a receptionist at the Center, throughout the 1990's I was a volunteer cook at two residential care facilities, The House of Light, and Our House. In 1994 friends helped me purchase a used Toyota, which I drove for two years. I called it the faith mobile. During that time I delivered meals to home bound PWAs under the auspices of Daily Bread Express, also a project of EMO.

My friend, Dave Porter, who had founded the gay newspaper The Northwest Fountain was a client at the HIV Day Center. One day Dave asked me if I had been tested for the HIV virus. My response was, "No, I'm afraid of what the results might be." Dave responded, "Where is that faith in God that you are always telling us to have?" He was right. Consequently, I made an appointment to be tested. The test result was negative.

Another friend, Terry, was a client at the House of Light. He had worked in the sound booth at Darcelle XV, and on my television crew. When Terry took his last breath in 1991, at 32 years of age, I held his hand. On the day following his death, I visited his empty room, with the traditional flower placed on his bed.

The powerful presence of the Holy Spirit filled that room and surrounded me. I started singing Amazing Grace. Suddenly, I became aware of the word 'amazing' in the title of the song. In that moment, I knew that Terry was in heaven. As I stood there by his empty bedside, God assured me that His amazing grace had been applied to Terry's soul. About four years later, new medications were devised that slowed down the HIV virus.

The clients in the various AIDS facilities enjoyed having me around. Not only did they respect my ministry as a TV preacher, they also loved my talents as an entertainer. My ability to make people laugh, helping to lift their spirits and forget their troubles, is every bit as spiritual as any preaching I do on television.

Throughout the 1990's, along with friends and relatives, I stood at the bedside of many as they were in the closing moments of their lives. It didn't take long for me to discover that, in many cases, God had placed me there for the visitors, more than for the clients themselves. Two of the deepest forms of emotional pain are the pain of unrequited love and the anguish of a mother losing a child. At Our House, I hugged many a mother as she cried on my shoulder. I also consoled many a grieving partner.

One morning, as I was preparing breakfast at Our House, the mother of a client told me that her son had just passed away. "Sister Paula," she said, "when you have a moment could you please come in and pray over him?" I said I would be glad to. About two hours later, when I finished up my duties in the kitchen, I joined this lady at the bedside of her son. As I had never prayed over anyone who had died, I silently asked the Holy Spirit to give me the words to say, words that would bring love and comfort to this woman who was experiencing a deep level of inner pain. Sitting across the bed, with her departed son lying there, we held hands as I prayed. I cannot recall what I said in that prayer. God's presence filled the room. When we opened our eyes at the conclusion of the prayer, we both noticed that there was a smile on the departed young man's face that was definitely NOT there when we entered that room.

Jerry was a chef at Darcelle XV. He was stricken with full-blown AIDS and was a client at Our House. During this time, our friend Katy, a drag performer at Darcelle XV, was doing volunteer work at the facility. In addition to her kitchen duties, Katy spent many hours at Jerry's bedside. When Jerry took his last breath, Katy was holding him in her arms. Later Katy shared with me, "When Jerry took his last breath I could feel the spirit leaving his body and he was lighter in weight after he passed on. Before working at Our House I did not believe in life after death. I do now."

As the latter part of the 1990's approached, I did not attend any particular church on a regular basis. My Sunday afternoons were spent watching renowned televangelists. This stirred up within me a spiritual hunger for charismatic worship.

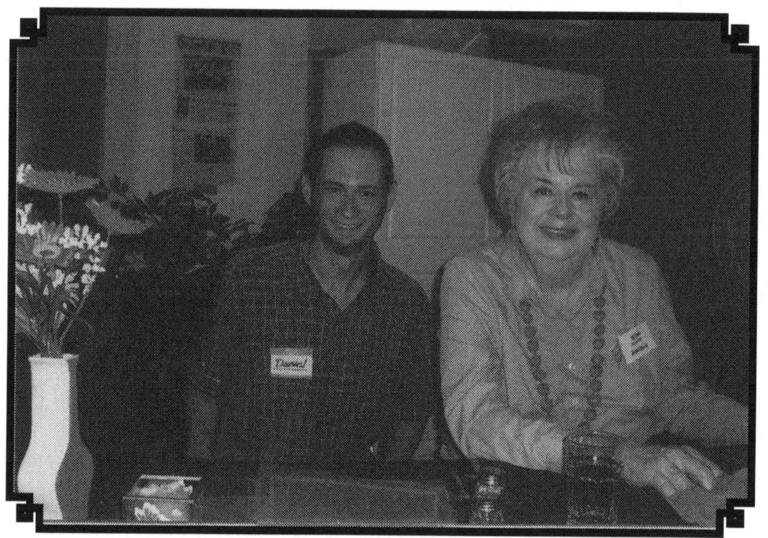

With Daniel, my producer on my
70th Birthday 2008

New Beginnings in a New Century

Ousted!

2001-2003

In the summer of 2000, Portland's Gay Pride organization publicly honored me with a prestigious Spirit of Pride award. When I accepted this honor, I shared with the crowed what it was like to live in Portland as an open gay person in the 1950's. As the first decade of the 21st Century got under way, little did I know what God had in store for me. I was about to face a very clear decision about who I was, and where I was going.

Who can forget the horrific events of September 11, 2001? On that fateful and historic morning, I heard the news of the attack on the Twin Towers in New York City from Katie Couric, while watching the Today Show. Many churches announced prayer services being held that evening on the television ticker tape, One such church was New Beginnings Christian Center, a large charismatic church in Portland.

Numb with shock, living on a fixed retirement income from Social Security and working part time as a telephone interviewer for a market research firm, I was fearful the Treasury Department in Washington DC would be attacked. I definitely felt the need to go to church. The evening 9/11 service at New Beginnings was very comforting. The Pastor, Larry Huch, said that the 9/11 attack was not God's judgment, as some televangelists were claiming. "It is," the Pastor said, "a spiritual war." Pastor Huch's springboard text was the same Old Testament Bible verse that I used the first time I preached in a church, when I was a teenager, in 1955:

"If my people, which are called by my name, shall humble themselves, and pray, and seek my face, and turn from their wicked ways; then will I hear from heaven, and will forgive their sin, and will heal their land." II Chronicles 7:14.

About six months later, I started attending New Beginnings

twice a week. I had a burden of prayer for a friend who was addicted to crystal meth. Prior to accepting Christ as his Savior, Pastor Huch himself had been a heroin addict. The apartment building where I was residing housed drug addicts, creating a very oppressive atmosphere. Walking into a charismatic church, with people smiling and happy, was like a breath of fresh air. I thoroughly enjoyed the worship services. One Sunday morning, there was a powerful move of the Holy Spirit in corporate worship. The emotional bondage that was keeping me bound to the oppressive atmosphere in my apartment building was broken off of me instantly.

Pastor Huch was also a prosperity preacher. He taught that it was not God's Will for Christians to be poor. This teaching, called "seed faith giving" by some, is based primarily on Luke 6:38:

Give, and it shall be given unto you; good measure, pressed down, and shaken together, and running over, shall men give into your bosom. For with the same measure that ye mete withal it shall be measured to you again.

Often, when receiving the offering, Pastor Huch's wife, Tiz, would say, "We are not trying to take money from you, we are trying to get money to you." I couldn't wait for the opportunity to walk down the aisle with my offering.

After attending New Beginnings for about six months, I signed up for a Monday night study entitled Old Testament Theology. One Sunday, after church, Pastor Tom Taylor, teacher of the Monday night class, approached me, and asked, "Are you on public access television?" I replied "Yes." Others in the congregation had recognized me from television. For the first time in my life, I was attending an evangelical heterosexual church, identified as Paula, where my trans-sexuality was known. What happened next would be devastating.

Pastor Tom invited me to remain after a Monday night study session, for "fellowship" in his office. There, he brought up my trans-sexuality. He wanted me to allow the ministers of the church to lay hands on me in a Sunday worship service and "cast that spirit out of me." At New Beginnings, they taught that GLBT people are controlled by an evil spirit. Their idea was for me to be "restored" to the person God created me to be. They wanted me to become a poster boy for their misdirected discrimination. Pastor Tom said: "This would be a tremendous testimony, and proof that someone can be delivered from this." He continued: "You will no longer have to wear makeup, and your hair will be cut like a man." He even offered to help me financially, "walking me through it," to purchase a new wardrobe of male attire. He said that I would have a "bright future" as a man.

Hoping to be able to continue to worship at New Beginnings, and to pacify Pastor Tom, I agreed to talk to someone at Portland Fellowship. This ministry was tied into Exodus International and the so-called "ex-gay" movement. After I met with them, they recommended to Pastor Tom that I be allowed to continue worshiping at New Beginnings and give God a chance to do a work in my life. Their recommendation was rejected. Pastor Tom told me, "You have two weeks in which to change. We will welcome you with open arms if you do. Otherwise," he continued, "don't come to church here at all." I chose to leave.

Pastor Tom said that Portland Fellowship wanted the same thing for me that New Beginnings did, only they came at it from a different approach. I responded, "You are right. They come at it with compassion; you come at it with condemnation." In a closing farewell letter to the ministerial staff at New Beginnings, I wrote:

"Your insistence that, within a few weeks, I have my hair cut like a man and come to church dressed in male attire, would not, in and of itself, change who I am one iota. I would merely be "restored" to being an unhappy gay man. I would rather be the happy transgender person that I have been for nearly 40 years. I fail to see how I could be "restored" to being heterosexual when I never have been heterosexual in the first place. God does not change one's person-hood; rather He anoints it and uses it for His glory."

In the letter, I also said:

"The easy thing for me to do would be to comply with your demands and start dressing in male attire, claiming to be 'delivered.' I would have the acceptance of your pastoral staff. Those pastoral staff members who have shunned me would embrace me as their brother. My testimony would bring me financial support and perhaps even impress Jan Crouch enough to give me a spot on Trinity Broadcast Network's global TV network. As you put it, I would have a 'bright future.' Interestingly enough, in exchange for the worship Jesus gave to God, Satan offered Jesus the same 'bright future' by offering Jesus the glory of the kingdoms of this world."

And the typed four page letter concluded:

"Whenever I have suffered the pain of rejection, Jesus has always been there for me. In my hour of loneliness He is right there, extending his nail-scarred hands; yea, my friend that sticketh closer than a brother. Thank God that His presence and supernatural power are not limited to the four walls of any particular church structure."

And Jesus said: "When I knocked at your door, you turned me away."

And the New Beginnings ministers said: "But Lord, when did we turn you away?" And Jesus replied: "When I came into your midst as a lonely old transgender preacher."

Jesus said: "And whosoever shall not receive you, nor hear your words, when ye depart out of that house or city, shake off the dust off your feet. Verily I say unto you, it shall be more tolerable for the land of Sodom and Gomorrah in the day of judgment, than for that city. "(Matthew 10:14, 15)."

Hurt and disappointed, yet knowing that God had a purpose in all of this, I shook the dust of New Beginnings off my feet, and moved on.

Sister Paula, Meet Daniel
2004

Upon my permanent, angry departure from New Beginnings Christian Center, I was deeply hurt. My human side wanted to ask my friend, Byron Beck, who wrote an opinion column for Willamette Week, a local tabloid, to write about my unloving and unjust expulsion from the charismatic church. I wanted him to decry the homophobic bigotry that is still rampant in some evangelical circles, and cite me as an example of unfair treatment and blatant discrimination. However, the Lord wouldn't let me do this. Being a sinner dependent on God's grace and forgiveness, I needed to extend forgiveness to this church for their unkindness to me. To harbor a long-time grudge and go on a mission of revenge would hinder my spiritual progress, my ministry, and my credibility. Even though I had been ousted from a church, the inner knowledge of my salvation remained intact.

In 2003 I canceled my public access television program. Financially, I could no longer afford to produce it. Since 1987, I had produced the program, on which I delivered messages of hope, forgiveness, and living a life in Christ. As the talent, the one in front of the camera, I provided the content for each program. For me, that was the easy part. The Bible, an unlimited goldmine of spiritual truth, provided me with all of the content I needed, and then some.

My frustration had focused mainly on my responsibilities as the producer. In addition to preparing the programs, I was constantly having to find replacements for crew members who would drop out. Sometimes on the night before a scheduled filming, a crew member would call in sick. Furthermore, while the air time itself was free, monies for other expenses came out of my own pocket. Public access forbade programs to ask for donations.

After my program went off the air the public access facility was bombarded with calls, asking when the Sister Paula show would be on. Folks on the street, and on the bus told me how much they missed the program. As I was walking down the street with a friend, a teenaged street person approached me and said how much my show meant to her. My friend said to me, "Paula, you made her feel that she has worth." A longtime friend called me "the only voice for the disenfranchised."

And I missed doing the programs. Three things that I love to do are preach, perform, and write. Yet, the cold fact remained: I could no longer afford to produce the program. I approached a couple of friends about producing my show; however, they had other commitments. I put up a notice on the bulletin board at the public access facility and got no response. And so, as the old gospel song says, I had a "little talk with Jesus." Here is what I said: "Lord, this is your ministry. If you want it to continue, then please send someone along to produce it." Now that I had turned it over to God, I put the need for a producer right out of my mind.

About four months later, on a warm spring afternoon in 2004, I had a social appointment to meet my friend Greg at an outdoor sidewalk coffee and doughnut shop. Greg was a Russian gay man who described me as "a beautiful person." As I approached the sidewalk tables, I noticed that Greg had brought along his roommate, a handsome and pleasant young man. "Sister Paula, meet Daniel," said Greg.

Daniel had relocated to Portland from San Francisco. I immediately felt comfortable around him. We became friends and occasionally met for coffee. It didn't take Daniel long to learn that I had preached on public access television, as an open trans-woman, for many years. When we were sitting at sidewalk tables, Daniel observed a wide diversity of people who would approach me, commenting on my television program -- either asking when it would air, or saying how much they missed it.

One day, Daniel said, “We are going to have to get you back on television.” Having experienced many disappointments with people, I thought within myself, “Oh yeah, yeah, yeah. I’ll believe that when I see it.” As it turned out, my skepticism was not only unfounded, it signified a lack of faith on my part. Sitting there at the sidewalk table was God’s answer to my “little talk with Jesus.” Years before, my friend Jack St. John had said to me, “Paula, you wouldn’t recognize love if it walked up and slapped you in the face.” God always answers our prayers. Sometimes we fail to recognize the answer when it comes.

And so -- I just love telling this part of the story -- with no television experience, armed with a little digital camera and an old laptop computer, Daniel started producing Sister Paula single programs. We filmed them on Portland’s waterfront, and other locations.

Eventually Daniel started talking about producing a documentary about my life and ministry. Three other people had previously approached me about producing a documentary, I declined. I often said to friends, “When the right person comes along to produce my documentary, I’ll know it.” Daniel was definitely that person. Even before I got to know him well, the inner voice of the Holy Spirit confirmed to my heart that Daniel would present my life story the way I wanted it told.

No longer did I have to concern myself with recruiting volunteer crew members. All I had to do was provide the content. Me in front of the camera with Daniel working behind the scenes was a perfect combination. Daniel purchased two Apple computers with editing programs and capabilities. I turned over the entire huge stack of tapes of my television programs to him. As time went on, the technical quality of the programs kept getting better and better. With the help of Rebecca Nay, a trans-woman activist and computer geek, Daniel created a beautiful website. In addition to audio and video podcasts of my public access programs, he has put up numerous YouTube clips for many years. Sir Darryl of the Sir Darryl Internet Radio Experience, advertised as "the most listened to radio program on the Internet," discovered me from my YouTube clip wherein I supported Hillary Clinton for President. Darryl then invited me to do ongoing bi-weekly interviews on his program.

David Kearns created a beautiful webpage - www.transevangelist.com - which is current in 2017. Included on this page is a link to the documentary film of my life and ministry produced originally by Daniel.

Years before, on one of my local television programs, I had predicted that my ministry would become worldwide. This prediction came true because I had that "little talk with Jesus" and turned the future of my ministry over to God. At this writing, from 2004 to 2012 and continuing, Daniel's friendship and loyalty have proven to be impeccable. Had I followed my human instinct to wage a media war on New Beginnings Christian Center, none of this would have happened. Painful at the time, taking the high road turned out to be far more effective.

Soon after Daniel came into my life, I received Divine direction to revisit two other churches from my teenage years.

Where Is The Lord God Of Elijah?
2003-2004

Jesus told his followers that "They will put you out of the synagogues," and that "whoever kills you will think that he offers God service." (John 16:2) In this same scripture passage, Jesus assured them that after his ascension into heaven, He would give them the gift of the Holy Spirit ("the Helper"). With God walking along beside them, and empowering them, they were able to forgive their persecutors. I had to do the same. And so, for the next two years, I attended different churches, some on a monthly basis. One of these churches went back to my teenage years as Larry in the mid-1950's and my early days living as Paula in the mid 1960's.

This was Portland Temple Wings of Healing. pastored by Dr. Max Wyatt until his passing in 1997. His father, Dr. Thomas Wyatt was the church's founding pastor. In 1959, Dr. Thomas Wyatt had relocated the world-wide Wings of Healing radio and missionary outreach ministry from Portland to Los Angeles. Dr. Wyatt's son, Max Wyatt, moved from his ministry in Salem, Oregon to pastor the Portland congregation. The original Wings of Healing Temple I had attended in Portland when I was a teenager, on SW 3rd Avenue & Mill Street, had been demolished to make way for urban renewal. Wings of Healing had purchased a 1950's style wood sanctuary at SE 20th Avenue & Hawthorne Boulevard, once used by the Open Bible Church. Upon Max Wyatt's demise, a long time Wings of Healing follower, Pastor George, took over the pulpit.

I will never forget my consternation the first time I walked into Portland Temple in 2003. To say the atmosphere was depressing would be putting it mildly. The small facility looked like it had not had a fresh coat of paint since it was built several decades earlier.

There was a small handful of people in attendance. The electric organ was not being used, simply because there was no one to play it. A long-time loyal member Phyllis Nash played the piano. If she was unable to attend, the pastor would call around, looking for a pianist.

This was a far cry from the 1950's when I had attended Wings of Healing and took a summer semester course at Bethesda Bible Institute. When the latter rain first fell in 1949, with a powerful outpouring of the Holy Spirit, people sang in the Spirit, also called "The Heavenly Choir." Throughout the decade, the large church conducted revival services every night. It had been vibrant and alive.

Now, in 2003, the revival cloud had moved on, and all that remained was a small remnant, meeting in the old and dilapidated facility, going through the motions of messages in tongues and their interpretation, with prophetic utterances. An old radio sermon of Dr. Thomas Wyatt came to mind, entitled Where Is The Lord God of Elijah? No more was the Shekinah -- the manifest presence of God -- hovering over the mercy seat of the Holy of Holies.

Pastor George, and his wife, Phyllis, were very cordial to me. I told him about my background with Wings of Healing. As soon as I started telling him about my transsexuality, he said, "I already know that. I've seen you on television."

In 2004 Pastor George watched my television program, filmed at Portland's waterfront park, on Gay Pride Day. He was not amused. In a Sunday service later in the year, that Daniel attended with me, the pastor preached on Romans 1:26, 27. Even though he told the congregation that the message was for everyone in the room, his sermon was obviously directed at me.

"You need to stop preaching that stuff. All of this Gay Pride. I am 'a-gin' it. God is against it. Tell them you were wrong. Dress like a man and start chasing women." He then commenced to talk about my conscience being "seared with a hot iron." He also said that he sincerely hoped that I had not committed the "unpardonable sin."

When I left that Sunday morning, I was livid with anger. I took it as a personal attack on my Christianity, my character, and, most of all, my ministry. This was a blatant misuse of the pulpit. Instead of lifting up Jesus Christ and the salvation He offers, he spent 40 minutes talking against me. Even Pastors Larry Huch and Tom Taylor at New Beginnings did not denounce me from the pulpit when I was given their ultimatum.

In the midst of applause by the group of about 20 people, an elderly lady rose from her seat and ranted against homosexuals. She cited Beverly LaHaye, stating that married heterosexual couples should not "do what those homosexuals do." I sat there stunned, finding it difficult to believe what I was hearing. If she were not so serious, I would have thought it was a joke!

That night I attended Liberation Street Church, a downtown mission which I was also attending monthly at that time. I told my friend Mike about my experience that morning at Portland Temple. He said, "Let go of it Paula," and I knew he was right. My inner knowledge and conviction that God accepted me as a trans-person was stronger than ever. Jesus said, "And ye shall be hated of all men for my name's sake; and he that endureth to the end shall be saved." (Matthew 10:22)

Let well-meaning and misguided preachers rant against me, it doesn't change my conviction and call from God one iota. I know that I am a Christian, meaning that Jesus Christ died for my sins and that I have eternal salvation, and that God has called me to preach, as an open trans-person.

That Monday morning, I wrote a poison-pen letter to Pastor George with copies to the grandson, Dr. Thomas Randolf Wyatt in Los Angeles. If awards were given for angry correspondence, this letter would have won, hands down. The Lord spoke to me and said, "Put this letter away, and if by next Monday you still want to mail it, then do so." By Friday of that week, I tore the letter up in little pieces. It was never sent.

Two Sundays later, I woke up with plans to attend a different church, when the inner voice of the Holy Spirit directed me to go to Portland Temple again. This I did not want to do, yet the guidance was clear.

When I arrived, the service had already began. During the time of fellowship, when everyone shakes hands, a lady walked up and introduced herself to me. It was Ruth, who had been the personal housekeeper for Dr. and Mrs. Wyatt back in the 1950's. When she heard me talking about my teenage years at Wings of Healing on my television program, she had written to me. Ruth, then pointed to a lady sitting two rows in front of me, and said, "That person in the purple outfit is Roberta."

Roberta knew me well when I attended Wings of Healing in the 1950's. She worked on the office staff, was editor of the March of Faith magazine, and ran the church bookstore. For well over 50 years, Roberta was loyal to Dr. and Mrs. Wyatt. Even though she preferred to remain in Portland, she had relocated to Los Angeles with the Wyatts in 1959. After Dr. Wyatt passed on in 1964, Roberta became the testimony lady, reading letters from listeners on the radio program. Evelyn Wyatt took over the international radio ministry, and kept it going until her passing in 2004 at age 91.

At the conclusion of the service, Pastor George's wife, Phyllis, told me that she assumed that the reason I was there was because of Roberta. When the Lord directed me to attend Portland Temple that day, I had no idea that Roberta would be there. There always has been, and always will be, a special place in my heart for Roberta.

When I left that day, I shook Pastor George's hand and said, on my way out the door, "I appreciate you." Unlike two weeks earlier, when I had exited that sanctuary filled with anger, this time I walked out the door with a smile on my face, feeling light as a feather. I never returned to Portland Temple again. That evening, I saw my friend Mike at the Liberation Street Church and I told him about this experience. He said, "Paula, you gave the devil a black eye."

It is interesting how fate works. Having already returned to a Church from my past, I was about to do it again. I had been active at Angelus Temple in Los Angeles; the headquarter church for the International Church of the Foursquare Gospel from 1964 through 1966. There they had only known me as Paula, and now God was directing me to the Portland Foursquare Church.

My Foursquare Days:
Then And Now
2003-2005

One would assume that, after my experience of being kicked out of New Beginnings Christian Center, I would be ready to either stop going to church altogether, or return to Metropolitan Community Church. I was not ready to do either. There surged within me a spiritual hunger for corporate Pentecostal worship. I visited Portland Foursquare (P4) for the first time on a Sunday morning in January 2003. As I was greeted warmly at the door, I wondered how I would be received as a well-known, transgender television preacher. As I entered the sanctuary, the memory of my Foursquare days at Angelus Temple came to mind. During the mid-1960's, I enjoyed my active involvement at the headquarter church for the denomination. When I was perceived as a biological woman in 1964, I was warmly received.

During my high school years in the mid 1950's, I had sometimes attended the Sunday night evangelistic service at P4. In those days the church had a full orchestra, a full robed choir, and enjoyed the largest Sunday School attendance in the City. During the 1960's, Angelus Temple also had a large robed choir, an orchestra and silver band.

When I started worshiping at P4 in 2003, it was hard for me to conceive that this was the same church I had attended in 1954, and the same denomination as when I attended the Los Angeles headquarter church in 1964. At P4 the church pipe organ was no longer used. For music, there was the piano, a saxophone player, drums, and two guitar players. Traditional hymns were no longer sung. Instead of a full robed choir there was a singing worship team of about six people, very casually dressed. In fact, the short miniskirts, colored hosiery, and boots worn by the women singing on the platform would have shocked Foursquare women of years gone by.

If the elderly lady at Angelus Temple who had publicly chastised me because my dress went about two inches above the knee when I was sitting on the platform were living today, she would have been aghast to see the skimpy platform attire worn by women in a Foursquare church in 2003. "The music in this church sounds like something you'd hear in a dive," complained a long-time P4 member. Another senior member said, "This church is going downhill with all that guitar strumming." There was definitely a generational rift within the congregation. The old timers felt that their spiritual needs were being overlooked. Many of them felt that it was their years of loyal giving that had paid the church's bills over the years. Church leadership, on the other hand, felt that in order to keep the church going in the future, the contemporary style of worship was needed to attract the younger generation.

As it was at New Beginnings, there were some who recognized me from television. A man who was serving food at a social function after Sunday worship said, "You are Sister Paula. I love your television program." He then said to the people in line, "This is Sister Paula. She preaches the Foursquare Gospel." I was delighted with this kind of feedback. This told me that my program was being watched and enjoyed by conservative evangelical people.

When P4's Pastor Larry Spousta called me to his office in for a talk, I shared with him that, in the mid-60's, I was secretary to Rev. Jean Darnall at Angelus Temple. I asked him how they would react if they had known back then that I was transsexual. "They probably would have rejected it," the pastor replied. He made it clear that he believed that I was, in fact, a Christian. He said that he would be in prayer for me that I would be in God's perfect Will, and that we would talk again in the future. Although Pastor Larry had told me I was welcome to worship there, I probably would not have been allowed to become an active member. I was happy to just enjoy the charismatic worship and be spiritually fed from the teaching and preaching and know nothing about the behind the scenes church politics.

Pastor Larry then expressed concern that someone had said to him that I am a man who uses the ladies' room. I assured him that I use a unisex toilet situated in a restaurant across the street. "Just so we have that understanding," he said. Later, a mentally disturbed man who disrupted the worship service when not on his medications was asked not to return. He complained to the pastor, "You throw me out and yet you let Sister Paula worship here".

From January, 2003 until August, 2004 I alternated between Portland Temple and P4. After that, I attended P4 every Sunday. I also enjoyed the Forerunners Sunday School class for seniors. The class was taught by a retired Foursquare minister, Rev. Jean Lund. Some folks in the class knew I was trans, and others did not. I loved Jean's teaching. She was an old timer in the Foursquare denomination and had pastored a Foursquare church in Idaho for many years.

On February 25, 2005, my life was suddenly turned upside down. During the time when I was attending P4 every Sunday, I collapsed on the street from cardiac arrest and plunged into a near death experience.

A Walking Miracle
2005

February 25, 2005 had started out like any other day. I had errands to run before going to my hairdresser and getting to my part time market research job at Market Strategies. I had been working there part time as a telephone interviewer doing surveys since 1994. The last thing I recall was alighting from a bus and walking up toward a payday loan place.

My memory of what transpired over the next 11 days is blank, except for a few hazy dream-like moments. Later, I was told, by friends what had transpired: I had collapsed on the street from cardiac arrest. A pedestrian with a cell phone called 911. Although it was difficult, the paramedics got my heart beating again with a defibrillator. Had they been five minutes later, it would have been too late. Or had I collapsed at home, I would have been discovered dead.

When I did not show up for my appointment with Tim my hairdresser, he knew that something was wrong. He walked up the street to Market Strategies where my shift was scheduled to start at 2 pm. My supervisor told him that they had not heard from me. "Paula never misses an appointment," Tim said. He knew something was wrong.

Tim called hospitals and soon discovered I had been brought into the emergency room of Emmanuel Hospital. He then called all over town telling of my plight. Within two hours people throughout the United States knew of my heart attack. He even called P4 and told them the grim forecast. The hospital switchboard received numerous calls asking about me.

News of my illness even reached Troy Perry in Los Angeles. He called the hospital and inquired about me, saying, "This is Rev. Perry." When he appeared as a guest on my TV program in January 2006, he said, "I wanted them to know that a minister was worried about you." They told Troy that they didn't think I was going to make it. They also said that to my mother.

I can only vaguely reconstruct events of that week. I recall a nurse walking into my room with pills. I threw the medications across the room. This is probably because of my dislike of being hospitalized. I vaguely remember a few seconds when I was pulling at cords that had me hooked up to paraphernalia. My body was hot with fever, so they put me on a bed of ice. Some of the time I was in an induced coma to prevent brain damage. I remained in intensive care for ten days.

Darcelle started arranging for my cremation. Darcelle and Roxy visited me during this period, only I do not remember this. A prayer request went out to MCC churches worldwide. My name was on the weekly prayer list of P4. My sister Teresa came to my hospital room and prayed over me every day.

I was unresponsive most of the time during this period. Later, Teresa said that on one of her daily visits I was feverish and unresponsive. She held my hand and asked God to remove the fever. Within minutes, she could feel my skin become cool and I began to respond. She brought in a beautiful bouquet of artificial roses that are a permanent memento of those days.

On March 8, 2005 I had a double quadruple open-heart bypass surgery. My first awareness of regained consciousness was when I was being wheeled down the hall from intensive care. I looked up and there were balloons! Among these colorful balloons was the cartoon figure SpongeBob Square Pants smiling down at me. In my room were several bouquets of flowers.

Not realizing all that happened over the past ten days, I arose from the bed to go to the bathroom. I immediately fell to the floor, and cried out for help. A nurse told me that I had just had open heart surgery. I had lost a whole week of time.

Mom called me and said that she had just read a newspaper article about the surgeon who performed the operation. He was considered a top heart surgeon in the state of Oregon. I realized that God had the right people there for me during this hour of crisis. It was definitely not my time to die. Several friends, both church and non-church people, said that my life was spared because my mission in my life was not yet fulfilled. (John 7:30)

Pastor Larry Spousta and Rev. Jean Lund of P4 visited me regularly and prayed with me. A man from P4's visitation outreach came to my room one day. He closed his prayer with the scripture:

"The eternal God is our refuge, and underneath are the everlasting arms." (Deuteronomy 33:27)

The comforting presence of the Holy Spirit enveloped me. I wept tears of gratitude. I felt that God spoke to me with words of assurance, and that throughout this entire ordeal His hand of protection remained on me. When I had collapsed on the street, I could have easily been seriously injured. Other bad things could have happened, such as brain damage or memory loss, but I was healing and I was whole.

I was hospitalized for nearly two weeks after the surgery, and then moved to a residential care facility for a seven day rehabilitation. There, the manager questioned me about my sexual identity. I told her I would prefer the word "trans" as my sex. "We are not that far advanced," she said. The place was depressing and I couldn't wait to get out of there.

When checking out to go home, I was given a cane, which I used for about a year. The therapist said, "Remember Paula, they cut you open. You take care of yourself." A male nurse admonished me, "Be careful that you don't fall and break your hip. If you do, you will be laid up with us in a cast for six months".

It was so good to be able to attend church once again. As I walked through the door of Portland Foursquare Church on a Sunday morning in early April 2005, assistant pastor Abe greeted me and said, "They say you are a walking miracle." Rev. Jean Lund welcomed me back to the Forerunners Sunday School class.

In addition to his duties as senior pastor at P4, Pastor Larry also served the NW District of the denomination, overseeing and counseling pastors. It got to the point where serving in both capacities was too much. Jean Lund advised him, "You are too good of a man to lose from burnout. You need to make a choice." Pastor Larry chose to resign as pastor and serve full time in the district position.

A Foursquare minister named Dennis Easter accepted the position as Senior Pastor of P4. I liked his preaching. He had grown up at Angelus Temple and often made reference to the same pastoral staff who were there in the 60's when I worshiped there.

Pastor Larry's wife Sue, and his secretary Bethany, had been very warm and friendly with me. Assistant Pastor Abe, who was very nice to me, resigned as assistant pastor to accept a pulpit in Colorado. On the other hand, both Rev. Easter's wife and his secretary were not friendly at all. It was definitely time to find another church.

Market Strategies would have welcomed me back with open arms. After the open heart surgery I felt that I could no longer handle the stress of telephone interviewing. So my only income was Social Security.

Upon my release from rehabilitation, Teresa brought me applications for apartment buildings that are in the federal government housing assistance subsidy program. Many people remain on a waiting list for two years before moving in. However, because of my health and below poverty level income, I was put on the top of the waiting list and got into a wonderful downtown apartment within two weeks after applying. It is situated close to downtown Portland's beautiful historic churches, and is the nicest apartment I have ever had. Every morning, I look out of my apartment at the scenic view of Portland's West Hills and thank God for the gift of being alive. Every day is a bonus.

Throughout the second half of 2005, I occasionally attended P4. I also checked out a couple of historic churches in the downtown area. The last time I attended a service at P4 was the annual Christmas Eve candlelight service of 2005. At this service a young man approached me and gave me a hug. He told me how much my television ministry blessed him.

In January 2006, my name was removed from the church mailing list.

A Church Vagabond Finds A Home

2006-2012 and continuing...

In his book of poetry, Passing Thoughts, the late Dr. Thomas Wyatt wrote:

Oh church of God, with power divine
and strength to bind and tie,
How can you strain at gnats so small,
when camels pass thereby?

There is nothing so cruel as religion without love. Many sound their trumpets, speak in tongues, prophesy, and yet they have no charity. This describes some church leaders who rejected me. To be fair, however, I must say that there are many people in evangelical churches who do manifest the Jesus kind of love called agape. It is a love that just loves. Yet, there are still some who do not understand the complexities of human sexuality issues.

After years of searching to find my place in life I wanted a Christian church in the heterosexual world that welcomes everyone to be a part of its ministry in full participation. I wanted a church environment where I would not have to hide anything; a place of worship where I am accepted as Paula. Accepted if even they know that Paula was born Larry. I wanted a real church family. People who are there for me when hard times come.

In my wanderings to various places of worship throughout the summer and fall of 2005, I found a mainline church that welcomes me as openly transsexual. By 2006, I was worshiping there every Sunday. It is located two blocks from where I live. This congregation is housed in a beautiful historic church structure in downtown Portland, with a fascinating history dating back to 1851. Since 1992, this congregation carries the banner 'Open and Affirming' (O&A), welcoming all people. In 1957, it became part of the United Church of Christ (UCC) along with three other Protestant groups. Maintaining its original name First Congregational Church, it is now called First Congregational United Church of Christ. (FC/UCC)

In the leering face of religious bigotry, FC/UCC has been bold in extending an invitation to all. This was the first mainline denomination to ordain a gay person (1972). I love their official statement:

"OUR FAITH IS 2,000 YEARS OLD OUR THINKING IS NOT."

To confirm commitment to justice and inclusiveness, in January, 1992 FC/UCC members adopted a Covenant of Openness and Affirmation. Included in this Covenant is this statement:

"Lesbian, Gay, Bisexual and Transgender people are welcome within the community of believers upon making the same affirmation of faith that all members make. We encourage all members to share their talents, gifts, and energy in the liturgy, employment, and leadership of the congregation."

On Sunday, November 19, 2006, along with others, I was received into membership at this church that practices true Christianity.

On Easter Sunday, April 8, 2007, the worship service culminated with the choir singing Handel's Hallelujah Chorus, with an open invitation for anyone to come to the platform and join in with the choir. This magnificent choral arrangement was accompanied by the church's historic pipe organ and a trumpet. While I was singing this familiar anthem with the choir in the bass section, the Shekinah Glory of God surrounded me, enveloping the entire congregation in triumphant resurrection power. My sister Teresa was in the congregation. She said, "Paula, I have never seen you so happy".

As I was feeling an upsurge of happiness and great joy, my memory flashed back to that Sunday evening of Christmas, 1963 when I was singing this same anthem with the Glad Tidings Assembly of God choir in San Francisco. Since they only knew me as Paula, I sang the alto part in falsetto in the women's section. Now, 44 years later, I stood on the platform of FC/UCC with the men in the bass section, still accepted as Paula. This was a liberating experience that I shall never forget.

In September, 2007 I joined the FC/UCC choir, and I continue to sing in it today. Not with a male voice, but with Paula's voice. A woman who was church shopping shared in a membership class, "Paula, when I saw you in the choir, I knew that I was in the right church."

Today I am still active in this church, serving on the Outreach Commission, helping serve meals to the homeless at Transition Projects, participating in the prayer chain, a weekly Bible study group, and numerous other activities. A church vagabond found a home. And not only a home, but also a church family.

The search to find my place in life has come full cycle.

EPILOGUE

The final verse in the Gospel According to John says:

"And there are also many other things that Jesus did, which if they were written one by one, I suppose that even the world itself could not contain the books that would be written. Amen." (John 21:25 NKJV)

Were I to tell everything I have done throughout my lifetime, and include everyone I have known or have interacted with, this book would be an encyclopedia.

When I first contemplated putting the story of my life in print, I asked a friend: "Do you think I should tell the readers about my sexual escapades?" He responded: "Just tell the truth". And this I have endeavored to do.

Now and then a sex scandal surrounding a celebrity preacher will erupt. When reading about the sins of Jim Bakker, Jimmy Swaggart, Ted Haggard, and others, I am reminded that preachers have human flaws just like everyone else. The great men and women of faith of the Bible were "subject to like passions as we are" (James 5:17) In sharing my life journey, I do not portray myself as a saint. In order to show how awesome God is, I include my sins and mistakes in the narrative.

I have gone through emotional storms when falling in love with someone who was not in love with me. To keep this book at a reasonable length, I have not told about all of my "unrequited love affairs" over the years. Some of these are heterosexual and bisexual street hustlers who would prefer not to be mentioned in this narrative, and I respect their desire for anonymity.

In this book I purposely made no mention of whether or not I have had sex change surgery. During the first ten years of living as Paula, I intended to have the operation. However, with experience and the passage of time, I discovered that a complex surgical procedure such as this had nothing to do with me being my true inner self. Some transsexuals see gender reassignment surgery as a "cure all" for their problems, and then become disillusioned to learn that surgically altering their genitals did not "change" anything. And yet, for others sex change surgery enabled them to be happy, living in the straight life.

Since 2006, I have gained acceptance in an increasing number of evangelical and charismatic circles, where my transsexuality is known. Many spiritual leaders are discovering that the prophet Joel's prophecy of the Holy Spirit being poured out on all flesh (Acts 2:16-18) includes gay, lesbian, bisexual and transgender people. When Rev. Troy Perry founded the first Christian denomination to openly accept gays, his dream was that some day gay people would be accepted in all churches. While this goal has not yet been fully attained, we are moving in that direction, as more and more congregations are becoming Open and Affirming. We are moving toward the fulfillment of prophecy when "The earth shall be full of the knowledge of the Lord, as the waters cover the sea." (Isaiah 11:9, Habakkuk 2:14)

My life has been especially blessed by the fact that I know that God created me to be a trans-person. Some day I shall stand before The Infinite One who knows the thoughts and intents of my heart from whom nothing is hidden (Hebrews 4:12 & 13) (Psalms 51:6, Psalms 139:7&8). The One who knows how many hairs are on my head (Matthew 10:30) shall judge me. This is the God who saved me and called me to preach. This is Jesus, my best friend, who walked beside me down the halls of Gresham Union High School when kids were jeering and making fun of me.

Even when I have sinned, and have made bad choices, God has bestowed unconditional forgiveness and pardon. When I have stumbled and fallen, God was right there to pick me up. "From the deep miry clay of degradation, God has always restored to me the joy of my salvation." (Psalm 51:10&12).

When I meet Jesus face to face, I will stand before God as a sinner totally dependent on the grace and mercy of God. Like Kathryn Kuhlman, I will say:

"Nothing in my hand I bring, simply to thy Cross I cling".

2010

AFTERWORD

During my high school days in the 1950's, there was no support groups of any kind for gay, lesbian, bisexual, transgender, and questioning youth.

Today, in the 21st century, this has changed. I am pleased to list herein six support groups available. A special thanks to my friend and GLBT ally, Joyce Liljeholm, for providing the following information.

PFLAG (Parents and Friends of Lesbians and Gays) started in the 1970's and now embraces transgender people as well. Parents and friends find support to understand and advocate for their GLBT loved ones. Visit www.pflag.org.

GLSEN (Gay Lesbian Straight Education Network) which started in the 1990's fostering Gay Straight Alliance Clubs for students in schools to promote a safe respectful climate in schools. GLSEN has done wonderful research which has been persuasive in changing attitudes of school administrators. GLSEN has empowered youth with a No Name-Calling Week. Visit www.glsen.org.

SMYRC (Sexual and Gender Minority Youth Resource Center) which started in Portland in 1998 as a safe place for GLBT youth. SMYRC offers activities and counseling. Visit www.smyrc.org.

OSSCC (Oregon Safe Schools and Communities Coalition) started in 2000 to improve school climate in Oregon. OSSCC offers funding and expertise to support youth led conferences called OQYS-Oregon Queer Youth Summit. Here, the "Q word" is how today's youth express their inclusion of lesbian, gay, bisexual and transgender, as well as youth who choose not to indicate gender. Fortunately the "gender stereotyping" that I grew up with is becoming non-existence with youth today. Visit www.oregonsafeschools.org.

TRANSACTIVE formed around 2005 and specifically supports gender-non-conforming children and youth as well as their parents. They provide advocacy to help the family embrace the inherent nature of their child and also work with the child's school and community. Visit www.transactiveonline.org.

THE TREVOR PROJECT is the leading national organization providing crisis intervention and suicide prevention services to lesbian, gay, bisexual, transgender, and questioning youth. They have a 24-hour hotline, as well as safe computer contact for GLBT youth. 866-488-7386. Visit www.thetrevorproject.org.

Paula may be reached through her website:

www.transevangelist.com

Colophon

TItles: Stage
Text: Calibri
Set in Adobe InDesign

Printed in the USA

www.onespiritpress.com
onespiritpress@gmail.com